Creativity Theory and Action in Education

Volume 5

Educational settings represent sites of creative possibility. They also represent the manifestation of some of the most persistent and dogmatic beliefs about teaching and learning. This series aims to push the frontiers of creativity theory, research, and practice in educational settings. Specifically, this series endeavors to provide a venue for disseminating the kinds of provocative thinking and cutting-edge research that can promote more creative approaches to teaching and learning. The focus of the series is on mainstream (rather than gifted or other specialized) educational settings. Another aspect worthy of exploration is domain specific or domain general view of creativity- one that has hitherto been the speculation of cognitive science but one that can be brought to the forefront of existing treatments of creativity. A final (and general) area of investigation is artistic, ecological, cultural and anthropological aspects of creativity that have been ignored by the community.

This Series:

- Capitalizes on the growing international interest and concern about the breakdown of creativity in everyday schools and classrooms
- Provides fresh thinking on complex issues and challenges pertaining to theory and practice aimed at promoting creativity in educational settings
- Challenges existing dogmas and overly narrow conceptions of teaching, learning, and creativity (e.g., creativity being separated from academic learning and linked to gifted education)
- Spotlights new theories, methodologies and approaches to studying and enacting creativity in a variety of domains, contexts, and levels (early childhood through higher education)

The Editors of this Series welcome proposals for edited and authored volumes that provide provocative and original explorations of creative theory, methodology and action in educational settings. This includes international and multidisciplinary perspectives on creativity across and within K-12, university, online and informal educational settings (e.g., museums, organizations, clubs, and groups). The audience for this series includes creativity and educational researchers, graduate students, practicing educators, and educational thought leaders.

Other Forthcoming volumes:
Reflections on the Future of Creativity, Technology and Education - In between the Good, the Bad, the Unimagined, and the Unintended, edited by Danah Henriksen and Punya Mishra (due early 2022)
    Uncertainty: A Catalyst for Creativity, Learning and Development, edited by Ronald A. Beghetto and Garrett J. Jaeger (due early 2023)

Proposal Review Process:
All proposals are reviewed by series and acquisition editors. There are two types of review: *expedited* and *extended*. Expedited reviews occur in cases where the series and acquisition editors have determined that a project should or should not move forward based on the fit and potential of proposal to contribute to the series.

Extended reviews occur in cases where proposals take on more specialized topics and would benefit from additional input provided by experts serving on the series advisory board and, in some cases, relevant external reviewers who can make a recommendation about the potential merit of a particular project. Extended reviews may also include an exit review of the completed work by board members or external reviewers.

More information about this series at http://www.springer.com/series/13904

Carol A. Mullen

Revealing Creativity

Exploration in Transnational Education
Cultures

 Springer

Carol A. Mullen
Blacksburg Campus
Virginia Tech
Blacksburg, VA, USA

ISSN 2509-5781   ISSN 2509-579X   (electronic)
Creativity Theory and Action in Education
ISBN 978-3-030-48164-3   ISBN 978-3-030-48165-0   (eBook)
https://doi.org/10.1007/978-3-030-48165-0

This Springer imprint is published by the registered company Springer Nature Switzerland AG.
The registered company address is: Gewerbestrasse 11, 6330 Cham, Switzerland

"Lock up your libraries if you like; but there is no gate, no lock, no bolt that you can set upon the freedom of my mind"

(Virginia Woolf, A Room of One's Own)

To Bill Kealy, my husband:
always loving, a bright light
For Wilson Mullen, my dad,
and Patricia Biggar, my mom,
always remembered, forever loved

~ Carol

Acknowledgments

Cheering me on, Ron said, "Yours will be the first sole-authored volume in our series!" Dr. Ronald Beghetto is series editor of Creativity Theory and Action in Education with Bharath (Dr. Sriraman). Encouraging my book proposal, Ron oversaw peer-review processes from beginning to end. Supportive in all circumstances, Ron is a remarkable mentor and coach.

I also appreciate the editorial board of outstanding creativity scholars whose collegial support and constructive feedback on the book manuscript helped improve it along key dimensions. Their anonymous commentary is highlighted at the end of my Introduction.

A special thanks to Natalie Rieborn, publishing editor of Springer International Publishing in the Netherlands, for being responsive and knowledgeable at every turn.

My husband Bill (Dr. William Kealy), always generous contributed his artistic talents and technology expertise, benefitting this book's graphical displays. And what an awesome barista!

Grant funding for this project came from various sources, awarded between 2015 and 2019. As senior Fulbright alumnus of two U.S. Fulbright Scholarships, I wish to acknowledge (1) the J. William Fulbright Foreign Scholarship Board, U.S. Department of State's Bureau of Education & Cultural Affairs, and (2) the Council for International Exchange of Scholars, and World Learning: Global Development & Exchange, a program of the U.S. Department of State, Bureau of Educational and Cultural Affairs.

A very special thanks to Virginia Tech, my university home in Virginia, for the research grants from the College of Liberal Arts and Human Sciences and the Institute for Society, Culture, and Environment for this exploratory international work. I also appreciate the School of Education's ongoing support of my creativity project, especially as it meant leaving the United States from time to time.

Virginia Tech   Carol A. Mullen
Blacksburg, VA, USA

Contents

About the Author

Carol A. Mullen PhD, is Professor of Educational Leadership at Virginia Tech, USA, and a J. William Fulbright Senior Scholar alumnus, awarded twice for research in China and Canada. Her recent books are *Canadian Indigenous Literature and Art: Decolonizing Education, Culture, and Society* (2020, Brill); *Creativity Under Duress in Education?* (2019, Springer, edited); *Creativity and Education in China* (2017, Routledge); and *Education Policy Perils* (2016, Routledge, coedited). Forthcoming is the *Handbook of Social Justice Interventions in Education* (Springer, edited). To date, she has published 25 academic books, 152 peer-reviewed journal articles and book chapters, 16 guest-edited special issues of journals, and many invited articles.

Crossing disciplinary boundaries in research, Carol is a multidisciplinary researcher whose scholarship extends to other social science domains, namely teacher education and higher education. She has served as President of two national-level professional associations and as department chair, director of a school of education, and associate dean in universities. A highly recognized teacher, supervisor, and scholar, she has received many awards, including Virginia Tech's Alumni Award for Excellence in Research, National Distinction Pool award, and Excellence in Research and Creative Scholarship. Additionally, she has been awarded the Jay D. Scribner Mentoring Award from the University Council for Educational Administration and the Living Legend Award from the International Council of Professors of Educational Leadership. With almost $5 million in funding, her external grants include two Fulbright Scholarships. Her PhD is from the University of Toronto/Ontario Institute for Studies in Education (Canada).

List of Figures

List of Tables

Chapter 1
Introduction

A timely topic these days is creativity and how to experience, express, and enliven it where restraints exist. In response, this book reveals dynamic creativity by fostering it under constraints and pressures in transnational cultures. For this purpose, Kaufman and Beghetto's (2009) Four C (4-C) Model of Creativity was adapted for use with students, faculty, and leaders. Here I set the scene with global issues pertinent to the exploratory study. Introduced are the 4-C creativity project, creative intervention, and glocal study contexts in the East and West. The structure of chapters is included.

Educators, institutions, organizations, and communities are being called upon to think and respond creatively to big problems. Global contexts are rapidly changing, and the problems we face in our educational capacities are complex and overwhelming. Globalization forces exacerbate creativity deficiencies in humans, cultures, and systems—a critical problem of our time. Counterproductive dynamics within accountability-oriented educational environments suppress creative potential. Constraints on creativity encompass much more than accountability regimes and are internal (Beghetto, 2019), which calls for creative interventions and solution-seeking endeavors in education. Exploring creativity with stakeholders in postsecondary settings can advance creative impact, inviting new pedagogies and methodological ventures.

With this book I offer one such creative intervention, with practical steps that support creative humanistic cultures inclusive of all. I operationalized creativity from the ground up through human interaction, practical engagement, and data-based interpretation. This challenging work, while a seed project, came to fruition because of people's willingness in different cultures to partake in theory-informed creative brainstorming and educational activity. In light of the creative responses elicited from academic contexts in three nations, dynamic creativity in regulatory policy cultures was awakened.

In *Revealing Creativity: Exploration in Transnational Education Cultures* my pedagogic research question is, Can diverse college students and educators discover creativity when encouraged under educational constraint? Also, what new ideas

© Springer Nature Switzerland AG 2020   1
C. A. Mullen, *Revealing Creativity*, Creativity Theory and Action in Education
5, https://doi.org/10.1007/978-3-030-48165-0_1

might be added to the social sciences canon, educational knowledge, and, specifi-cally, the creativity paradigm? An unknown is whether creativity can be rediscov-ered, even with the support of theory-steeped practical guidance, when restraints are present, including in the research sense. As applicable to my project, limited access to stakeholders and time permitted for engagement was a constant barrier, yet cre-ativity was both experienced and expressed. In the following pages, I tell this trans-national story, revealing creativity against all odds.

In a snapshot, this book:

- Offers longitudinal glocal study of creativity within three countries, all subjected to high-stakes standardized testing
- Provides insight into the recovery and fostering of creativity under educational constraint and pressure within accountability-bound competitive cultures
- Bridges theory with method, and practice with action, through an innovative treatment of creativity theory that engages diverse college populations
- Illustrates a new methodological framework and tool that serve as a translation, interpretation, and application of the 4-C creativity theory
- Reveals the power of creative intervention and methods for uncovering as well as releasing creativity in difficult situations
- Brings to the fore Hidden-c—belief in one's creative capacity—through a pro-cess whereby students are guided to uncover their latent potential as creators
- Also introduces a continuum of creativity described as Experience, Express, and Enliven Creativity (E^3C) that can trigger Hidden-c

Chapters were informed by creativity theory and dynamic pedagogical explora-tion in three industrial global economies dominated by educational performance measures and a high-stakes testing ethos. They are organized thematically as three parts:

- Framing the Longitudinal Glocal Study as Creative Action (Part I)
- Applying the 4-C Creativity Model in Three Global Cultures (Part II)
- Enlivening Creativity-Deficit Educational Settings Worldwide (Part III)

Chapter 2 introduces the 4-C project's purposes and goals, main concepts and linkages among them, and the creative intervention and glocal setting.

Toward framing creativity for this book, Chap. 3 presents salient concepts and pertinent theories that support the creative intervention and glocal contexts in which it unfolded; beyond this, specialized terms like *glocal* are descriptively defined. *Glocal* describes a phenomenon that is particular and universal at the same time—it's essentially a hybrid of *global* and *local*. I use this term to refer to a local environ-ment that is impacted globally, such as by test-centric accountability trends (see Chap. 3). Glocal (and *glocalization*), an educational policy term as used by Brooks and Normore (2009), refers to "a meaningful integration of local and global forces" (p. 52). The concepts and theories that shaped my inquiry offer ways of viewing the central creativity model, the 4-C typology. Along with its 4-Cs, in addition to my notion of a fifth c (i.e., Hidden-c), the framework is advanced as a lead construct.

Chapter 4 outlines the methodological frames and creative pedagogic methods in accordance with dynamic processes and strategies. Specifically, it presents a qualitative methodological translation of the 4-C typology and adaptation for discovery in three glocal contexts. The features of case study applicable to the investigation over time are outlined. Global influences (creativity crisis, curriculum shortfalls, and creativity constraints) on creativity and the creative intervention are also introduced.

Part II, the heart of this creativity project, consists of three empirical case studies, taking readers from Chongqing, China (Chap. 5), to Toronto, Canada (Chap. 6), and then Sydney, Australia (Chap. 7). Each transnational portrait of an educational urban setting offers a multilayered narrative and analysis. Application of the creativity model within learning environments is key to all three cases. The accounts contain descriptions of glocal dynamics, participant perspectives, creative actions organized around the 4-Cs, and thematic results. In regard to the creativity–accountability dilemma illustrated, creativity and accountability dynamics are culturally steeped. Cultural connections are made in the case narratives.

Part III takes up the challenge of enlivening creativity-deficit educational settings worldwide. Chap. 8's synthesis of outcomes advances analyses of the three glocal case studies relative to commonalities and variations within them and study implications. Also discussed theoretically and practically is the Hidden-c concept that draws attention to creators' personal powers for being creative despite, or in light of, restraints and pressures. The idea is that when creativity is released, this does not somehow occur apart from constraints (Beghetto, 2019).

Creativity that is experienced, expressed, and enlivened can renew creativity where absent or subjugated within accountability-laden educational places is advanced in this chapter (i.e., Chap. 8). The conjecture that creativity can manifest under duress has been "tested," albeit to a limited extent, owing to the highly exploratory nature of this work and eclectic approaches used. Creativity-deficit cultures need to be able to benefit from enrichment. Theory-building around creativity and promising, if not empowering, creative risk-taking and practice offer direction, stimulation, and hope.

Takeaways (Chap. 9) from this international creativity project wrap up the book. Three major global influences that affected the 4-C program and outcomes are described in tension with counterforces. As is explained, the influences tend to magnify within educational places undergoing change, and counterforces can nonetheless be exerted so that creativity can be revealed. Meta-perspectives are highlighted and for anyone interested in studying creativity and applying models to invigorate creative action.

The writing ahead represents my narrative as a creativity researcher who moves along the mainstream narratives of creativity researchers while attempting to refine the existing narratives based on my own explorations. The anonymous reviewers of this book expressed this thought, stating that "it represents a narration from a researcher who is willing to deepen her understanding of a theory of creativity—the 4-Cs—and to broaden her understanding with responses and experiences from different cultural contexts." An elaboration was that this book will most likely appeal to creativity researchers with interest in how the 4-C theory is applied and how responses from qualitative research broaden the meanings of the existing concepts or, in this case, the types of creativity. They also wrote that my contribution makes an original contribution to the field within the context of the framework of 4-Cs proposed by Kaufman and Beghetto (2009) over a decade ago. Readers, they added, can expect to encounter an application and expansion of the 4-Cs beyond the familiar vocabularies. A final point made by the reviewers is that the articulation of the 4-Cs and beyond can stimulate people's realization that the boundary of theorizing creativity is indeed beyond the capacity of counting the number of Cs.

References

Beghetto, R. A. (2019). Structured uncertainty: How creativity thrives under constraints and uncertainty. In C. A. Mullen (Ed.), *Creativity under duress in education? Resistive theories, practices, and actions* (pp. 27–40). Cham, Switzerland: Springer.

Brooks, J. S., & Normore, A. H. (2009). Educational leadership and globalization: Literacy for a glocal perspective. *Educational Policy, 24*(1), 52–82.

Kaufman, J. C., & Beghetto, R. A. (2009). Beyond big and little: The Four C Model of Creativity. *Review of General Psychology, 13*(1), 1–12.

Chapter 2
Exploring Dynamic Creativity in Accountability Cultures

2.1 Overview

To optimize intelligent and effective action, we understand creativity as theory, practice, and action—not as a craft for passing the time. Illustrating this logic, leading creativity theorists (e.g., Beghetto & Corazza, 2019; Karwowski, Han, & Beghetto, 2019; Kaufman & Beghetto, 2009, 2013; Kaufman & Sternberg, 2019) promote awareness by emphasizing the importance of generating and validating creativity theory, as well as developing and facilitating personal creativity. Construct-oriented developmental interventions rooted in validated theory-informed frameworks can enrich disciplines, societies, and lives. As such, creativity is more than an essential performance skill—it's vital to dynamic processes of self-actualization and becoming "world class learners" who contribute to global societies (Zhao, 2012). Besides this, creativity provides leverage for the viability of global education, academic programs, and the disciplines (Tienken & Mullen, 2016; Wagner, 2012; World Economic Forum, 2013; Zhao, 2014) (Fig. 2.1).

Creativity's advancement of human reflection and development is through creative risk-taking, problem-solving, expression, innovation, novelty, usefulness, collaboration, and effectiveness. Beghetto (2019) of Arizona State University has asked, Can the development and expression of creativity be cultivated in the face of constraints and conventions that expect conformity to curricular mandates and more? To illustrate, he invited consideration of a familiar enough classroom scenario involving

a teacher who wants students to express creativity in their science fair projects. Before assigning students to create their own projects, the teacher discusses the scientific conventions and requirements of the project. (For example, each project must pose a hypothesis, gather evidence to test the hypothesis, and explain whether the hypothesis has been supported.) Students are then invited to work within these conventions to create their own original, personally meaningful science fair projects. (para. 5)

© Springer Nature Switzerland AG 2020
C. A. Mullen, *Revealing Creativity*, Creativity Theory and Action in Education 5, https://doi.org/10.1007/978-3-030-48165-0_2

Fig. 2.1 Beghetto discussing essential ideas on creativity with a school practitioner audience (Ronald A. Beghetto, presenter)

Importantly, as illustrated through this vignette and in the academic discourse on this topic, creativity can and does thrive even in constraining circumstances, policy climates, and accountability-bound cultures—a game-changing idea (e.g., Beghetto, 2019; Beghetto & Kaufman, 2013; Mullen, 2019a, b, c). Influenced by thought and action, context and flux, when creativity is dynamically experienced, it can affect the quality of human life, improving difficult circumstances and inspiring hope. Moreover, dynamic creativity changes situations and is changed by them—it enables transformation even in accountability-laden cultures and repressive policy climates (Beghetto & Corazza, 2019; Mullen, 2019d).

This book bridges theory and practice where creativity is suppressed and authentic engagement is infrequent. It enlivens generative possibilities for creativity-deficit educational settings worldwide, providing strategies and ways forward. A key contribution of the book is its validation and promotion of theory-enriched creativity and creative intervention in education for anyone seeking to release creativity and transform education.

Unique elements comprising the pedagogic research and book are:

1. Methodological framework for applying and extending the Four C (4-C) Model of Creativity (Kaufman & Beghetto, 2009)
2. Longitudinal glocal study with detailed case studies conveying transnational education aspects
3. Sense-making of creativity in college settings, relative to the 4-Cs and unique cultural and accountability contexts

4. Hidden-c, dynamic creativity, and the Experience, Express, and Enliven Creativity (E³C) Continuum—all forces for empowering self-discovery (Mullen, 2018, 2019d)

Responses from diverse university stakeholders about creativity in transnational educational cultures could prove revealing. As such, the thrust of the work under present consideration is whether students, faculty, and leaders in education can experience creativity and reveal it, despite interferences that may burden them. For this purpose, I use Kaufman and Beghetto's (2009, 2013) classic educational theory the 4-C creativity model.

Revealing Creativity: Exploration in Transnational Education Cultures also considers what new ideas and knowledge can be gleaned through an exploratory study of this nature. An empirical case study, this project reflects "creativity under duress in education"—as taken up in a book with this title (i.e., Mullen, 2019a). The work builds on existing literature on dynamic creativity in education and attempts to make a contribution to it (e.g., Beghetto, 2019; Beghetto & Corazza, 2019; Beghetto & Sriraman, 2017; Corazza, 2016; Mullen, 2017, 2018).

A creativity–accountability dilemma spurs dynamics of possibility and constraint. Although it may seem counterintuitive, constraints also arouse creative thought and action. For example, when teachers overcome self-doubts about the value of creativity content, they have been known to effectively facilitate student development and take another creative leap by building assessment into the process (Beghetto, 2005, 2019; Mullen, 2018; Schmidt & Charney, 2018). Through creative openings, opportunities, and interventions in classrooms, creativity can be renewed individually, interpersonally, and collectively (Beghetto, 2016). As such, an assumption guiding this book is that "creativity always operates in constraints … creative expression emerges from structured experiences with uncertainty"; while constraints do "[stifle] creativity, … they actually serve as a supportive structure for creative thought and action in educational settings" (Beghetto, 2019, p. 27). In any profession and at all grade levels, creators can tap into the creativity that is hidden even from themselves—we all have the potential to do creative work within difficult circumstances (Mullen, 2017, 2018).

Another epistemological belief of mine is that creative programming needs to be internationally reclaimed in public education's accountability culture and practiced within a wide range of learning spaces. Given that more people worldwide are interested in cultivating creativity (Tan, 2013) and learning about it (Beghetto, 2016), *Revealing Creativity* comes at an ideal time. Translating creativity theory into a method, I designed creative engagement activities, including an immersive encounter, operationalizing Kaufman and Beghetto's (2009) 4-C creativity model. (Chap. 3 describes this theory and its validation in educational psychology; also Mullen, 2019d.) Ward and Kennedy (2017) recognized the 4-C model's value in pursuing "big questions." How creativity as a global trend influences education in specific cultural contexts is such question, I believe. Creativity theories, especially those that have been tested, no matter how preliminarily (e.g., Kaufman & Beghetto, 2013), can be mined for potentially executable ideas leading to the implementation of programs that not only foster engagement but also bolster creative confidence. The 4-C typology also offers a viable alternative to commercial models of creativity that commodify creativity and advance corporate interests.

This book bridges theory and practice where creativity is suppressed and authentic engagement is infrequent. It also validates and promotes theory-enriched creativity and creative intervention in education for anyone seeking to release creativity and transform education, no matter the magnitude. Diverse stakeholders were guided to interpret the 4-C classification system within their cultural contexts. In different testing cultures, participants, mostly undergraduate and graduate students, expressed their creativity in ways explicitly influenced by theory and the theme: creativity and accountability in education. Across disparate settings, they not only shared perspectives on creativity under duress but also gave culturally specific examples, even producing artifacts where time permitted. Students both experienced and expressed creativity guided by the 4-C theory-informed methodology. And across all stakeholders and sites, there were hints that creativity would be enlivened in future contexts. In what follows, I elaborate on project purposes and goals, and the creative intervention and context.

2.2   Purposes and Goals of Project

The main purpose of this book was to reveal creativity with and beyond the 4-C creativity typology by applying this theory from Kaufman and Beghetto's body of work (e.g., Kaufman & Beghetto, 2009, 2013). Exploring the 4-Cs internationally in transnational education cultures was critical to the overall direction for the study aimed at obtaining responses from qualitative research that could broaden the meanings of existing concepts or, in this case, the types of creativity. I was driven to deepen my understanding of a theory of creativity—the 4-Cs—and enrich my perspectives with responses and experiences from different cultural contexts. Wanting to provide guidance to readers interested in utilizing or adapting my research program and activities was of interest.

Acting on these purposes set in motion the primary methodological goal to learn how college educators interpret and respond to the 4-C creativity model within their learning environments. How they regard and experience creativity when it seems beyond reach, even impossible perhaps, in accountability-bound, high-pressure cultures was a source of intrigue.

Operationalizing this aim involved developing a methodological framework and activating creativity in accountability cultures within postsecondary educational settings facing twenty-first-century hardships. Spending time thinking about creativity and being creative with cultural inhabitants who are teaching, learning, and leading in repressive test-centric nations was an aspiration. My hope was to offer a glocal investigation of creativity that potentially supports others in exploring possibilities for applying theory-informed models in these difficult times. A motivation is to hopefully enhance educational literature with a theory-supported application involving people who directly experienced the intervention from which others can benefit.

A desire was to expand this project with multidisciplinary perspectives on creativity, culture, and accountability. The study interest was in creativity in tension with accountability in relationship to culture within glocalities. Of particular value was translating a popular creativity theory (the 4-C model) into a creative method within three policy-dominant high-stakes accountability nations in the East and West, and producing glocalized case studies. Taking the time to think through an innovative process for addressing obstacles to creativity is one thing, but it is quite another to spend years seeking to spark creative learning in world cultures.

2.3   Longitudinal Glocal Study

The thrust of this longitudinal glocal study is people's capacity for experiencing, expressing, and enlivening creativity within the challenging constraints of educational contexts. Educators' perspectives on creativity in transnational, accountability-driven educational environments can be tapped for insight. Even though it may seem counterintuitive, creativity can be understood and directly experienced where authority, control, and restraint are active threats.

As evidenced by other emergent research, creativity under duress in education is a pressing contemporary issue (e.g., Beghetto, 2019; Mullen, 2019a). *Revealing Creativity* uniquely contributes to this emergence a longitudinal glocal study, which is my name for this spinoff on the more familiar genre, longitudinal qualitative research. This type of research provides an opportunity to learn how participants make meaning of particular phenomena and trends of interest like aging, health, and development with respect to the human lifespan (see Shanahan, Mortimer, & Johnson, 2016).

Much varies in how longitudinal research is envisioned, designed, and approached. Researchers' "operating assumptions about creative thought and action" (Beghetto & Karwowski, 2019, p. 8) also differ. Study of creativity can proceed in more dynamic or static ways. And, longitudinal designs can be used with qualitative or quantitative data. Besides the focus and purpose, the time element greatly varies, with some research taking many years to complete. However, study episodes are organized in such a way as to make time for data to be collected and interpreted, and for insights to be gained about creativity phenomena, whether by creativity researchers like myself, developmental psychologists, sociologists, or others. Longitudinal approaches to investigating educational creativity are considered favorable to dynamic creativity in that they require study of the phenomenon of interest over time and as long, moderate, or small periods. Regarding the current study, the longitudinal design involved the observation, elicitation, documentation, and interpretation of qualitative data over months and years. Periods were set aside in the United States for reflecting, writing, and refining procedures, and for learning as much as possible about the country yet to be visited. In contrast, micro-longitudinal approaches to creativity research involve shorter, even rapid, intervals of data collection, but these also "take into account the dynamic and emergent nature of creative expression in classrooms" (Beghetto & Karwowski, 2019, p. 13).

In Shanahan et al.'s (2016) edited collection, one of the longitudinal approaches reported was an investigation of "familial generations." Parents and children within intergenerational structures attracted research interest, especially the parenting process. Longitudinal research can track the same people (considered a "cohort") and be strictly observational, neither of which characterized my qualitative design. The educators in my study were not the same inhabitants in each country and people unknown to me agreed to participate within the transnational locations. The glocal participants ranged from being mainly homogeneous in one educational setting to heterogeneous in the other two, with differences in race, ethnicity, culture, gender, age, language, institutional role and status, and educational discipline. While the research design required observation, it called for action relative to participatory engagement and leadership on the part of participating educators and me. The design I created was prospective and thus relied on the collection of new data, which is another feature of longitudinal studies (just like the retrospective design that depends on existing data). While additional elements distinguish longitudinal qualitative studies from other types of research, it should be mentioned that large numbers of participants are optional; in fact, there may only be a few (Shanahan et al., 2016). My 4-year study had a fairly large number ($N = 152$; $n = 34$ in China, $n = 80$ in Canada, and $n = 38$ in Australia), especially considering that data collection was time-intensive and activity-based in all three locations, and that interviews were accommodated in two of them.

Longitudinal glocal study, then, seems apt for describing the research I envisioned, designed, executed, interpreted, and narrated as case study. Time was a critically important element for completing these steps. Consideration was given to time at the outset, upon having decided to turn my study aspirations into Fulbright applications without knowing when decisions would be rendered. Sponsored scholarships eventually ensued in support of this project and its framing around creativity and accountability in education. For the applications, spaced years apart, I articulated the research project flexibly, seeking to pursue creativity-in-action that would be responsive to cultural differences. I also anchored this work in the 4-C creativity model, indicating that it had yet to be applied with educators who were navigating accountability dynamics in high-stakes standardized countries. It turned out that my creativity study covered a 4-year period (from 2015 to 2019) with physical travel to, and research within, three nations in the East and West. However, realities are that the project planning (and Fulbright application process) occurred well before the year 2015, and that this book took into 2020 to complete.

My rationale for choosing this research design (longitudinal glocal study) was to discover if educators (students, professors, and leaders) in different accountability cultures can discover creativity where encouraged in a global climate of educational constraint. Because China, Canada, and Australia were high-stakes testing nations that shape priorities for teaching and learning, it was unknown whether creativity was available or could be sparked locally in college spaces (e.g., classrooms) within such globally affected places. In select glocal sites in which creativity and accountability seemed incompatible as perspectives on, and approaches to, creative learning, I was allowed to intensively engage others within universities in China (2015), Canada (2017), and Australia (2019).

Before each visit to a country, I spent time researching global and national trends and my Fulbright institutions, as well as networking with the hosts and their teams. I also obtained feedback from creativity researchers that helped improve my study design and methodologies. Additionally, I interpreted the data collected from the glocalities and wrote the case studies, which benefitted from the astute reactions researchers generously provided. The study design, including procedures, materials, and activities, were all kept consistent to the extent possible, with variations occurring in response to cultural situations and demands, such as the need for dual language usage (English and Mandarin) on study materials in the Chinese educational setting, and in the verbal sharing of all printed documents, including activity instructions. Targeted data collection for this book was tied to participants' responses to my original 4-C creativity activities and interview protocol; beyond this, crucial sources of information were educational creativity theories and models, and accountability reforms, policies, and discourse. Through the various processes, developments, and steps described, creativity emerged, revealed and released within burdened cultures.

Readers may find it helpful to consult another source for an extended discussion of the steps, decisions, and critical incidents involved in this real-world international investigation that led up to the China research visit and view it in hindsight (see Mullen, 2020b). In that publication, I narrate more details relative to the first (China) phase of the longitudinal study in relation to my model Globally Active Learning (GAL), and the phases of initiation, engagement, implementation, and aftermath.

2.4 Creativity–Accountability–Culture Linkages

For this book, pursuing creative links between creativity and accountability necessitated a cultural lens. Like creativity, accountability morphs and takes on different meanings from one setting to the next. Participating educators' perspectives on creativity were culturally and contextually nestled. Thus, I strove to mine creativity's and accountability's connotations for cultural and contextual variations. A social justice take on accountability triggers systemic issues like inequity and the responsibility of higher education institutions to decolonize policies and structures and eliminate disparities (racial, social, etc.; e.g., Mullen, 2019b, 2020a).

Culture and creativity also share an intriguing relationship. Cultivating creativity has long been recognized as a sociocultural process involving psychological and cultural change (Tan, 2013). However, creativity in relation to culture is an emergent topic in creativity research, as is accountability within these domains. Of interest is creativity's role in invigorating glocal cultures, and in turn being transformed by culture. Devoted to creativity and culture, Glăveanu's (2016) far-reaching collection goes a step further not only by making this relationship the centerpiece of an entire work but also by engaging its complexities and underexplored tensions. His handbook is among the publications addressing the culture gap in creativity research, like Tan's, thereby legitimizing culture and creativity as an exciting multidisciplinary area of study.

New knowledge generation around creativity in high-stakes testing cultures in the West and the East was an aspiration for this project. China, Canada, and Australia—wherein my study was situated—are being profoundly shaped by cultural, political, and educational dynamics. These countries were counted among the world's 72 Programme for International Student Assessment (PISA) nations in 2018 (Australian Council for Educational Research, 2019). PISA is overseen by the Organization for Economic Co-operation and Development (OECD, 2019), a powerful economic body. The OECD's mission is to grow market economies through innovation, recommend policy, and measure nations' productivity. Its rankings based on comparative assessments spark governments' goals and policies, and it seems zeal to compete as a global leader in education (Harris & Jones, 2017; Tienken & Mullen, 2016; Zhao, 2012, 2014). PISA's accountability benchmark continues to have severe consequences for poorly performing testing cultures, despite the excessive time spent on tested subjects (Sjøberg, 2016).

PISA-testing nations' documented creativity deficit attracts global criticism, particularly for China (Zhao, 2014). Yet, at the micro level of public and private Chinese schooling, creativity has actually been witnessed and revealed (e.g., Mullen, 2017, 2018, 2019a, 2019b, 2019c). A promising outcome, I was eager to build on my discoveries with exploratory work in three nations, as detailed in the case study chapters. Creativity, innovation, and entrepreneurship, and even collaboration and critical thinking, exist on the periphery of many PISA-tested schools, despite these global competencies being needed in workforces (Tienken & Mullen, 2016; Zhao, 2012, 2014). High-stakes standardized tests have an incalculable effect on creativity and human growth, as well as educational and social equity, and workforce readiness and performance (Frick, 2013). Theoretically, constraints on creativity may be glaring among immigrant, refugee, Indigenous, and other vulnerable cultural ethnic groups subjected to policies of the dominant culture, so it's likely that much more monitoring is needed by researchers of inequities and exclusions (see, e.g., Mullen, 2020a; Narey, 2019).

Pervasive barriers to creative and innovative thought are increasingly evident in classrooms. The climate of education has been dramatically changing, with a conspicuous reduction in creative thought and performance within elementary, secondary, and postsecondary grades (Frick, 2013; Kim, 2011; Kim & Chae, 2019; Narey, 2019). Frick asserted, "Performance-oriented atmospheres created by high-stakes testing—a focus on student scores, rote memorization, and drills—can decrease students' intrinsic motivation and ability to think creatively" (p. 231). Testing regimes perpetuate colonizing dynamics, resulting in low achievement for vulnerable student populations and reduced life opportunities, as well as stark social equity gaps (McCarty, 2018; Mullen, 2019b, 2020a; Sjøberg, 2016; Tienken & Mullen, 2016; Zhao, 2014).

Obstacles to teacher and learner creativity have also been widely identified. To generate creative opportunities in the social interaction of teaching and learning, many educational researchers provide creativity frameworks and models for classroom application in the early years (e.g., Kim & Chae, 2019) and college years (e.g., Narey, 2019). Working resourcefully and creatively with difficult issues and non-negotiable constraints, educators are strongly urged to nurture their creative selves, extending to creativity goals, opportunities, engagement, expression, content, and assessment in the classroom (Beghetto, 2005, 2016, 2019; Beghetto & Corazza, 2019; Frick, 2013; Mullen, 2018, 2019c, 2019d; Schmidt & Charney, 2018). Solution-seeking interventionist dynamics from these and other creativity studies abound. They include self-reflective knowledge seeking, creative and holistic pedagogic approaches, authentic practices and assessments (e.g., demonstrations and performances), intrinsic motivation and learning goals, and barrier identification and personal change. Such democratic practices presume responsibility on the part of educational communities to rise to the occasion on behalf of excellence and equity. Accountability from this perspective relies on educators' creative adaptation despite duress (Mullen, 2019a) and everyday constraints (Beghetto, 2019).

2.5   Creative Intervention and Glocal Context

Anchoring my interventionist approach to creativity theory is longitudinal glocal study of education populations in China (2015), Canada (2017), and Australia (2019). Across the educational domains, information was collected within leading research universities located in populous mega-cities: Chongqing, Toronto, and Sydney, respectively (Chap. 4 contains details about creative methodology). These settings were sequentially "disrupted" in the process of revealing creativity over a 4-year period. The three locations are simultaneously localized and globalized in relation to accountability and cultural creativity dynamics (and trends).

Two U.S. Fulbright Scholarships and internal grants sponsored the China and Canada trips, and grant funding from my home institution endorsed the Australia trip, with generous support from all institutional hosts. These investigations depended on my capacity as researcher/pedagogue/facilitator/interviewer to effectively navigate the different systems before and during the onsite work. Often, I was called upon to persuasively describe my project and the fit of its educational activities with existing missions, programs, and courses. Two years after this process was initiated in 2013, all governing boards and concerned parties authorized my project with China; Canada and Australia were both negotiated and sponsored separately with new stakeholders. The boards and officials responsible for overseeing international visits from professors had interest in creativity as a topic and source of exploration, and thus my study.

Creativity that is construed as progressive and developmental throughout the human lifespan (e.g., Hammond, Skidmore, Wilcox-Herzog, & Kaufman, 2013) oriented my approach to the project as an opportunity for professional development. In the data collection sessions, strategies were triggered for potentially enriching educators' twenty-first-century understandings of global trends within their milieu. Seeking authentic responses, I devised methods to prompt thinking about creativity relative to the types (i.e., Mini-c, Little-c, Pro-C, and Big-C; Kaufman & Beghetto, 2009), with linkages to educational accountability. Classes, seminars, interviews, and conversations all facilitated thinking, interaction, and documentation in dynamic ways. Engagement was high by those who see themselves as activists and participate in movements.

Propelling the interventionist creative work was my adaptation of the 4-C typology in places neither exposed to creativity in the curriculum nor benefitting from knowledge of creativity. Methodological translation of this framework centered on a qualitative intervention that, while structured, was very open ended, thereby inviting ownership of the creative process as well as unexpected responses and countless possibilities. The creative intervention provoked understandings and applications of creativity tied to culture and context, time and space, within settings where global trends impact life at the micro level. In the urban sociocultural environments of Chongqing, Toronto, and Sydney, human actors' views of creativity and the 4-Cs were elicited. The idea was for participants to reflectively and spontaneously "story" creativity and accountability dynamics within their cultures. In this way and over time, my original method (i.e., a translation and practical application of the 4-C model) was piloted, implemented, and refined, albeit in an emergent form to this day. Eclectic, not replicable, approaches to data collection characterize the methods and results, owing to the need to creatively adapt from one site to the next.

2.6   Summary

This chapter introduced the longitudinal glocal study with respect to 4-C project purposes, and the creative intervention and transnational context. Also, unique elements comprising the pedagogic research were briefly discussed. Hopefully, the creative pedagogic research and results will spark insights, methods, and discoveries so that creativity scholars and practitioners can engage anew or more fully in the creative process. Readers are invited to find something stimulating to ponder and try. Chapter 3 is where creativity frameworks are described, along with definitional descriptions, theories, and the 4-Cs.

References

Australian Council for Educational Research (ACER). (2019). *PISA*. Retrieved from https://www.acer.org/ozpisa

Beghetto, R. A. (2005). Does assessment kill student creativity? *The Educational Forum, 69*(3), 254–263.

Beghetto, R. A. (2016). Creative openings in the social interactions of teaching. *Creativity: Theories–research–applications, 3*(2), 261–273.

Beghetto, R. A. (2019). Structured uncertainty: How creativity thrives under constraints and uncertainty. In C. A. Mullen (Ed.), *Creativity under duress in education? Resistive theories, practices, and actions* (pp. 27–40). Cham, Switzerland: Springer.

Beghetto, R. A., & Corazza, G. E. (Eds.). (2019). *Dynamic perspectives on creativity: New directions for theory, research, and practice in education* (pp. 137–164). Cham, Switzerland: Springer.

Beghetto, R. A., & Karwowski, M. (2019). Unfreezing creativity: A dynamic micro-longitudinal approach. In R. A. Beghetto & G. E. Corazza (Eds.), *Dynamic perspectives on creativity: New directions for theory, research, and practice in education* (pp. 7–25). Cham, Switzerland: Springer.

Beghetto, R. A., & Kaufman, J. C. (2013). Fundamentals of creativity. *Educational Leadership*. Retrieved from http://www.ascd.org/publications/educational-leadership/feb13/vol70/num05/Fundamentals-of-Creativity.aspx

Beghetto, R. A., & Sriraman, B. (2017). *Creative contradictions in education: Cross disciplinary paradoxes and perspectives*. Cham, Switzerland: Springer.

Corazza, G. E. (2016). Potential originality and effectiveness: The dynamic definition of creativity. *Creativity Research Journal, 28*(3), 258–267.

Frick, B. (2013). Fostering student creativity in the era of high-stakes testing. In J. Hattie & E. M. Anderman (Eds.), *International guide to student achievement* (pp. 231–233). New York, NY: Routledge.

Glăveanu, V. P. (Ed.). (2016). *The Palgrave handbook of creativity and culture research*. London, UK: Palgrave Macmillan.

Hammond, H. L., Skidmore, L. E., Wilcox-Herzog, A., & Kaufman, J. C. (2013). Creativity and creativity programs. In J. Hattie & E. M. Anderman (Eds.), *International guide to student achievement* (pp. 292–295). New York, NY: Routledge.

Harris, A., & Jones, M. (2017). Leading educational change and improvement at scale: Some inconvenient truths about system performance. *International Journal of Leadership in Education, 20*(5), 632–641.

Karwowski, M., Han, M.-H., & Beghetto, R. A. (2019). Toward dynamizing the measurement of creative confidence beliefs. *Psychology of Aesthetics, Creativity, and the Arts, 13*(2), 193–202.

Kaufman, J. C., & Beghetto, R. A. (2009). Beyond big and little: The Four C Model of Creativity. *Review of General Psychology, 13*(1), 1–12.

Kaufman, J. C., & Beghetto, R. A. (2013). Do people recognize the Four Cs? Examining layperson conceptions of creativity. *Psychology of Aesthetics, Creativity, and the Arts, 7*, 229–236.

Kaufman, J. C., & Sternberg, R. J. (2019). *The Cambridge handbook of creativity* (2nd ed.). Cambridge, UK: Cambridge University Press.

Kim, K. H. (2011). The creativity crisis: The decrease in creative thinking scores on the Torrance tests of creative thinking. *Creativity Research Journal, 23*(4), 285–295.

Kim, K. H., & Chae, N. (2019). Recapturing American innovation through education: The creativity challenge for schools. In C. A. Mullen (Ed.), *Creativity under duress in education? Resistive theories, practices, and actions* (pp. 215–233). Cham, Switzerland: Springer.

McCarty, T. L. (2018). So that any child may succeed: Indigenous pathways toward justice and the promise of *Brown*. *Educational Researcher, 47*(5), 271–283.

Mullen, C. A. (2017). *Creativity and education in China: Paradox and possibilities for an era of accountability*. New York, NY: Routledge & Kappa Delta Pi.

Mullen, C. A. (2018). Creative learning: Paradox or possibility in China's restrictive preservice teacher classrooms? *Action in Teacher Education, 40*(2), 186–202.

Mullen, C. A. (Ed.). (2019a). *Creativity under duress in education? Resistive theories, practices, and actions.* Cham, Switzerland: Springer.

Mullen, C. A. (2019b). De/colonization: Perspectives on/by Indigenous populations in global Canadian contexts. *International Journal of Leadership in Education*, 1–20. https://doi.org/1 0.1080/13603124.2019.1631986

Mullen, C. A. (2019c). Dynamic creativity: Influential theory, public discourse, and generative possibility. In R. A. Beghetto & G. E. Corazza (Eds.), *Dynamic perspectives on creativity: New directions for theory, research, and practice in education* (pp. 137–164). Cham, Switzerland: Springer.

Mullen, C. A. (2019d). Global leadership: Competitiveness, tolerance, and creativity—a Canadian provincial example. *International Journal of Leadership in Education, 22*(5), 629–643.

Mullen, C. A. (2020a). *Canadian Indigenous literature and art: Decolonizing education, culture, and society.* Leiden, The Netherlands: Brill.

Mullen, C. A. (2020b). Mentoring in a globally active learning context: Initiation, engagement, implementation, and aftermath. In B. J. Irby, J. N. Boswell, L. J. Searby, F. Kochan, R. Garza, & N. Abdelrahman (Eds.), *The Wiley international handbook of mentoring* (pp. 115–135). Malden, MA: Wiley.

Narey, M. J. (2019). Who stands for what is right? Teachers' creative capacity and change agency in the struggle for educational quality. In C. A. Mullen (Ed.), *Creativity under duress in education? Resistive theories, practices, and actions* (pp. 313–337). Cham, Switzerland: Springer.

Organization for Economic Co-operation and Development (OECD). (2019). *About the OECD.* Retrieved from oecd.org/about

Schmidt, M., & Charney, M. (2018). Assessing creativity as a student learning outcome in theatre education. In S. Burgoyne (Ed.), *Creativity in theatre* (pp. 271–287). Cham, Switzerland: Springer.

Shanahan, M. J., Mortimer, J. T., & Johnson, M. K. (Eds.). (2016). *Handbook of the life course* (Vol. 2). Cham, Switzerland: Springer.

Sjøberg, S. (2016). OECD, PISA, and globalization: The influence of the international assessment regime. In C. H. Tienken & C. A. Mullen (Eds.), *Education policy perils: Tackling the tough issues* (pp. 102–133). New York, NY: Routledge & Kappa Delta Pi.

Tan, A.-G. (Ed.). (2013). *Creativity, talent, and excellence.* London, UK: Springer.

Tienken, C. H., & Mullen, C. A. (Eds.). (2016). *Education policy perils: Tackling the tough issues.* New York, NY: Routledge & Kappa Delta Pi.

Ward, T. B., & Kennedy, E. S. (2017). Creativity research: More studies, greater sophistication and the importance of "big" questions. *Journal of Creative Behavior, 51*(4), 285–288.

World Economic Forum. (2013). *The global competitiveness report: 2013–2014.* Geneva, Switzerland: Author. Retrieved from http://www3.weforum.org/docs/wef_globalcompetitive-nessreport_2013-14.pdf

Zhao, Y. (2012). *World class learners: Educating creative and entrepreneurial students.* Thousand Oaks, CA: Corwin.

Zhao, Y. (2014). *Who's afraid of the big bad dragon?* Thousand Oaks, CA: Jossey-Bass.

Part I
Framing the Longitudinal Glocal Study
as Creative Action

Chapter 3
Creativity Framed: Definitional Descriptions, Theories, and the 4-Cs

3.1 Introduction

The context-setting question for this chapter is, What definitions and theories advance knowledge, practice, and action that potentially allow creativity to be recovered and fostered under educational constraint? To quote Beghetto (2016), "As our understanding of the phenomenon of creativity continues to grow, it is becoming more and more evident that researchers need new ways of conceptualizing, identifying and studying creativity in the midst of social practices" (p. 270). In his body of work, he has theorized and demonstrated that "creativity can and does thrive under pressure, constraints, and other forms of uncertainty," including "accountability mandates" (see Beghetto, 2019, p. 27).

To Tan (2013), "interest" in promoting creativity is increasing in different nations. Confirming this, Cropley and Patston (2019) referred to a call for "a more creative education paradigm" (p. 267) from educational policy entities in Australia, Hong Kong, and elsewhere. Beghetto (2016), too, noting a global shift toward creative education, away from standardized testing and regimented pedagogy, asserted that it beckons "a timely reflective analysis on knowledge of creativity and cultivating creativity" (p. 27). Adding to this dialogue, I take readers on my journey to high-stakes testing cultures where such creativity ideals are difficult to realize.

To discover educational and cultural ways of seeing creativity while identifying political overtones, I engage in theory-building. *Accountability, creative economy, creativity, dynamic creativity, glocal(ity), Hidden-c, culture, social justice,* and the *Four C (4-C) Model of Creativity*—key concepts in this book—are defined. In this chapter, I advance the 4-C theory in preparation for my methodological, pedagogical, and contextual translations (Chap. 4) and case studies (Chaps. 5, 6, and 7). Hidden-c, introduced here, makes a unique contribution to the creativity literature. (Hidden-c, while mentioned in different places, is discussed in Chap. 8 relative to its embedded concepts of creative self-belief and action, and dynamic creativity.)

© Springer Nature Switzerland AG 2020
C. A. Mullen, *Revealing Creativity*, Creativity Theory and Action in Education 5, https://doi.org/10.1007/978-3-030-48165-0_3

Creativity and culture within educational settings constitute complex, changing domains of knowledge. Numerous definitions and multiple conceptualizations exist of the main ideas described in this writing (e.g., dynamic creativity). Academic creativity theories abound in the literature; in *Revealing Creativity*, the 4-C creativity theory is pivotal to both understanding and exploring creativity in education. Definitions of specialized terms are elaborated, with context and citations, and at the same time they are not intended to be comprehensive in that they are all shaped around the book's topic, purpose, and study. As conceived for this writing, each definition and theory is anchored to creativity that fosters seeing and experiencing creativity in dynamic ways within regulatory accountability-bound policy cultures. The descriptors that follow overlap to some extent, as do the examples; for the sake of clarification, I offer differentiations.

Literature review methods pertaining to the 4-C theory and its popularity immediately follow. Creative research methods used for the longitudinal glocal study are covered in Chap. 4. The individualized methodological approaches used in each nation are taken up in the cases. With contextual–cultural relevance, the three case study chapters recount creativity and its meanings, as well as it associated models and their paramount importance to the theory-building, decision-making, and action undertaken in the particular glocalized cultures.

3.2   Popularity of the 4-C Theory

Regarding its academic origins, the 4-C has its influence in a broad array of previous theories and perspectives discussed by the originators in various articles (Beghetto & Kaufman, 2007, 2014; Kaufman & Beghetto, 2009, 2014). In their 2019 publication, Kaufman and Beghetto (2009) proposed four creativity types/levels for their developmental 4-C Model. (For the 4-C differentiations, see section, "4-C Model of Creativity.")

Reviewing the creativity research that describes the 4-C typology (or select aspects)—citing one of Kaufman and Beghetto's (e.g., 2009, 2013) or Beghetto and Kaufman's (e.g., 2007) publications that explains this theory—I have tentatively settled on six criteria. These arose from evidence pointing to their salience:

1. *Reference point.* Creativity researchers worldwide describe this popular theory, using it as point of reference for contributing to the conversation about creativity within the field and future directions for exploration, particularly in educational sites for children, youth, and adults and across all grade levels, given its developmental emphasis (e.g., Celik & Lubart, 2016; Collard & Looney, 2014; Cropley & Patston, 2019; Glăveanu & Tanggaard, 2014; Hui, 2015; Mullen, 2017a, 2017b, 2018, 2019c; Neber & Neuhaus, 2013; Plucker, Guo, & Dilley, 2018; Stoeger, 2003; Zhou, Shen, Wang, Neber, & Johji, 2013; Zittoun & Gillespie, 2016).

2. *Cultural and cross-cultural.* Cultural and cross-cultural research are grounded within the 4-C framework/conception of creativity, allowing for cultural–contextual comparison, local or glocal in nature, relative to the complex role of culture in shaping creative thought and behavior within different cultures in the East and West (e.g., Celik & Lubart, 2016; Hui, 2015; Zhou et al., 2013).

3. *Knowledge-building.* A popular theory, the 4-C typology advances knowledge-building and theorizing about creativity. Paying tribute to Mini-c and Little-c for promoting everyday creativity within learning spaces (e.g., classrooms) allows creators to express themselves creatively, make discoveries, and experience their creative development in ways that may foster continued creativity, even recognized contributions in the realm of Pro-C and, albeit rarely, Big-C (e.g., Doyle, 2019; Karwowski, 2016; Mullen, 2018; Noice & Noice, 2018; Schmidt & Charney, 2018; Stoeger, 2003; Zhou et al., 2013).

4. *Pedagogic application.* Application to pedagogical and learning contexts extends the recognized theory's influence and value in such areas as the nurturing of creativity within classrooms subjected to high-stakes testing and bereft of creative approaches; creative breakthrough in everyday and professional creativity are desirable pursuits within investigative contexts spanning local and global settings (e.g., Collard & Looney, 2014; Mullen, 2017a, b, 2018, 2019c).

5. *Impactful forces.* This recognized theory is central to the ongoing debate around complexities involved in the individual creator's (creative self) relationship to, and dynamic interplay with, impactful cultural and environmental forces (e.g., Glăveanu & Tanggaard, 2014; Mullen, 2019c).

6. *Disciplinary Crossovers.* Scholars from wide-ranging academic disciplines (e.g., theatre/ drama and other arts; business and business education; economics; educational leadership, teacher education, and other social science areas) utilize the 4-C theory from educational psychology for descriptive, exploratory, aesthetic, empirical, and/or appraisal purposes in the study of creativity (e.g., Berlin, Tavani, & Beasançon, 2016; Dawson, 2018, Neber & Neuhaus, 2013; Noice & Noice, 2018; Mullen, 2018, 2019c; Schmidt & Charney, 2018).

To clarify, this is an abbreviated list only of scholars matched with each of the six criteria. Numerous creativity researchers around the world have described, analyzed, or applied the 4-C theory, thereby validating it. (Many researchers also reference Kaufman and Beghetto's other conceptualizations of creativity, such as metacognitive creativity and creative self-beliefs.)

Based on my synthesis of publications in education, I discovered that the popularity of the 4-C theory was owing, in particular, to its utilization as a reference point in discourse on creativity. Varying and budding attention has been given to the other areas, with a clear need for much more pedagogic application, including in cultural and cross-cultural contexts. It is within these particular domains that I aim for my book to contribute to the vibrant conversation occurring around this framework, particularly involving knowledge-building in relation to pedagogic application cross culturally. Expressions from the creativity research community convey that the 4-C model is appreciated for offering a typology of creativity, emphasizing developmental and progressive creativity, and valuing everyday creativity that is personal and meaningful but unrecognized (Mini-c) or recognized but in an informal or limited way (e.g., by a student's teacher or peers; Little-c).

Thus, I give weighted attention to Kaufman and Beghetto's (2009) creativity theory, adding my own voice to disciplinary experts from various nations. Beyond the far-reaching acknowledgment of this model in the literature, I translate it into a creative method within three glocalized settings (see Chaps. 5, 6, and 7). In the methods chapter (Chap. 4), my description of methods pertaining to locating relevant literature is summarized (Table 4.1).

Tapping into the creative impact of the 4-C theory for its conceptualization of creativity and creative phenomena, I also benefitted from empirically grounding it through my application in glocal research sites. For example, Kaufman and Beghetto's (2013) preliminary testing of their 4-C model indicated that "people can recognize and differentiate levels of creativity" (p. 234). The 1364 college undergraduates they surveyed did, in fact, "perceive nuances in different levels of accomplishment," and even though Pro-C and Little-c merged in their responses, Big-C and Mini-c were "distinguishable" (p. 229). These researchers' statistical analysis of results indicated that the students were able "to recognize Mini-c as a distinct category of creativity" as well as "differences in the higher forms of creative expression (albeit in a somewhat less distinct way than as specified by the Four C model)." While "[this] model posits more fine-grained distinctions between Big-C, Pro-C, and Little-c" than was suggested by the students, who "view[ed] these categories at a larger grain size," "Pro-C and Little-c [proved] somewhat indistinguishable and [they strongly associated] Big-C and Pro/little-c creativity" (p. 233). The discovery—that college students could productively engage in sense-making around the 4-Cs—proved encouraging, inspiring me to see what I might learn from an international inquiry.

3.3 Definitions of Key Terms and Concepts

In the following section, major concepts—creative economy, creativity, dynamic creativity, Hidden-c, and culture—in this book constitute complex, changing domains of knowledge in academia. Each definition is elaborated with source substantiation and illustrations. My description of the 4-C Model of Creativity follows the definitional descriptions.

3.3.1 Accountability

Accountability in education means different things, including "answerability, blameworthiness, liability, and the expectation of account-giving" ("Accountability," 2020). Examples of accountability are educational policy reform, required content, standardized testing, test-centered curriculum, responsibility for balanced teaching, and calls to action to promote cultural change and social equity. Thus, creativity and accountability are not always at odds; the ideas may be mutually reinforcing, exist on a continuum, or have place-bound meaning.

Revealing Creativity focuses exclusively on meanings and manifestations of accountability as related to creativity in education. As a creativity restraint, accountability and its affect can vary widely, and it may be negative, positive, normative, or too ambiguous or complex to judge. Accountability takes such forms as high-stakes testing; accountability-bound policies and mandates; and parameters within programs, curricula, and activities.

3.3.2 Creative Economy

With widespread currency, *creative economy* pairs creativity with economies and globalization. This term recognizes creativity more explicitly than other favored usages for defining modern civilization, notably *knowledge economy* and *global economy*. These concepts as presented in policy documents and other public sources also acknowledge creativity, as in for aiding influential aspects of globalization, namely, global competitiveness, high-stakes accountability, national prosperity, and cultural tolerance (see, e.g., Mullen, 2019c, d). *Cultural economy* is another such term that deserves pause, especially as Australian researchers O'Connor and Gibson (n.d.) chose it over *creative economy* because the latter "reduces cultural value to economic value, and indeed defines this economic value rather narrowly around 'innovation effects' [whereas] cultural economy has an international currency, providing a strong base for comparison" (p. 6). However, this is the very problematical policy context that is being identified in my use of creative economy.

While there is no consensus, corporations and governments across nations increasingly use the term *creative economy* (e.g., World Economic Forum, 2013). The choice of *economy* for describing contemporary life on this planet and the coupling of it with *economy* in policy and public discourse suggest that a movement may be afoot to turn creativity into a tool that further politicizes and commodifies both the economy and human worth. Creativity—tied to labor markets and creative industries (e.g., arts)—conjures a picture of creativity's role of ensuring world economies' vigor, wealth, and value and capacity to compete in the global marketplace (Boily, Chapdelaine, Hartley, Kent, Suurkask, & Wong, 2014; Ibbitson, 2014; Johnson, 2010; O'Connor & Gibson, n.d.).

Globalization, a powerful world trend, significantly shapes creativity and its forms. Creative and innovative productivity apparently increases when residents live in bustling cities (like my research sites of Chongqing, Toronto, and Sydney) (Johnson, 2010). To illustrate, Canada has long broadcast that it's a "dominant force in today's world economy" (Boily et al., 2014, p. 1). The nation had a historic breakthrough in international testing in 2017 (BBC, 2017), which was preceded by the priority placed on economic success. Creativity was widely identified as the means to this end, "requir[ing] a shift in culture" favoring "tolerant and flexible environments" (p. 12). An assertion in this Canadian report (i.e., Boily et al.) is that "creative minds" must be "incubate[d]" so they "can thrive," with the demand for new jobs and, presumably, global-ready graduates.

Concerned with prosperity, Canadian policy "looks beyond traditional economic metrics to … the development of people's creative potential" (Boily et al., 2014, p. 2). Acknowledged is the intangible type of creativity whereby citizens collaborate on new ideas leading to the design of creative products, albeit to advance national wealth. Canada's "greatest resource" is "its people" is a refrain in many sources; accordingly, a strategy called for was the rewriting of innovation policies and "high-impact federal initiatives … in building a more competitive and creative Canada" (Boily et al., p. 1).

In the creativity era, have we truly come to embrace dynamic creativity? Within many globally competitive cultures, commercialization of creativity is apparent in economic policy that casts creativity as innovation (creative innovation) for capital-generating purposes (O'Connor & Gibson, n.d.). A related economic goal in the Canadian economy is to boost "creative industries" financially (Canadian Heritage, 2017). And, in such global cultures, teachers and learners reportedly suffer from testing circumstances and stifling pedagogies that promote a creative "brain drain" (Mullen, 2018, 2019d).

High-stakes accountability cultures neglect opportunities to exercise the imagination and creative capacity across elementary, secondary, and university levels (Mullen, 2017a, b, 2019a). Imitation and literal comprehension, competencies valued in the nineteenth century, cannot advance global education (World Economic Forum, 2013) or creative education. As Zhao (2014) attested, even the best schools are not usually working with the global competencies of creativity and entrepreneurship. As commonly stated in the educational literature, global-ready graduates are definitely underrepresented among postsecondary populations; unlike their peers, they possess creative capacities and creatively generate meaning, problem-solve, actively reflect, produce collaboratively, and work collectively (e.g., Narey, 2019; Tienken & Mullen, 2016; Zhao, 2012, 2014)

3.3.3   Creativity

A highly complex notion that attracts proliferating definitions, some creativity researchers think that *creativity* is too indescribable or mysterious to define (see Corazza, 2016). It involves a "mysterious process" by which people "come up with new ideas and new things," thereby "bring[ing] into existence something genuinely new that is valued enough to be added to the culture" (Csikszentmihalyi, 1996, pp. 6, 25). Educational philosopher Dewey (1934) wrote that art (also, aesthetic creativity), like the imagination, "accepts life and experience in all its uncertainty, mystery, doubt, and half knowledge" (p. 34).

Besides being recognized as mysterious, some creativity researchers define *creativity* as not a thing like a personal belonging or special attribute but rather a "distinction" attributed to "particular experiences, ideas, actions, and artifacts" (Beghetto, 2019). As such, creativity—when not summed up (or dismissed) as mysterious—likely has knowable dimensions when viewed as an "attribute" instead of an "entity" (Beghetto, 2019).

A Western perspective on *creativity* refers to something new that is tangible (e.g., a literary work) or intangible (e.g., a theory) and has two concepts or criteria: the action or product must be (1) unique or unusual and (2) valuable or useful (e.g., Corazza, 2016; Cropley & Cropley, 2010; Diedrich, Benedek, Jauk, & Neubauer, 2015; Hammond, Skidmore, Wilcox-Herzog, & Kaufman, 2013; Mumford, 2003). In fact, many researchers concur that creativity requires both originality/newness/ novelty and usefulness/meaningfulness/task appropriateness. These two elements occur within particular contexts; according to Helfand, Kaufman, and Beghetto (2016), an "interdependent relationship" exists among novelty, appropriateness, and context, thereby highlighting the role and value of context in shaping what is considered novel and useful. Importantly, creativity, as defined by Beghetto (2019) and other researchers upon whom he builds, "involves contextually defined originality and meeting task constraints" in classrooms or activities through which students find ways to balance their original ideas with the expectations of tasks (p. 28). Context and constraint, built into the bones of creativity, are not simply influences on creativity; rather, they serve as dual criteria for defining creativity.

Regarding the fundamental product aspect of creativity, process trumps product when it comes to children and their healthy creative development (e.g., Hammond et al., 2013, p. 293). Creative process is important for promoting young people's engagement in creative activities, which supports an "indirect approach" to "teaching creativity." (The direct approach, in contrast, supports the creation of products.) Teachers' "encouragement and feedback" and capacity for promoting pupils' "intrinsic motivation," and balancing this with "extrinsic motivation" as warranted, all matter. Numerous other elements of importance to student learning and achievement include environments in which children feel safe, have choices, and can make mistakes (Hammond et al., p. 293). Additionally, creativity is developmental, involving "exploration and imagination," "cognitive abilities," and "experience," all of "which are associated with overall academic achievement" in "language" and "cognition" (Hammond et al., p. 292).

Importantly, a point worthy of emphasis is that this definition of creativity is culturally rooted—it's a "prevalent Western concept" that American developmental psychologist Gardner (1991), among others, has pointed out. Creativity, like the arts, does not exist in a cultural vacuum. In his comparison of the West, particularly the United States, and China (arising from his research journeys to China and encounter with his own cultural bias and assumptions about creativity), Gardner painted a series of contrasts. To Western minds, creativity (and the arts) can be "best described as the human capacity regularly to solve problems or to fashion products in a domain in a way that is initially novel but ultimately acceptable in a culture"; elaborating, he stated, creative "achievements … radically alter our understanding of scientific phenomena or our conceptions of the personal or social world" (p. 14). Another element of his definition is that a "transformative" climate fosters creativity, unlike rigid routine.

China poses a challenge to these views wherein creative activity is likened to the "re-creation of traditional beautiful forms and the engendering of moral behavior" (p. 14). Learning to play musical instruments from a young age and with pose, dignity, and integrity is one such example (as explained in Chap. 4). Changes are recognized in China and have merit, but the Chinese worldview about creativity (and the arts) neither looks to novelty and the remarkable rethinking of something nor prizes "cognitive, problem-finding, world-remaking activities" (p. 14). Helping to explain these differences, Gardner noted that because China is an ancient country, Chinese sensibilities are "evolutionary," not dramatic, which can be expected from much younger countries.

Resonances from the literature bolster these observations about creativity from a cultural–historical perspective. Building on the creativity research of collaborators Niu and Sternberg (2001), Kaufman and Beghetto (2009) explained, "Eastern conceptions, much more than Westerners, value the characteristic of 'goodness,' including 'moral goodness,' 'contribution to the society,' as well as the 'connections between old and new knowledge'"; expectations according to "standard Chinese traditions," they added, are that exceptional human beings satisfy not only their own needs and interests but also those of others and society (p. 3).

Creativity, a strength that comes from within, involves making, building, or doing something. The power of imagination allows us to see in unconventional ways and find different ways to solve problems. Creative people make ordinary, unrelated things extraordinary; by conveying what they see, they enrich or transform their local contexts (Craft, 2002) or take their disciplines, professions, and even societies in a new direction (Csikszentmihalyi, 1996; Kaufman & Beghetto, 2009; Li & Gerstl-Pepin, 2014).

Not restricted to the individual level, creativity occurs at group and organizational levels (Mumford, 2012) and within systems (Csikszentmihalyi, 1996). Also, creativity's association is with creative collaboration and problem-solving performances; thus, it encompasses the collaborative process of arriving at creative (re) solutions to complex problems and performances, for example (Sawyer, 2012). In such group situations, the "collective social product" cannot be attributed to individual contributors, for it transcends any one person's effort (Sawyer, p. 67).

Creativity spans originality and regeneration in limitless forms. To Corazza (2016), however, "originality" and "effectiveness" are essential cornerstones to creativity. Creativity research offers the example of "reiniation," where creators try "to move the field to a new (as-yet-unreached) starting point and then progress from there" (Kaufman & Beghetto, 2009, p. 6). It follows that original work and transformation of thoughts or things into something not pre-existing is considered a dynamic creative process and achievement. Continually upheld, novel creation is the definitional quintessence and fundamental character of creativity (e.g., Bandura, 1997; Corazza).

Novelty, not left to the creator's judgment, depends on the view of experts (e.g., peer reviewer) and is time based, contextually determined, and culturally informed. Both originality and effectiveness are subjected to a group's requirements/criteria/assessments like those belonging to a field or discipline (Csikszentmihalyi, 1996). Corazza (2016) explained that while authenticity is a significant component of originality—meaning that the work was not pre-existing—effectiveness refers to the outcomes of creative processes (e.g., "transformation of knowledge," p. 261). Thus, experts' judgments in relationship to creators' work occur subjectively in particular circumstances and periods. Given these realities, effectiveness must be cast as a "pragmatist requirement for the definition of creativity" that "should scientifically account for the … subjectivity of judgment," itself dependent on time and context (Corazza, p. 260).

A foremost assumption in creativity theory, then, is that an idea's creativity is determined by its "novelty and usefulness" (Diedrich et al., 2015, p. 35; Corazza, 2016; Richards, 2007). In Diedrich et al.'s study that evaluated ideas, it makes sense that novelty had greater importance than usefulness for predicting creativity: "If an idea is not novel its usefulness does not matter much, but if an idea is novel its usefulness will additionally determine its actual creativity" (p. 35). A distinction has been made of first- and second-order criteria of creativity (novelty followed by utility) in a live setting.

From a different perspective, the re-creation or reinvention of that which exists is also creative and potentially dynamic and noteworthy. Contributions in this vein widely vary and include the replication and improvement of pre-existing products in the creative economy. For example, China's globally recognized capacity for improving upon products at a pace never before seen is judged to be creative and innovative (Woetzel & Towson, 2013). The Public Republic of China's (PRC) adaptability in its economy, a "real manifestation of Chinese brainpower," is "cost innovation": China has mastered the art of "making incremental improvements to existing products—and at making them cheaper" (Woetzel & Towson, 2013, p. 95; also Abrami, Kirby, & McFarlan, 2014). Cost innovation has created new foreign markets for the PRC, although the "made in China" label has mixed reviews around the world (Mullen, 2017a). While creativity (and innovation) has been universally recognized as a global competency, the capacity for imitation is insufficient for forwarding global education, according to many sources (e.g., Wagner, 2012; World Economic Forum, 2013; Zhao, 2012).

Throughout history and in different nations, originality and reproduction are subjected to debate when it comes to what creativity is (and is not). In support of including reproduction as creativity—an unpopular stance in the creativity canon of the West—US-based lecturer Gasca (2014) surmised, "Creative minds [have] embraced the idea that to be creative, you need not necessarily be original," among them French writer Voltaire, who wrote "originality is nothing but judicious imitation." Citing other philosopher–authors, Gasca asserted that it's a mistaken belief that creativity demands unique ideas when in actuality new ones often reiterate, improve, or simply clarify what already exists. Creative acts, he explained, include the synthesizing of ideas that seem disconnected or unrelated and looking at things in a fresh or unconventional way by breaking out of patterns. Thus, improving on an idea, making it easier to use or understand, or presenting an alternate perspective can also be considered creativity or innovation. Ferguson (2012) has gone so far as to claim that originality does not exist.

Arguably, creativity is more dimensional than just making something, seeing differently, and solving problems, for it extends to innovating and inventing, question-posing and meaning-making, and change and transformation. A snapshot of the creative person is someone who approaches problems flexibly and manages decision-making that is not already structured (Li & Gerstl-Pepin, 2014). While problem-solving is important, question-posing is more so, Eisner (2004) contended, so the creative person who pursues amorphous problems is asking open-ended questions. Such questions invoke creativity, and complex problem identification and problem-solving enhance it. Knowledge-building can also be creative (Tan, 2013), as can applying knowledge in practical pedagogic contexts (Beghetto, 2006) and thoughtfully appraising knowledge (Robinson, 2015). These approaches to creativity contrast with constraints. Pervasive examples of constraint are problems already posed (to students) through direct instruction and testing (Eisner, 2004) and autocratic leadership and leading that censor opportunities for independent, creative thought and action (Sawyer, 2012).

The value attributed by experts, policymakers, societies, and public institutions to tangible, concrete products of creativity has likely cast creativity's entanglements with innovation and invention. On the one hand, for thinkers like curriculum theorist Schwab (2004), *creativity* is interchangeable with *innovation* and *invention*: "Creativity implies some measure of invention" (p. 114). On the other hand, Hunter (2013) is among those who distinguish creativity from these other types: *Creativity* is the "capability/act of conceiving something original or unusual," *innovation* is the "implementation of something new," and *invention* is the "creation of something that has never been made before" (p. 9). An implication is that creativity has a lesser purpose and status, in effect only serving as a catalyst for innovations and inventions, which is consistent with the competitive and monetary values of a creative economy.

Alternatively, Tan (2013) described something other than a creativity–innovation–invention hierarchy. Conceived as a continuum relative to its dynamic role, creativity "includes actions and interactions that lead to human development, innovations, civilizations, inventions, breakthroughs, discoveries, revolutions, and evolutions" (p. 28). Specifically, creativity can be a discovery or adaptation: "*Breakthrough* creativity" involves the "search for new ideas," whereas "*adaptive* creativity is the result of responding creatively to breakthroughs [such as] to transform them for applications in everyday life" (p. 28; italics are in the original). Further, "discovery, invention, and innovation in varying degrees are related to creativity" (p. 28).

Perhaps having inspired such conceptualizations, Bandura (1997) affirmed creativity and its relationship to innovation: "Creativity constitutes one of the highest forms of human expression," subtly differentiating it from innovation while casting it as somehow integral to creativity. He asserted, "Innovativeness largely involves restructuring and synthesizing knowledge into new ways of thinking and of doing things," which importantly depends on "cognitive facility [in the exploration of] novel ideas and search for new knowledge" (p. 239).

To underscore the points raised about context in relation to creativity, an assertion is that not only is it important to understanding creativity but also that "context largely determines what is written, painted, sculpted, sung, or performed" (Byrne, 2012, p. 13). The explanation, according to this social scientist–musician, is that "conventional wisdom" dictates otherwise—"maintain[ing] that creation emerges out of some interior emotion"; while "passion" plays a role in creativity, "the form that one's work will take is predetermined and opportunistic," meaning that creators act upon opportunities that are available (p. 13).

3.3.4 Dynamic Creativity

To present a working definition of *dynamic creativity*, I turn to sources that resonate with my intended meanings: Corazza's (2016) notion of dynamic creativity as a phenomenon extending well beyond "static creative achievement" (p. 261) and Glăveanu and Tanggaard's (2014) description of creative identity as always changing, possibly regenerating. *Dynamic creativity*, then, is thought to have "inconclusive outcomes" for people engaging in, and persisting with, creativity. Like *creativity*, according to Corazza (2016),

> The fundamental element that should be at the core of the definition of [dynamic] creativity is … the search for potential originality and effectiveness, much before any attribution of creative achievement (or inconclusiveness) has materialized. This is extremely important both to reflect the overall experiential evidence of the phenomenon … and to effectively educate new innovators in their approach to the process. (p. 261)

Dynamic's etymology comes from ancient Greek to denote power/ful and able. Complex, dynamic interplays among individuals, systems, and cultures stimulate change or progress within a system ("Dynamic," 2020). Csikszentmihalyi's (1996) leading systems model of creativity seeks to explain micro (creative individual's psychology) and macro (social system) interrelationships. Hennessey (2017) thinks such "social and cultural influences" should be understood dynamically, given that creativity arises from "forces operating at multiple levels" (pp. 341–342); exploring creativity as a "system in action," then, allows for study of small and big cultures— classrooms and societies, respectively—as a dynamic system.

Conceived dynamically, creativity involves constant activity, change, or progress. Continuous creative activity or change within systems and cultures has been conceptualized as *dynamic creativity* (Mullen, 2019c). Adopting "a dynamic approach in creativity studies," explained Corazza (2019), allows for a "macroscopic" view of creativity processes as dynamic, open ended, and inconclusive— creativity as limited to an episode, time, place, product, creator, and so forth amounts to reductionism, for "[we cannot] foresee all the possible future implications of an innovative idea," pp. 300–301). Seen as a Dynamic Universal Creativity Process (as named by Corazza [2019]), creativity episodes from a "universal wide-sense view of creativity" (p. 299) are always changing. "A creativity episod[e] in the evolution of our cosmos" (Corazza, 2019, p. 297), creative identity, as conceived by Craft (1997), comes to mind as an example. From a wide angle, even creative identity would "transcend" its "agents" of personhood—the teacher self—within the "psycho-social" domain (Corazza, 2019, p. 297).

Dynamic creativity can come from disequilibrium of selves, systems, and cultures. Instability and uncertainty propel creativity in ways that are emergent, even chaotic—productive upheaval can be sparked by addressing weighty problems and challenges to preconceived ideas (Collard & Looney, 2014). "Signs of meta-creativity" as such arise from "questioning assumptions" and examining values (Runco, 2017, p. 311). When we scrutinize our assumptions and values, we potentially enact creativity at entirely new levels. Also intrinsic to the dynamic process of creativity and outcomes are "subjectivity and the imagination," which has incited disagreement among stakeholders (e.g., experts) where original outcomes question or violate norms and paradigms (Corazza, 2016, p. 262).

Quite possibly, stasis can block creative action and progress. For example, a student's original perspective or work may be discounted in the closely controlled classroom. If this situation should change and the unique contribution becomes recognized (by peers or teachers), creativity's "inconclusive and dynamic nature" is animated (Beghetto & Corazza, 2019, p. 1). Also connoting stasis are narrow definitions of creativity that "privilege" successful outcomes and productivity in the realm of creative achievement, in effect shortchanging a multitude of dynamics involved in creators' generative process (e.g., "search[ing] for original ideas" and "explor[ing] multiple alternatives"; Corazza, 2016, p. 261).

From this perspective, disruptions, complexities, and unknowns—integral to active engagement—should be credited as having creative value. A richer definition of creativity incorporates the word *potential* in the standard definition: "Creativity requires potential originality and effectiveness" (Corazza, 2016, p. 262). The inclusion of this one word arguably invokes a different perspective—creativity's dynamism depends on the development of hidden abilities or qualities that may lead to success or usefulness, and it involves uncertainty, indetermination, and risk-taking in the process.

In fact, "disequilibrium may spur creative processes"; consider the study finding that "learners (including teachers) were most likely to benefit from creative processes that addressed significant problems or … that challenged their previous conceptions" (Collard & Looney, 2014, p. 350). Systems like educational organizations that are stable, as in motionless yet paradoxically perpetuating tradition or the status quo ("Stasis," 2020), then, are not necessarily where human dynamics suitable to creativity best thrive.

Dynamic creativity depends on potentiality (Corazza, 2016) combined with an attitude of possibility (Craft, Cremin, Burnard, Dragovic, & Chappell, 2012). Craft has long described creativity as possibility thinking, driven by "what-if" formulations. She even forwarded possibility thinking as an evidence-based concept driving creativity. With everyone being capable of questioning and imagining, as children do through "self-initiated play" (Craft, McConnon, & Matthews, 2012), possibility thinking, like potentiality, could influence thinking within systems and effect change.

From the life science discipline, systems theorist Wheatley (1992) also asserted that a "what-if" mindset disrupts a "fix-it" mentality. To her, the possibility attitude is a catalyst for change and renewal of organizational systems. If possibility is conducive to change, as Ferdig and Ludema (2005) also contended, then it makes sense that generative possibility fuels dynamic creativity's existence. (See Mullen [2019c] for an elaboration on these forces.)

With reference to dynamic creativity in Canada, creative dynamics are involved in its world standing. In a state of flux, just 3 years after much self-blaming as a tolerant–globally uncompetitive nation, in 2017 its global education status dramatically changed. Canada was ranked in the top on the Programme for International Student Assessment tests for math, science, and reading (BBC, 2017).

Racial tolerance remains a quintessential aspect of Canada's national identity. Accepting more immigrants than other nations, its national parties have even competed for recognition as "more pro-immigrant" than any other party (Ibbitson, 2014). In current times, Canada accepts droves of migrants and refugees despite backlash from Canadian anti-immigrationists whose intolerance is largely attributed to US President Trump's depictions of "outsiders as a frightening threat" (Ball, 2016). Beyond Canada's overall diversity mindset, the positive impact of immigrants on economic growth apparently helps explain the general receptivity to outsiders (Ibbitson).

Canada constantly re-creates itself, striving to turn problems like colonization of Canadian Indigenous peoples into solutions while, paradoxically, evidencing greater cultural inclusion of immigrants and refugees (Mullen, 2020). Creative products arising from its culturally diverse identity include less tangible creativity through "restorative" (rather than "punitive") justice. For example, "innovative expression in memorials" honors Aboriginal assertion of identity and activism (pp. 1–2). Besides these memorials, tangible creative production extends to "sustainable communities" that "address critical housing inadequacies … based on legacy Intuit knowledge of changing climate and respect for the unique traditions of community" (pp. 1–2).

Stasis also characterizes the dynamic Canadian context. Colonization of Indigenous populations is still rampant across educational, medical, social, and political domains. Negative stereotypes of tribes and Aboriginal knowledges in official educational policy, extending to classroom curricula, serve as a quick but convoluted example of dominating/subjugating relations. Such dynamics ensure the continuation of racial bigotry and a White/Indigenous binary paradigm of race. The pushback of tribal nations and teacher educators among other faculty in Canada is changing conditions in specific contexts through racial consciousness and tribally inclusive policy and curricula (Mullen, 2020). Given the pervasiveness of de/colonial tensions, the (re)making of cultural creative identity in Canada vividly illustrates dynamic creativity on a historic and modern scale (Glăveanu & Tanggaard, 2014; Mullen, 2019b).

3.3.5   Glocal(ity)

Places can be simultaneously local and global. "Local and global interconnectedness" (Espinoza-Gonzalez et al., 2014, p. 57; Mullen, 2019b) is the essence of what makes something glocal. I add *glocality* as an identifier of glocalized phenomena, as in globally specific locations.

Permeating the glocal study contexts in this book is the pervasive high-stakes testing ethos and global pressure on schools to competitively perform according to quantifiable metrics considered by many researchers to be narrow and biased in favor of some content areas at the expense of others (see Mullen, 2019d). The curricular exclusion of creativity and the arts, and repression of creative and artistic expression within learning environments, is felt worldwide; alternatively, creative expression can be enacted in less than ideal circumstances when intentionally orchestrated, despite constraints and uncertainties, through curricular "creative openings" in pedagogic contexts (Beghetto, 2016, 2019). Glocalized cultural contexts vary tremendously from one nation to another; for, complexities and nuances are associated with educational creativity and accountability phenomena. As such, glocal systems are influenced by accountability and economic trends. Standardized testing and educational policies and practices that include high-stakes accountability tests have been widely criticized for colonizing underrepresented groups at a sociocultural disadvantage and for homogenizing difference, thereby invalidating cultural distinctions (Mullen, 2019b, c, 2020; Narey, 2019; Robinson, 2015; Zhao, 2012, 2014).

"Doing" creativity in glocalities wherein local and global worlds intersect expands Dewey's (1934) criterion of authenticity in creative engagement. For Dewey, creativity (or art) is authentic when experienced in the system in which it is created and when produced thoughtfully and by the imagination from which it stems. A contribution the glocal concept makes to creativity research is system as local–global and the perspectives of creators on creativity and world issues. At one end of the glocal continuum, Craft (2002) is among those who realize the importance and weight of locality in the transformation of things, contexts, and humans. Along this continuum, the micro-longitudinal context is also attributed value in the creativity research—Beghetto and Karwowski (2019) describe it as a methodological approach that involves "taking multiple measurements of the phenomena of interest over a small period of time" at "rapid intervals" (e.g., minutes; pp. 13–14). As explained, it allows for study of dynamic, ephemeral phenomena, such as "creative confidence beliefs" (p. 7), and it differs from classic longitudinal designs.

Contrasting with the micro-longitudinal concept, my context and approach can be aptly described as glocal. Glocality as a common denominator enabled study of dynamic creativity within three accountability-bound transnational settings over a 4-year period. During that time, using eclectic qualitative strategies, creativity was guided, observed, and enacted in minutes, hours, and days and framed as an intentional encounter through classes, sessions, and interviews.

3.3.6 Hidden-c

A fifth C, *Hidden-c* refers to the personal power of creativity emanating from belief in one's creative capacity, and it is closely associated with established theory in the creativity literature. As emergent term of mine introduced elsewhere (Mullen, 2018, 2019c), Hidden-c is expanded upon and unpacked relative to the case studies; also, it's an implication of the present research.

3.3.7 Culture

Culture and creativity are inextricably linked. "Culture shapes creativity"—ideas of creativity are distinct from one culture to the next; individuals' creativity preferences differ, especially "from individualist and collectivist cultures"; and accuracy of creativity assessments depends on their being "culturally appropriate" (Shao, Zhang, Zhou, Gu, & Yuan, 2019; also, Hondzel & Gulliksen, 2015; Kaufman & Beghetto, 2009; Niu & Sternberg, 2001). Definitions of creativity are therefore influenced by culture and its conceptualization: "Western, individualistic social framework tend to place emphasis on creative products and use novelty and appropriateness as criteria for judging creative work" whereas "Eastern cultures, which tend toward collectivism, often value creativity as an aspect of personal fulfillment, with guidance and reverence for authority and traditions" (Hondzel & Gulliksen, 2015, p. 2); additionally, "usefulness seems more important than novelty in the East" (Shao et al., 2019). My research method necessitated making connections between creativity and culture. To explore creativity, I culturally translated the 4-C model (from Kaufman & Beghetto, 2009) as a strategy for eliciting postsecondary educators' perspectives on creativity in relation to accountability within three transnational settings.

The tendency to overgeneralize cultural differences between China and America's social behavior, and reduce culture to logical explanations (based on psychological constructs and variables like beliefs) for the sake of transparency, has long been cautioned by Bond. His cross-cultural theorizing and scientific research in psychology demonstrate specificity of thought and analysis, and how to unpack differences at the cultural level while continuing to build on theory. An exemplar can be found in Bond's discussion around psychological constructs (e.g., "self-esteem") in which he framed specific questions and performed research analyses aimed at discerning cultural differentiation without robbing culture of its "nimbus" qualities or "*magnum mysterium*" (i.e., "great mystery") (see Bond & van de Vijver, 2011).

Seen as an "ecosystem," culture encompasses nations' social and political life and economy, with complex webbings involving art and creativity, and "identity, tradition, ritual, and social bonding, etc." (O'Connor & Gibson, n.d., p. 27) Emotion should not be left out of this conceptualization in that culture has also been understood as a "repository of emotional knowledge" (p. 3)—Sundararajan (2015) utilized this definition of emotion, translating it into a research method for theorizing emotion (like intimacy) as nuance within Chinese collectivist cultures and as connected to Confucius for whom the development of emotion was considered the aim of education fulfilled by poetry.

Influential creative works come from radically different cultures and worldviews (e.g., Kaufman & Beghetto, 2009; Sundararajan, 2015), supporting the claim that dynamic creativity occurs within dissimilar sociopolitical systems, while likely amenable to liberal democracies. To have cultural impact, from a Western perspective, a creative idea must be affirmed by experts and "included in the cultural domain to which it belongs" (Csikszentmihalyi, 1996, p. 27; Corazza, 2016).

Another idea of culture from the creativity discipline is the bias of global cultures toward "eminent creativity" (Kaufman & Beghetto, 2009, p. 1), favoring cultural icons (broadly speaking, celebrated innovations and inventions, and famous people and places). This lopsided view may help to explain why the "quality of creative products in schools" does not attract much attention. Consequently, because these lack "clear reference standards," creativity goes without a common definition in education policy and curricula (Collard & Looney, 2014, pp. 3, 351).

Within testing cultures creativity is a challenge to foster, as these have been characterized as stymied environments or life systems (Zhao, 2014). Creative expression and innovation in such uniform curricular contexts, spanning the West and the East, is a struggle to both cultivate and guide. A pedagogic problem is "teachers' desire to avoid discouraging learners' self-expression," thereby giving "little guidance"; consequently, "neither teachers nor learners are encouraged to develop their own sense of what counts as high-quality creative work" (Collard & Looney, 2014, p. 351).

To illustrate pertinent cultural ideas with reference to China's testing milieu, teachers are expected to help students achieve high scores on tests and socialize them to unquestioningly respect authority (Lee & Pang, 2011. This is considered highly exploitive of the universal respect for authority presumed in the culture. Zhao (2014) has also explained that low scores on entrance exams limit future possibilities for Chinese citizens, with severe consequences being poor quality of life and even suicide owing to a strong feeling of cultural shame. China's global competitive mindset dominates, undermining such collectivist strengths as social belonging and familial kinship (Staats, 2011; Zhao, 2014).

Paradoxically, while China's labor markets control education systems and hinder creativity (Staats, 2011), the nation accredits the collective with being creative (Sternberg, 2006). The collectivist tradition should make it amenable to collaborative expressions of creativity and cooperative groupings in educational institutions, but another constraint is that classes are typically large and teacher centered (Starr, 2010).

In mainstream China, owing to cultural constraints, it's difficult to teach a twenty-first-century curriculum that advances global competencies. Classroom pedagogies must align with rote-based testing goals even though the World Economic Forum (2013) identifies creativity and entrepreneurship as proficiencies needed for global literacy. However, generative possibilities exist within this test-centric environment where Chinese students—presumed to lack creativity (Li & Gerstl-Pepin, 2014)—have opportunities to experience creative interventions. In one such case, 34 Chinese education undergraduates produced dynamic cultural work in direct response to Kaufman and Beghetto's (2009) 4-C creativity typology (Mullen, 2017a; also, see Chap. 5 herein). Explicit instructions, cooperative groups, and a collectivist orientation all supported the creative learning.

Chinese students' reduced creativity more generally likely reflects not their human capacity but their culture, learning environment, or teacher pedagogy. In Niu and Sternberg's (2001) study, evaluators rated the creativity of Chinese and American college students, finding the American artwork more creative and aesthetic. Negative influences in China are the learning environment's task constraints and teacher absence of directives to be creative. Similarly, Niu, Zhang, and Yang (2007) attributed performance-based differences between college students in the United States and Hong Kong to cultural influences. (Americans proved stronger in creative thinking on creative writing and problem-solving tasks involving insight.) Such study results challenge the racist stereotype that Asians are not creative (based on perceived talents, etc.).

Unfortunately, a prevailing belief is that Chinese learners are uncreative, even robotized (Mullen, 2019c). China's government believes its citizens lack creativity and are incapable of flexible and divergent thinking, critical thinking, and higher order thinking. The global news and even published research perpetuate this stereotype. All such influences probably interfere with creative behavior and expression. In China, students take direction from teachers whose signals are from authorities, all carriers of the regime. Given its millions of followers, Confucianism has likely reinforced allegiance to the nation's government. Chinese students have had to become very good at tested subjects, sacrificing development in open-ended problem-solving. However, despite the generalization that this population is creativity-poor and math-smart, creative expression and innovation do exist not only in China's entrepreneurial sector (e.g., Woetzel & Towson, 2013) but also in its educational sector (e.g., Mullen, 2017a, b, 2018a, 2019c).

3.3.8 Social Justice

Seeking to make the world a better, more inclusive and equitable place, a social justice view of creativity, and creative capacities in particular, is that it has the power to change the environments that influence it (e.g., Charmaz, Thornberg, & Keane, 2018; Mullen, 2020; Narey, 2019). Creativity is conceptualized as a social justice construct in this volume, casting it in the role of helping to imagine, and act on, the world as it should and could be (Charmaz et al.). Further, I describe *tribal justice* and *climate justice* and explain them in relation to theories, events, and creative actions within the Australian context (Chap. 7).

Operationalizing social justice tenets, to the extent possible, I make transparent assumptions, beliefs, and interpretations in my creativity discourse. The creative tensions taken up in *Revealing Creativity* exploit the binary of creativity and accountability, such as justice and injustice, freedom and inhibition, opportunity and threat, possibility and impossibility, equality and inequality, and power and powerlessness. Even disclosure and concealment emerged as a creative dynamic in the storylines narrated. The assumption that creativity is automatically just and accountability unjust is a simple binary that does not hold up at all times, which forces attention on context, complexity, nuance, and ambiguity. Ideological differences inherent in Western and Eastern worldviews are included as appropriate.

Theorists acknowledge that no consensus exists around the meaning of social justice, including in education (e.g., Bogotch & Shields, 2014). Described as a broad construct, social justice encompasses macro-level (in)justices and actual or material inequities that produce suffering for groups whose rights have been violated or not upheld, and whose education, life, and history are colonized (Fredericks, Maynor, White, English, & Ehrich, 2014; Mullen, 2020).

Indigenous scholars, like Tuck and Yang (2012), who debate the use of social justice theory to advance tribal equity, similarly describe social justice. Social justice has been viewed as a "generic term for struggle against oppressive conditions and outcomes" and "a philanthropic process of 'helping' the at-risk and alleviating suffering" (Tuck & Yang, p. 21). The focus on oppression and the oppressed owing to systemic injustices, despite social agreements/contracts, possibly points to an overlap in social justice and tribal justice theories. Social injustices toward Aboriginal people, worldwide, are identified in the literature and public discourse. Examples include dispossession and gaps in wealth and governmental policies, and an education that reduces them to poverty without their cultures, homes, languages, and sometimes their own children (e.g., Fredericks et al., 2014; Tuck & Yang). At times, Indigenous-produced creativity in literature and art thrives in the midst of tumultuous constraints (Mullen, 2020).

In the qualitative interpretationist tradition of Charmaz et al. (2018), I reflect the view that creativity research can provide a window onto socio-political conditions. Case study examples are the role of hierarchy, family, culture, and heritage in students' (inter)subjective understandings and treatments of creativity, and implicit racism in the law and national identity.

3.3.9 Four C Creativity Model

As previously stated, an influential academic theory that quintessentially informs dynamic perspectives on creativity is the Four C Model of Creativity (Beghetto, 2019; Beghetto & Kaufman, 2007). Kaufman and Beghetto's (2009) typology includes the Mini-c and Pro-C categories they developed. They added Pro-C to their 2007 model, reintroducing it in 2009 as the 4-Cs of creativity. The 4-C framework differentiates creativity as

- inherent in personal meaning-making and learning (Mini-c)

- recognition of a creator's Mini-c idea or creation (Little-c)
- professional expertise in an area of creativity that has value to a community (Pro-C)
- eminent creativity reserved for greatness (Big-C)

Owing to their importance in this book, each of the 4-Cs is next described.

3.3.9.1 Mini-C

Mini-c involves novel and personally meaningful experiences of creativity. Creative ideas and insights that are subjectively judged as "new and meaningful (i.e., creative)" by the creator is the determining factor, not what others may (or may not) see or think (Beghetto, 2019, p. 29). Some Mini-c experiences can grow in "creative magnitude" (Beghetto, 2019) and become Little-c and quite possibly Pro-C, even Big-C (Kaufman & Beghetto, 2009). It has been said that "some of the outcomes of imagining are microgenetic: they affect how a situation keeps unfolding leading to everyday creativity with a 'mini-c'" (Zittoun & Gillespie, 2016, p. 234; Mullen, 2018). Eisner (2004), too, described meaning-making itself an aesthetic process; private and elusive, it's often overlooked. Creative beings do not just *have* experiences—we make sense of them. Creative development can be dynamic and transformative: A situation becomes Mini-c, which progresses to Little-c, and Little-c manifests as Pro-C, and Pro-C develops into Big-C (4-C model).

Conveying our creative discoveries, we may creatively render these using images, schemas, and more, and as art/ifacts, performances, and so forth. Artists have long "convey[ed] their visions in new technologies such as cinema [and] virtual realities," wrote Gardner (2011, p. 65), endorsing digital self-expression as generative. Creativity also lives in the social sciences.

3.3.9.2 Little-C

Little-c is recognition of Mini-c in a social context, such as school or work. For example, when a student's original take on an event or history project is acknowledged by a teacher, peer, or someone else, creative confidence can benefit. The Little-c creator who creatively used physical or digital objects and tools without much thought about personal artistry is now attuned to creativity at a different level. When a teacher or another acknowledges the originality and usefulness of a creator's idea or solution for resolving a problem, creativity is given value beyond the self. Teachers (and influential others) who provide opportunities for expressing Mini-c's latent potential facilitate Little-c, theoretically planting seeds for Pro-C and Big-C (Beghetto, 2019; Mullen, 2018). Feedback in some form is key, then, to the transition from one type of creativity to the next (Beghetto, 2019).

Humans constantly encounter problems, and being recognized for identifying or solving a problem or seeing an existing problem differently imbue Little-c, although

Little-c is not restricted to problems and problem contexts. It may arise from help-ing others with something or conveying a new way of thinking for which one's creativity is appreciated (Beghetto, 2019).

In everyday problem-solving, creativity has endless possibilities—even the word *problem* is multifaceted. When we puzzle over something, we are trying to solve a problem. And when we make inferences and decisions and arrive at a solution or judgment, we might very well be creatively problem-solving. Many of us simply react to problems rather than anticipating them, which arguably takes greater cre-ative capacity. A creative person might ask, what does *problem* mean in this con-text? What is the nature of this problem that I am *anticipating*? (Schwab, 2004). Sophisticated dialogue can set in motion a smaller c becoming a bigger C.

3.3.9.3   Pro-C

A professional's creativity or creative contribution is Pro-C if it is recognized by the community (e.g., academic discipline, field, profession) for its value. Creative con-tributions of merit/worth, distinguished creative achievements, and highly accom-plished creativity all make the cut. Theory and/or practice can be enriched, modified, or even changed prominently by the creative contribution. Doyle (2019) defines Pro-C, based on her reading of Kaufman and Beghetto's 2009 schema, as "not domain changing, but adding to the domain within its current structures," such as an experiment that clarifies another's innovation (pp. 43–44). If it can be said that Pro-C is associated with pre-existing parameters, accomplishments of professional cre-ativity can vary widely, from replication or improvement of pre-existing products to "reiniation," where creators try "to move the field to a new (as-yet-unreached) start-ing point and then progress from there (e.g., Lavoisier inventing a radical, new type of chemistry"; Kaufman & Beghetto, 2009, p. 6).

Likely, creative professionals who study unsystematic, difficult problems beat others to them by not sticking with problems already evident in the domain. Schwab's (2004) take is that the "eye" of creative (e.g., Pro-C) individuals is illumi-nated "by possible fresh solutions to problems, new modes of attack, and new rec-ognitions of degrees of freedom for change [to occur]"; they don't miss the "novel features of new problems" (pp. 114–115). Attraction to novelty and originality may lead to creative breakthroughs that have influence beyond one's reach. Pro-C cre-ative risk-takers use, disrupt, or remake structures of knowledge—described by Csikszentmihalyi (1996) as the rules and procedures (symbolic knowledge) of a field or domain.

3.3.9.4   Big-C

Creativity of great magnitude on the scale of famous achievements that transform cultures or societies is Big-C. Eminent creativity can even change the world. The imagination once again plays a central role. Zittoun and Gillespie (2016) use humankind's story of the moon to illustrate Big-C and how it transpired through progressive creativity, owing to "a continuation of imagination" manifesting creative "or social innovation." The "imagination can have sociogenetic outcomes," as in when people dreamed of "flying to the moon," which sparked others' imaginations, thereby turning the imagination into "a social project"; from that point, the goal was attainable, profoundly changing society (p. 234). The Big-C invention transpired through the vision of the moon landing and Apollo program's enabling of human spaceflight. Big-C, like Pro-C, is not restricted to an accomplished person—it can be a many peopled space, even though someone (e.g., astronaut) or something (e.g., NASA) may become "the face."

Big-C artwork, as another example, comes from Mini-c, Little-c, and Pro-C, yet the humanity it embodies can be lost. According to Dewey (1934), Big-C art can be "isolated from the human conditions under which it was brought into being and from the human consequences it engenders in actual life-experience" (p. 3). Aesthetic creativity and value emerge from daily life, experience, and emotion, and art is connected to everyday life through human nature and the environment. Daily conditions and influences (e.g., activities) that imaginatively inform aspects of life should count as part of the cultural treasury—such storylines are intrinsic to the aesthetics of art-making and art of doing. Enlivening creativity to the point of achieving classic status can, ironically, lose touch with the very personal and social creativities that gave rise to it.

In fact, researchers building on the 4-C theory acknowledge that while "extraordinary accomplishments" (in science, art, technology, etc.) are remarkable, Big-C breakthroughs originate in smaller acts of creativity. Eminent creativity has traces in "myriads of Little-c creativity accomplishments;" notably, "numerous creative learning decisions" are involved as we set goals, deal with obstacles, and become more efficient with learning (Stoeger, 2003, p. 3).

A study of "Big-C" music composers (Mozart, Beethoven, and Liszt) by economist Borowiecki (2017) brings these ideas to life. It was found that major events (e.g., achievement and illness) affected their emotions (e.g., sadness) and activity levels. Text analyses of 1400 letters they wrote suggested that these "giants" are similarly affected by life's challenges as other people and that they proved no less human (and probably that much more relatable).

Cryptanalyst Alan Turing, a Big-C British contributor to science for having cracked the German Enigma code with his team in WWII—whom U.S. President Barack Obama singled out as a revolutionary genius—sparked the computer age. He invented an electromagnetic machine (the modern computer) and generated the idea of artificial intelligence. Biographer Hodges (2014) animated what I see as Mini-c being revealed in such ways as Turing's creative capacity for quickly solving crossword puzzles. Recognition of Mini-c (Little-c) came when he was hired for his puzzle-solving expertise and mathematical prowess; also, he was granted permission to assemble a talented team, designing a challenging puzzle for candidates to solve. Pro-C evolved out of his theorizing about the capacity of machines to think and perform by solving problems; in 1936, his article on "computable numbers" became the foundation of computer science. Persecuted for his scientific ideas and morality, he persevered in the face of adversity and saved many lives during the war (ironically ending his own life after years of clashing with the state).

3.3.9.5 Discussion of the 4-Cs

Kaufman and Beghetto's (2009) Western theory of creativity has been extensively described by educational psychology researchers and others. Over time, this pattern has solidified the value, influence, and modern currency of the 4-C creativity model (as explained in the "Literature Review Methods" section). Their four creativity types and overarching framework offer a unique take on the creativity of the individual(s) and influences from the milieu. To Kaufman and Beghetto, external forces are indeed highly influential on a person's creativity and potential impact, as indicative in the scholarly dialogue they bring to the table along with other creativity experts. Corazza (2016) describes particularly well the dependency on judgment processes and judges themselves of creative accomplishment being credited.

As stated, breakthroughs spring from generativity's seeds (i.e., Mini-c and Little-c), directing theoretical and investigatory attention to modest forms of creativity. In fact, an impetus behind the 4-Cs is to raise awareness of creativity that's *not* about Big-C breakthroughs but rather daily occurrences. Everyday creativity (also identified as Mini-c, Little-c, and personal creativity) is widely recognized across disciplines as a vital and influential creative source. When the everyday world unfolds as a dynamic place–space of creativity, growth (of students and others) is cultivated, creative practice is explored and assessed, and glocalities are creatively enlivened (Craft, 2002; Dewey, 1934; Mullen, 2017a, 2018; Richards, 2007; Schmidt & Charney, 2018; Reilly, Lilly, Bramwell, & Kronis, 2011; Stoeger, 2003). Western researchers commonly associate everyday creativity with problems that are met with novel and useful solutions.

Inquiring into everyday creativity, Reilly et al. (2011) researched teaching in 12 Canadian elementary, secondary, and university classrooms. Commonplace teacher creativity involved identifying teaching issues, choosing tactics to address them, and assessing teachers' actions and results through research. Site-based creativity brought forth teacher awareness in service of teaching and learning, teacher values for guiding creative instruction and choices, and teacher community that builds networks for students and professionals.

Of interest, then, is the nearly invisible, barely detectable Mini-c and Little-c creative learning process belonging to teachers, students, and others. Creativity researchers have long faced the challenge of "teaching for creativity" not being practiced in many preK–12 schools, thereby expending energy on designing models and strategies for enriching creativity in classrooms, research, and the knowledge base (e.g., Plucker, Guo, & Dilley, 2018; Reilly et al., 2011). Reilly et al. added that creative teaching and learning are less visible in the North American creativity literature than UK-produced research. A concern they expressed is that even within education fewer studies are available than expected of teachers' creative practice. They call for instructional research on creativity knowledge in association with classroom practice, effective creative pedagogy, and interpersonal and social creativity.

3.4 Summary

This chapter addressed definitions and theories that advance knowledge, practice, and action and allow creativity to surface despite (or because of) constraint. Literature review methods were explained. Defined descriptively, key terms were anchored to salient conceptualizations and studies. Also, the 4-C creativity model was brought forward and its influence and importance validated relative to research. This typology was discussed in detail to lay the foundation for the rest of the chapters. Next, I present the study methods used for my treatment of the literature and approach to the sites, with practical translation of the 4-C theory, in preparation of the cases.

References

Abrami, R. M., Kirby, W. C., & McFarlan, F. W. (2014). Why China can't innovate. *Harvard Business Review*, 1–11. Retrieved from https://hbr.org/2014/03/why-china-cant-innovate

Accountability. (2020). *Wikipedia*. Retrieved from https://en.wikipedia.org/wiki/accountability

Ball, M. (2016, September 2). Donald Trump and the politics of fear. *The Atlantic*. Retrieved from https://www.theatlantic.com/politics/archive/2016/09/donald-trump-and-the-politics-of-fear/498116

Bandura, A. (1997). *Self-efficacy: The exercise of control*. New York, NY: Freeman.

BBC. (2017, August 3). How Canada became an education superpower. *Education News*. Retrieved from http://www.educationviews.org/canada-education-superpower

Beghetto, R. A. (2006). Creative self-efficacy: Correlates in middle and secondary students. *Creativity Research Journal, 18*(4), 447–457.

Beghetto, R. A. (2016). Creative openings in the social interactions of teaching. *Creativity: Theories–research–applications, 3*(2), 261–273.

Beghetto, R. A. (2019). Structured uncertainty: How creativity thrives under constraints and uncertainty. In C. A. Mullen (Ed.), *Creativity under duress in education? Resistive theories, practices, and actions* (pp. 27–40). Cham, Switzerland: Springer.

Beghetto, R. A., & Corazza, G. E. (2019). Introduction to the volume. In R. A. Beghetto & G. E. Corazza (Eds.), *Dynamic perspectives on creativity: New directions for theory, research, and practice in education* (pp. 1–3). Cham, Switzerland: Springer.

Beghetto, R. A., & Karwowski, M. (2019). Unfreezing creativity: A dynamic micro-longitudinal approach. In R. A. Beghetto & G. E. Corazza (Eds.), *Dynamic perspectives on creativity: New directions for theory, research, and practice in education* (pp. 7–25). Cham, Switzerland: Springer.

Beghetto, R. A., & Kaufman, J. C. (2007). Toward a broader conception of creativity: A case for "mini-c" creativity. *Psychology of Aesthetics, Creativity, and the Arts, 1*, 73–79.

Berlin, N., Tavani, J.-L., & Beasançon, M. (2016). An exploratory study of creativity, personality and schooling achievement. *Education Economics, 24*(5), 536–556.

Bogotch, I., & Shields, C. M. (Eds.). (2014). *International handbook of educational leadership and social [in]justice*. New York, NY: Springer.

Boily, P., Chapdelaine, N., Hartley, M., Kent, L., Suurkask, K., & Wong, J. C. (2014). *Creativity unleashed: Taking innovation out of the laboratory and into the labour force.* Retrieved from http://www.actioncanada.ca/wp-content/uploads/2014/04/ac-tf3-creativity-report-en-web.pdf

Bond, M. H., & van de Vijver, F. J. R. (2011). Making scientific sense of cultural differences in psychological outcomes: Unpacking the *magnum mysterium.* In D. Matsumoto & F. J. R. van de Vijver (Eds.), *Cross-cultural research methods in psychology* (pp. 75–100). New York, NY: Cambridge University Press.

Borowiecki, K. J. (2017). How are you, my dearest Mozart? Well-being and creativity of three famous composers based on their letters. *The Review of Economics and Statistics, 99*(4), 591–605.

Byrne, D. (2012). *How music works.* San Francisco, CA: McSweeney's.

Canadian Heritage. (2017). *Creative Canada: Policy framework.* Retrieved from canada.ca/content/dam/pch/documents/campaigns/creative-canada/cccadreframework-en.pdf

Celik, P., & Lubart, T. (2016). When East meets West. In V. P. Glăveanu (Ed.), *The Palgrave handbook of creativity and culture research* (pp. 37–55). London, UK: Palgrave Macmillan.

Charmaz, K., Thornberg, R., & Keane, E. (2018). Evolving grounded theory and social justice inquiry. In N. K. Denzin & Y. S. Lincoln (Eds.), *The Sage handbook of qualitative research* (5th ed., pp. 411–440). Thousand Oaks, CA: Sage.

Collard, P., & Looney, J. (2014). Nurturing creativity in education. *European Journal of Education, 49*(3), 348–364.

Corazza, G. E. (2016). Potential originality and effectiveness: The dynamic definition of creativity. *Creativity Research Journal, 28*(3), 258–267.

Corazza, G. E. (2019). The Dynamic Universal Creativity Process. In R. A. Beghetto & G. E. Corazza (Eds.), *Dynamic perspectives on creativity: New directions for theory, research, and practice in education* (pp. 297–319). Cham, Switzerland: Springer.

Craft, A. (1997). Identity and creativity: Educating teachers for postmodernism? *Teacher Development, 1*(1), 83–96.

Craft, A. (2002). *Creativity and early years education.* London, UK: Continuum.

Craft, A., Cremin, T., Burnard, P., Dragovic, T., & Chappell, K. (2012). Possibility thinking: Culminative studies of an evidence-based concept driving creativity? *International Journal of Primary, Elementary and Early Years Education, 41*(5), 538–556.

Craft, A., McConnon, L., & Matthews, A. (2012). Creativity and child-initiated play: Fostering possibility thinking in four-year-olds. *Thinking Skills and Creativity, 7*(1), 48–61.

Cropley, D. H., & Cropley, A. (2010). Functional creativity: "Products" and the generation of effective novelty. In J. C. Kaufman & R. J. Sternberg (Eds.), *The Cambridge handbook of creativity* (pp. 301–317). New York, NY: Cambridge University Press.

Cropley, D. H., & Patston, T. J. (2019). Supporting creative teaching and learning in the classroom: Myths, models, and measures. In C. A. Mullen (Ed.), *Creativity under duress in education? Resistive theories, practices, and actions* (pp. 267–288). Cham, Switzerland: Springer.

Csikszentmihalyi, M. (1996). *Creativity: The psychology of discovery and invention.* London, England: HarperPerennial.

Dawson, K. (2018). Performative embodiment as learning catalyst: Exploring the use of drama/theatre practices in an arts integration course for non-majors. In S. Burgoyne (Ed.), *Creativity in theatre* (pp. 67–87). Cham, Switzerland: Springer.

Dewey, J. (1934). *Art as experience.* New York, NY: Perigee Books.

Diedrich, J., Benedek, M., Jauk, E., & Neubauer, A. C. (2015). Are creative ideas novel and useful? *Psychology of Aesthetics, Creativity, and the Arts, 9*(1), 35–40.

Doyle, C. L. (2019). Speaking of creativity: Frameworks, models, and meanings. In C. A. Mullen (Ed.), *Creativity under duress in education? Resistive theories, practices, and actions* (pp. 41–62). Cham, Switzerland: Springer.

Dynamic. (2020). *Wiktionary.* Retrieved from https://en.wiktionary.org/wiki/dynamic

Eisner, E. W. (2004). What does it mean to say that a school is doing well? In D. J. Flinders & S. J. Thornton (Eds.), *The curriculum studies reader* (2nd ed., pp. 297–305). New York, NY: Routledge.

Espinoza-Gonzalez, D., French, K. B., Gallardo, S., Glemaker, E., Noel, S., Marsura, M., … Thaw, C. (2014). Decolonizing the classroom through critical consciousness: Navigating solidarity *en la Lucha* for Mexican American studies. *The Educational Forum, 78*(1), 54–67.

Ferdig, M. A., & Ludema, J. D. (2005). Transformative interactions: Qualities of conversation that heighten the vitality of self-organizing change. *Research in Organizational Change and Development, 15*, 171–207.

Ferguson, K. (2012). Embrace the remix. *TEDGlobal 2012*. [Recorded talk]. Retrieved from https://www.ted.com/talks/kirby_ferguson_embrace_the_remix?language=en

Fredericks, B., Maynor, P., White, N., English, F. W., & Ehrich, L. C. (2014). Living with the legacy of conquest and culture: Social justice leadership in education and the Indigenous peoples of Australia and America. In I. Bogotch & C. Shields (Eds.), *International handbook of educational leadership and social [in]justice* (Vol. 2, pp. 751–780). New York, NY: Springer.

Gardner, H. E. (1991). *To open minds*. New York, NY: Basic Books.

Gardner, H. E. (2011). *Truth, beauty, and goodness reframed: Educating for the virtues in the age of truthiness and Twitter*. New York, NY: Basic Books.

Gasca, P. (2014). History's inventive minds say you don't have to be original to be creative. *Entrepreneur*. Retrieved from https://www.entrepreneur.com/article/237050

Glăveanu, V. P., & Tanggaard, L. (2014). Creativity, identity, and representation: Towards a socio-cultural theory of creative identity. *New Ideas in Psychology, 34*, 12–21.

Hammond, H. L., Skidmore, L. E., Wilcox-Herzog, A., & Kaufman, J. C. (2013). Creativity and creativity programs. In J. Hattie & E. M. Anderman (Eds.), *International guide to student achievement* (pp. 292–295). New York, NY: Routledge.

Helfand, M., Kaufman, J. C., & Beghetto, R. A. (2016). The Four-C Model of Creativity: Culture and context. In V. P. Glăveanu (Ed.), *The Palgrave handbook of creativity and culture research* (pp. 15–36). London, UK: Palgrave Macmillan.

Hennessey, B. A. (2017). Taking a systems view of creativity: On the right path toward understanding. *Journal of Creative Behavior, 51*(4), 341–344.

Hodges, A. (2014). *Alan Turing: The enigma*. Princeton, NJ: Princeton University Press.

Hondzel, C. D., & Gulliksen, M. S. (2015). Culture and creativity: Examining variations in divergent thinking within Norwegian and Canadian Communities. *SAGE Open*, 1–13. https://doi.org/10.1177/2158244015611448

Hui, A. N.-N. (2015). Is relational theory a better answer to the psychology of creativity? In A.-G. Tan & C. Perleth (Eds.), *Creativity, culture, and development* (pp. 161–178). Singapore: Springer.

Hunter, G. S. (2013). *Out think: How innovative leaders drive exceptional outcomes*. Mississauga, ON: Wiley Canada.

Ibbitson, J. (2014, July 2). Why is Canada the most tolerant country in the world? Luck. *Globe and Mail*. Retrieved from https://www.theglobeandmail.com/news/politics/why-is-canada-the-most-tolerant-country-in-the-world-luck/article19427921

Johnson, S. (2010). *Where good ideas come from: The natural history of innovation*. New York, NY: Penguin Group.

Karwowski, M. (2016). Culture and psychometric studies of creativity. In V. P. Glăveanu (Ed.), *The Palgrave handbook of creativity and culture research* (pp. 159–186). London, UK: Palgrave Macmillan.

Kaufman, J. C., & Beghetto, R. A. (2009). Beyond big and little: The Four C Model of Creativity. *Review of General Psychology, 13*(1), 1–12.

Kaufman, J. C., & Beghetto, R. A. (2013). Do people recognize the Four Cs? Examining layperson conceptions of creativity. *Psychology of Aesthetics, Creativity, and the Arts, 7*, 229–236.

Kaufman, J. C., & Beghetto, R. A. (2014). *The Four C Model of Creativity*. [Utube video]. Available from https://www.youtube.com/watch?v=oR70dV53jBM

Lee, J. C. K., & Pang, N. S. K. (2011). Educational leadership in China: Contexts and issues. *Frontiers of Education in China, 6*(3), 331–241.

Li, Q., & Gerstl-Pepin, C. (Eds.). (2014). *Survival of the fittest: The shifting contours of higher education in China and the United States.* Heidelberg, Baden-Württemberg, Germany: Springer-Verlag GmbH Press.

Mullen, C. A. (2017a). *Creativity and education in China: Paradox and possibilities for an era of accountability.* New York, NY: Routledge & Kappa Delta Pi.

Mullen, C. A. (2017b). Creativity in Chinese schools: Perspectival frames of paradox and possibility. *International Journal of Chinese Education, 6*(1), 27–56.

Mullen, C. A. (2018). Creative learning: Paradox or possibility in China's restrictive preservice teacher classrooms? *Action in Teacher Education, 40*(2), 186–202.

Mullen, C. A. (Ed.). (2019a). *Creativity under duress in education? Resistive theories, practices, and actions.* Cham, Switzerland: Springer.

Mullen, C. A. (2019b). De/colonization: Perspectives on/by Indigenous populations in global Canadian contexts. *International Journal of Leadership in Education,* 1–20. https://doi.org/1 0.1080/13603124.2019.1631986

Mullen, C. A. (2019c). Dynamic creativity: Influential theory, public discourse, and generative possibility. In R. A. Beghetto & G. E. Corazza (Eds.), *Dynamic perspectives on creativity: New directions for theory, research, and practice in education* (pp. 137–164). Cham, Switzerland: Springer.

Mullen, C. A. (2019d). Global leadership: Competitiveness, tolerance, and creativity—a Canadian provincial example. *International Journal of Leadership in Education, 22*(5), 629–643.

Mullen, C. A. (2020). *Canadian Indigenous literature and art: Decolonizing education, culture, and society.* Leiden, The Netherlands: Brill.

Mumford, M. D. (2003). Where have we been, where are we going? Taking stock in creativity research. *Creativity Research Journal, 15,* 107–120.

Mumford, M. D. (Ed.). (2012). *Handbook of organizational creativity.* London, UK: Elsevier.

Narey, M. J. (2019). Who stands for what is right? Teachers' creative capacity and change agency in the struggle for educational quality. In C. A. Mullen (Ed.), *Creativity under duress in education? Resistive theories, practices, and actions* (pp. 313–337). Cham, Switzerland: Springer.

Neber, H., & Neuhaus, B. J. (2013). Creativity and problem-based learning (PBL): A neglected relation. In A.-G. Tan (Ed.), *Creativity, talent, and excellence* (pp. 43–56). New York, NY: Springer.

Niu, W., & Sternberg, R. J. (2001). Cultural influences on artistic creativity and its evaluation. *International Journal of Psychology, 36*(4), 225–241.

Niu, W., Zhang, J. X., & Yang, Y. (2007). Deductive reasoning and creativity: A cross-cultural study. *Psychological Reports, 100*(2), 509–519.

Noice, T., & Noice, H. (2018). The actor's real role on the production team. In S. Burgoyne (Ed.), *Creativity in theatre* (pp. 3–17). Cham, Switzerland: Springer.

O'Connor, J., & Gibson, M. (n.d.). *Culture, creativity, cultural economy: A review.* [report.] Retrieved from https://acola.org/wp-content/uploads/2018/08/06-culture-creativity-cultural-economy.pdf

Plucker, J. A., Guo, J., & Dilley, A. (2018). Research-guided programs and strategies for nurturing creativity. In S. I. Pfeiffer, M. Foley-Nicpon, & E. Shaunessy-Dedrick (Eds.), *APA handbook of giftedness and talent* (pp. 387–397). Washington, DC: American Psychological Association.

Reilly, R. C., Lilly, F., Bramwell, G., & Kronish, N. (2011). A synthesis of research concerning creative teachers in a Canadian context. *Teaching and Teacher Education, 27*(3), 533–542.

Richards, R. (Ed.). (2007). *Everyday creativity and new views of human nature.* Washington, DC: American Psychological Association.

Robinson, K. (2015). *Creative schools: The grassroots revolution that's transforming education.* New York, NY: Viking.

Runco, M. A. (2017). Comments on where the creativity research has been and where is it going. *Journal of Creative Behavior, 51*(4), 308–313.

Sawyer, R. K. (2012). Extending sociocultural theory to group creativity. *Vocations and Learning, 5,* 59–75.

Schmidt, M., & Charney, M. (2018). Assessing creativity as a student learning outcome in theatre education. In S. Burgoyne (Ed.), *Creativity in theatre* (pp. 271–287). Cham, Switzerland: Springer.

Schwab, J. (2004). The practical: A language for curriculum. In D. J. Flinders & S. J. Thornton (Eds.), *The curriculum studies reader* (2nd ed., pp. 103–117). New York, NY: Routledge.

Shao, Y., Zhang, C., Zhou, J., Gu, T., & Yuan, Y. (2019). How does culture shape creativity? A mini-review. *Frontiers in Psychology, 10*(1219). https://doi.org/10.3389/fpsyg.2019.01219

Staats, L. K. (2011). The cultivation of creativity in the Chinese culture—past, present, and future. *Journal of Strategic Leadership, 3*(1), 45–53.

Starr, J. B. (2010). *Understanding China: A guide to China's economy, history, and political culture* (3rd ed.). New York, NY: Farrar, Straus and Giroux.

Stasis. (2020). *Merriam-Webster.* Retrieved from https://www.merriam-webster.com/dictionary/stasis

Sternberg, R. J. (2006). Introduction. In J. C. Kaufman & R. J. Sternberg (Eds.), *The international handbook of creativity* (pp. 1–9). Cambridge, UK: Cambridge University Press.

Stoeger, H. (2003). Learning as a creative process. In A.-G. Tan (Ed.), *Creativity, talent, and excellence* (pp. 1–11). New York, NY: Springer.

Sundararajan, L. (2015). *Understanding emotion in Chinese culture: Thinking through psychology.* Cham, Switzerland: Springer.

Tan, A.-G. (2013). Psychology of cultivating creativity in teaching and learning. In A.-G. Tan (Ed.), *Creativity, talent, and excellence* (pp. 27–42). New York, NY: Springer.

Tienken, C. H., & Mullen, C. A. (Eds.). (2016). *Education policy perils: Tackling the tough issues.* New York, NY: Routledge & Kappa Delta Pi.

Wagner, T. (2012). *Creating innovators: The making of young people who will change the world.* New York, NY: Scribner.

Wheatley, M. J. (1992). *Leadership and the new science: Learning about organization from an orderly universe.* Oakland, CA: Berrett-Koehler.

Woetzel, J., & Towson, J. (2013). *The 1 hour China book.* Cayman Islands: Towson Group LLC.

World Economic Forum. (2013). *The global competitiveness report: 2013–2014.* Geneva, Switzerland: Author. Retrieved from http://www3.weforum.org/docs/wef_globalcompetitivenessreport_2013-14.pdf

Zhao, Y. (2012). *World class learners: Educating creative and entrepreneurial students.* Thousand Oaks, CA: Corwin.

Zhao, Y. (2014). *Who's afraid of the big bad dragon?* Thousand Oaks, CA: Jossey-Bass.

Zhou, J., Shen, J., Wang, X., Neber, H., & Johji, I. (2013). A cross-cultural comparison: Teachers' conceptualizations of creativity. *Creativity Research Journal, 25*(3), 239–247.

Zittoun, T., & Gillespie, A. (2016). Imagination: Creating alternatives in everyday life. In V. P. Glăveanu (Ed.), *The Palgrave handbook of creativity and culture research* (pp. 225–242). London, UK: Palgrave Macmillan.

Chapter 4
Creative Pedagogic Methods: Dynamic Processes and Strategies

4.1 Overview: Research Questions and Objectives

Stimulating creative intervention in glocal universities, the central research question was, Can diverse college students and educators discover creativity when encouraged under educational constraint? Rather than assuming that creative education lacks a pulse in accountability-bound cultures, being open minded (and willing to engage in creative risk-taking) allows for the possibility of creative thought, expression, and action. Other questions included:

- What does the discovery process entail in this context, and what can be learned from it?
- What insights might participants have about creativity and creative ideas/theories/ models/ processes/methods/artifacts?
- What do participant responses to the 4-C creativity model as an instrument/template/ framework convey about creativity and accountability in education as cultural phenomena?
- What notions of creativity embedded within high-accountability education settings are reflected in context-laden ideas, policies, and practices?
- What potential context-specific relationships among Australia, China, and Canada exist in the data with ramifications for creativity and accountability phenomena?
- What new ideas might be added to the social sciences, educational knowledge, and creativity research?

Approaching creativity as theory-informed practice and action was the primary objective expected to have numerous benefits. Not only can this approach advance and deepen theorizing about creativity, it can also support creative development in learning environments. A methodological view and treatment of creativity theory offers educational theory enrichment while revealing creative capacities inherent in human learning. Creativity researchers continue to find that in university-based

C. A. Mullen, *Revealing Creativity*, Creativity Theory and Action in Education 5, https://doi.org/10.1007/978-3-030-48165-0_4

teacher education programs, attention on creativity is inadequate, as is accountability for the creative development of future teachers and leaders (e.g., Narey, 2019). At the college level, creativity-steeped theorizing in education, combined with exercises, interventions, and programs, is sorely needed (in light of the emphasis on the preK–12 schooling domain by creativity researchers). Current demonstrative contributions in the literature originate in creativity and arts-based educational research fields (e.g., Cancienne, 2019; Kaufman & Beghetto, 2013; Kauper & Jacobs, 2019; Mullen, 2017, 2018; Narey, 2019). Creative pedagogic methods for transnational exploratory study—the basis of this chapter—grew out of the recognized need for creativity in university classrooms and programs that prepare future teachers and leaders.

A presupposition of mine is that creativity needs to be revealed to potential creators using validated creativity models. Another presupposition is that accountability, a complex phenomenon that takes many forms, is a significant influencer on creativity and education policy. The importance of culture in shaping, and being shaped by, forces of creativity and accountability was another assumption. As such, all three constructs—creativity, accountability, and culture—were cast as intertwining phenomena, extending to their dynamic interplay in glocalities within China, Canada, and Australia.

My interest in perspectives on creativity takes into account understandings of creativity in relation to accountability within cultural contexts. I wondered how postsecondary educators might interpret a creativity theory presented to them for reflection and response, and in some cases, rendering and performance (i.e., Kaufman and Beghetto's [2009] Four C [4-C] Model of Creativity). Educators worldwide navigate public policy contexts and negotiate reforms, but little is known about their sense-making around creativity, extending to how it is influenced by, and even embedded in, modern accountability paradigms. We know that many teachers and schools are expected to be accountable to creativity, such as by introducing creative practices (Cropley & Patston, 2019), but what do they do (and not do), and how do they conceptualize creativity and accountability? Parsing educators' thoughts within lived policy domains and making their voices heard is encouraged (e.g., Ciuffetelli Parker & Craig, 2015). Thus, I was keen to seek engagement in college contexts with a creative intervention built upon the 4-C theory. Statements made by participants about policies and the policy landscape in education are reflective of their perceived/experiential realities, as demonstrated in the case study Chaps. (5, 6, and 7).

The heart of this chapter is my methodological translation of the 4-C creativity theory and its adaptation for study in three urban glocal cultures. Creative pedagogic methods spurred dynamic processes and strategies to aid theorizing, researching, and teaching. Multiple data collection sessions occurred using validated protocols: Individuals (students, faculty, and leaders) partook in group sessions (classes and workshops/seminars) and one-on-one interviews dealing with creativity and accountability within familiar cultural contexts. The qualitative methodology was multifaceted (and amenable to changing situations), with its three aspects addressed here. The case studies were conducted in glocalities (Chongqing, Toronto, and Sydney), respectively. Six data sources are also covered.

As such, a practical goal of this pedagogic research project was to design a common set of methodologies and adapt them to fit the transnational university contexts. All three case studies build on shared methods, to varying degrees. Besides having a shared focus, the methodologies and strategies used for data collection are eclectic—they diverged in response to the unique dynamics (possibilities and constraints) in each location; as examples, the opportunity to teach a course (and use the 4-C creativity program in it) at one site was not available in the other two; also, access, albeit highly restricted, to classes taught by instructors in two of the sites was simply not available in a third one. Because of such variability, an explanation appears in the case chapters where additional details and modifications are concerned; otherwise, what is stated in this chapter holds across the cases. While methodological variations are covered in each case study, I provide brief illustrations herein to assist with the transition to them.

An energizing, fertile thought in creativity research is that the creativity–culture relationship can promote dynamic creativity in educational settings (e.g., Glăveanu, 2016; Tan, 2013). However, when cultures have high-pressure, external accountability expectations for performance, barriers to creativity can escalate and intensify. This leads me to wonder what conditions make it possible for educators to understand theory-enriched creativity and creative learning. In this vein, I set forth the objective of revealing creativity in test-centered places.

When seen as a dynamic occurrence, creativity manifests despite or even because of constraints (Beghetto & Corazza, 2019). In addition, researchers can not only seek creativity but can also create the conditions for others to develop, experience, and recognize their own creative potential. As such, according to Burnett's Five-Point Star model, schoolteachers who "recognize[e] their own creativity" may develop "a creative environment," "integrat[e] creativity into content delivery," and "teach classes in creativity" (as cited in Burnett & Smith, 2019, p. 180; Fig. 10.1). Her model offers a flexible, open-ended framework for taking creativity research to the next level. The idea is that pedagogic researchers studying learning environments can introduce a theory-enriched creativity program or process to encourage awareness of creativity and support others' professional development (PD) and creative learning, as well as their own. (Later, I describe the role of my own PD and creative learning in this book project.)

Let us assume that dynamic creative processes are needed at all levels of education, worldwide, for eliciting creativity in real-world practice. Pressures, policies, conditions, circumstances, philosophies, beliefs, norms, and socialization all influence (and can enliven or dampen) creativity. As repeatedly observed in the educational creativity literature, such constraints on creativity are glaring in test-centric, accountability-obsessed cultures (e.g., Henriksen, Creely, & Henderson, 2019; Kim & Chae, 2019; Li & Gerstl-Pepin, 2014; Mullen, 2018, 2019a, 2019b; Mullet,

Willerson, Lamb, & Kettler, 2016; Tienken & Mullen, 2016). But what about post-secondary education and dynamics of creativity and accountability in different world cultures? How might any of us pursue potentialities for recovering, as well as fostering, dynamic creativity in policy reform settings?

Stimulating creative intervention in glocal universities, the central research question was, Can diverse college students and educators discover creativity when encouraged under educational constraint? Rather than assuming that creative education lacks a pulse in accountability-bound cultures, being open minded (and willing to engage in creative risk-taking) allows for the possibility of creative thought, expression, and action. Other questions included:

- What does the discovery process entail in this context, and what can be learned from it?
- What insights might participants have about creativity and creative ideas/theories/ models/processes/methods/artifacts?
- What do participant responses to the 4-C creativity model as an instrument/template/framework convey about creativity and accountability in education as cultural phenomena?
- What notions of creativity embedded within high-accountability education settings are reflected in context-laden ideas, policies, and practices?
- What potential context-specific relationships among Australia, China, and Canada exist in the data with ramifications for creativity and accountability phenomena?
- What new ideas might be added to the social sciences, educational knowledge, and creativity research?

4.2   Methods, Processes, and Strategies

Steering my conceptualization of methodology for the three international field studies was my desire to explicitly connect creativity and accountability while drawing out cultural connections. Of interest were participants' perspectives on creativity and what forms creativity and accountability take within lived cultural contexts. Is it that creativity and accountability are like oil and water, metaphorically speaking, and do not mix, and that, no matter what, creativity cannot thrive under constraint? Can any creativity be expected in inflexible, stifling situations where students and faculty are highly accountable to prescriptive curriculum, learning outcomes, and performance measures? What about the role of internal (personal) accountability for engaging in creative activity, having choices, performing activities, and making discoveries? The strategy adopted for gaining access to student perspectives was my 4-C creative intervention within classrooms; other stakeholders' views were tapped within individual and group settings.

4.2.1 Literature-Informed Methodology

Contemporary literature on creativity informs this writing's conceptual methodology regarding global educational trends and associated constructs. Sought in the knowledge canon were scholars' creativity theories in psychology and education, with particular interest in postsecondary education, specifically teacher and leadership education and cultural and policy studies. As mentioned, methodological support for theory-building and exploration particularly came from Kaufman and Beghetto's (2009) 4-C creativity model and their topically related discourse (e.g., Beghetto & Kaufman 2007; Kaufman & Beghetto, 2013).

Another step involved reviewing topical academic literature on creativity in high-impact journals and (hand)books spanning 1996 to 2019. (Cambridge University Press and Springer are among the sponsoring publishers.) Online databases searched included the full text holdings of publishers and the libraries of my home university and those in the three glocalities. ERIC from WorldCat and Education Research Complete from EBSCOhost yielded topical articles from academic journals and pertinent books. Documents were also accessed via Google Scholar.

Discourse about creativity appeared in diverse sources: academic journals devoted to the topic of creativity (e.g., *Creativity Research Journal*), book series (e.g., Creativity Theory and Action in Education, published by Springer), and edited books. Within these parameters, influential theoretical and empirical sources were located using the search term *creativity* (also, *Mini-c, Little-c, Pro-C,* and *Big-C*), in association with *accountability, Australia, Canada, China, creative economy, culture, dynamic creativity, educational policy, Four C Model of Creativity, globalization, glocal(ity), Hidden-c, social justice, testing,* and other concepts.

In an earlier literature review of creativity frameworks (Mullen, 2019d), educational psychology was particularly well represented among the academic disciplines as a prolific contributor to the creativity paradigm. Moreover, educational psychology is multidisciplinary and transdisciplinary (as opposed to insular) in both the conception and treatment of creativity. Beyond this, creativity models stemming from psychology are frequently adopted and described, (re)theorized, and/or applied by other disciplinary scholars, including Kaufman and Beghetto's (2009) popular 4-C theory. Csikszentmihalyi (1996) described creativity itself as "crossing the boundaries of domains" (p. 9). Increasingly, creativity researchers are disciplinary boundary crossers and explorers of "new paradigms of creativity" (Tan, 2013, p. 27).

Crossing the disciplinary boundary into teacher education is not new for educational psychologists, as my illustrations suggest in the current chapter and full-blown case studies. (As a multidisciplinary scholar in educational leadership, I have a history of publishing scholarship in educational psychology and teacher education.) Border-crossing's forays are into early childhood education (Craft, Cremin, Burnard, Dragovic, & Chappell, 2012; Craft, McConnon, & Matthews, 2012), cultural studies (e.g., Sternberg, 2006), systems thinking/science, sociology

(Csikszentmihalyi, 1996, 1999), and more. Thus, *educational psychology* served as a baseline descriptor for searching databases and extending into other disciplines.

4.2.2 Case Study Research Design

Here, I address the case study research design used for this project. "Single-case design" (Yin, 2018) describes this small-scale within-case and cross-case educational analysis. The three chapters that follow are devoted to within-case descriptions of the phenomena under study—methodological application of the 4-C model in policy-dominant high-stakes accountability nations' educational settings at the college level. The cross-case synthesis of the sites appears in Chap. 8.

The case study method is conducive to qualitative study of "complex social phenomena" (e.g., "small group behavior" and "interpersonal relations"; Yin, 2018, p. 4). Creativity is complex and unfolds within sociocultural contexts (Sawyer, 2017; Tan, 2013), satisfying Yin's criterion that the boundaries of a case be informed and enriched by complexity and context.

These cases have identifiable boundaries (Yin, 2018), including particular locations in different countries, an established theory (4-C creativity model), and specific interrelated phenomena—creativity, accountability, context, and culture. However, the boundaries between a case and its context are typically vague; in my situation, the close attention paid to context and culture added detail to my methodological plan. As such, each case study evidences an eclectic arrangement of methods and data sources suitable to its contextual and cultural features.

Case study boundaries were derived from numerous commonalities allowing each site to qualify for exploratory analysis. All three countries are members of the G20 (Group of Twenty)—an international forum for governments and banks founded to foster worldwide financial stability. China, Canada, and Australia are among the largest 20 global economies. Collectively, the G20 economies account for "90% of the gross world product, 80% of world trade, two-thirds of the world population, and [about 50% of Earth's] land area" ("G20," 2020).

The physical location (the city and country) is identified, but not the specific university, in keeping with the terms and protections afforded via my home institution in the United States. All three were research universities with a strong teaching and educational mission in bustling mega-cities dotted with higher education institutions. International and study-abroad students were disproportionally high.

Each research site represents a phase of my research journey between 2015 and 2019, with 1 month spent at each location. Even though I live and work in the United States, my movement was from the East to the West: Chongqing, China—2015; Toronto, Canada—2017; and Sydney, Australia—2019. (The time-frame was influenced by the conditions of the Fulbright specialist program.) Nonetheless, all three glocalities allowed for time-intensive data collection onsite via postsecondary educational programs. Other commonalities allowed for my broadly conceived methods and data sources to take shape in each glocality, relative to what was possible at that time and in that place. As such, the data collected from classes and interviews were mixed across the sites, depending on my negotiations with leaders hosting my visit and, as applicable, faculty.

Being self-directed in carrying out the study and advocating for what was needed sparked negotiations around such constraints as how best to engage classes in creativity given the heavy demands on courses and schedules. It was necessary to get to know which key insiders (e.g., institutional hosts and student-centered faculty) might be available and to what end. It became quickly apparent that I had to proactively seek opportunities for accessing faculty and students (through their course professors) and interviewing stakeholders. Because I was not a member of the community or personally known, it was essential to cultivate interest and buy-in.

Boundary entities I imposed at the outset were "people's conceptions of creativity" and their potential for "recogniz[ing] the four Cs" (Kaufman & Beghetto, 2013, p. 229). Whether participants could go further to identify modern dynamics of accountability relevant to creativity and their culture was another complexity. Additionally, the guided instruction around creative learning meant that creativity under constraint was ever-present in the very context in which I was encouraging student teams to reveal creativity (to themselves and others) through challenging 4-C work. All considered *educators* in my study, I was drawn to education students, faculty, and leaders' capacity to make sense of the 4-C theory by applying the 4-Cs within their cultural contexts. This led me to wonder, What is the human capacity for culturally and contextually interpreting creativity in meaningful ways when faced with daunting pressure? A dynamic rendition of lived tensions within the educational settings had to be part of the story.

4.2.3 Glocal Research Sites

With deep conflict in their educational systems, the pull between traditional and creative education paradigms is ever present in the three sites. While they are exposed to national education boards and reform-based policies that set the tone for creativity and innovation to be vigorously promoted in classrooms (e.g., Cropley & Patston, 2019; Henriksen et al., 2019), the educational culture is itself beset with standardized testing and, consequently, intense scrutiny. PreK–12 teachers responsible for standardized testing outcomes have described a loss of pedagogic freedom and drain on decision-making, to the detriment of students who are expected to be creative in accordance with twenty-first-century expectations of workforce employees (Au, 2011; Kim, 2011). Consequently, creative pedagogies are not as likely to be infused in education by human "products of the high-stakes testing culture" (Kim & Chae, 2019, p. 217).

High school graduates should possess the capacities to think critically, create, and collaborate on complex social problems (Au, 2011; Tienken & Mullen, 2016; Zhao, 2012). Across democratic and autocratic educational systems around the world, the thinking is that Australia (Henriksen et al., 2019), Canada (Mullen,

2019b, 2019c), and China (Zhao, 2014) suffer, albeit to varying degrees, from creativity and innovation deficits—just like the United States (Kauper & Jacobs, 2019; Kim & Chae, 2019; Mullet et al., 2016). In many schools and universities, creativity in teaching and learning appears disappointingly weak (Narey, 2019), despite counterforces. In Toronto, strong teacher unions oppose damage to creativity in classrooms burdened with provincial standardized testing (Mullen, 2019b; Chap. 6 herein).

Of significance, China, Canada, and Australia are all adopters of the Programme for International Student Assessment (PISA), a high-stakes international testing (of science, mathematics, reading literacy, collaborative problem-solving, and financial literacy) and assessment regimen. According to countless sources, PISA tests provoke fear in schools; dampen creativity, innovation, and critical thinking; and attract criticism from the public and academics, worldwide (e.g., Au, 2011; Kim & Chae, 2019; Tienken & Mullen, 2016; Zhao, 2012).

A social justice consequence of PISA and testing cultures is that they produce, if not justify, educational and social inequities (e.g., Kempf, 2016; Tienken & Mullen, 2016). As the achievement gap widens, students' futures suffer; they often lack enriching opportunities to develop their creative capacity in the classroom, which is essential for thinking creatively, engaging in open-ended problem-solving, and expressing originality and individuality (e.g., Kim & Chae, 2019; Mullen, 2019a; Narey, 2019). However, even when schools "focus too narrowly on meeting task constraints," generative creativity is nonetheless possible, for "even in such [restrictive] situations, small openings do emerge on occasion [that] offer opportunities for students and teachers to think and act in new and meaningful ways" (Beghetto, 2019, p. 38).

At the postsecondary level, teachers and leaders are responsible for building a successful future for others. But in PISA nations—where standardized test scores greatly matter—any wiggle room for seizing creative moments and developing creativity is limited. College students in education, having grown up with standardized testing, may not have benefitted from creative activities that demand a conceptual and analytical response (Kim & Chae, 2019). In a review of the literature (i.e., Mullet et al., 2016), it was found that education students in teacher preservice programs, like practicing teachers, do not feel confident enough to facilitate creativity, and classroom teachers judge themselves incapable of identifying creative works. Anecdotally, teacher educators like Kauper and Jacobs (2019) "notic[ed] a decline in what we would describe as creative expression in our classes of undergraduate students in the United States"—besides seeking correct answers, their students are risk avoidant and lack imagination (p. 340). Another significant constraint on creative expression in classrooms is described by many creativity and arts-based educational researchers as negative myths and misconceptions about creativity; at the top of this list, perhaps, educators commonly believe that creativity is synonymous with the arts (e.g., Cropley & Patston, 2019; Kauper & Jacobs). Creativity, then, is misunderstood.

Should the question arise as to why I did not include the United States as a research site given that it is also a PISA nation, I wanted to put myself in a situation of extremes to see if creativity could be released under duress. In part this meant that I would want to be in places where I lacked firsthand experience, reliable networks, and social capital. Of course, the nature of a Fulbright is such that it locates the awardee in a "foreign," environment, and I was eager for a creative challenge and new adventure. Eligible glocal research sites were places where creativity would prove challenging to understand and reveal, and where the viability of my 4-C creative intervention could be put to the test.

Besides these criteria, the nations I selected were "foreign" to me, a citizen of the United States where I've lived since 1995. China, Canada, and Australia all allowed for not only exploratory study but also creative risk-taking. While I was born and schooled in Canada, it had changed greatly since my move. On the one hand, Canada's booming multicultural diversity owing to strong liberal leanings set it apart from many nations, but on the other hand, its PISA adoption signaled a radical move toward "educational standardization" and a "testing" pedagogy (Kempf, 2016; also, Mullen, 2019b). In fact, Toronto and Canada as a whole had become much more culturally and internationally diverse over the past few decades. All of these factors justified being placed in Toronto for my second Fulbright award. Finally, my own networks proved vital in forging the connections that led to my stay. However, advanced planning for data collection was not accommodated in the locations, so I sought opportunities and openings onsite.

4.3   Data Collection

Now I describe the creative pedagogic methods utilized in terms of their breadth, specificity, and approvals. Then I move to the data sources that proved suitable for this project.

4.3.1   Creative Pedagogic Methods

1. Broad literature review for locating relevant sources for creativity and accountability in education and within cultures, as summarized in Table 4.1. (Chap. 3 has the description.)
2. Tailored literature review for identifying select sources on educational creativity and accountability within creative/global economies: China (Chap. 5), Canada (Chap. 6), and Australia (Chap. 7).
3. Case study treatments of my creative intervention within three glocalities. Crucial elements of the cases are the previously stated phenomena (creativity in relation to accountability within a global culture) and the creative curriculum that was built on the 4-C creativity model and literature reviewed. (All three cases include a table delineating the 4Cs—Mini-c, Little-c, Pro-C, and Big-C—and reflecting aspects of site-based data collection and analysis.) Additional

Table 4.1 Broad methods used for locating relevant literature on creativity in education (C. A. Mullen)

PRIMARY RESEARCH QUESTION
Can diverse students and educators discover creativity where encouraged with pedagogic guidance under constraint?
INCLUSION CRITERIA
Research: Empirical studies, theoretical essays, books and book series (e.g., Springer's Creativity Theory and Action in Education), and public sources published from 1996 to 2019; the earliest year of publication regarding creativity research from educational psychology only for the present book was 1996, with Csikszentmihalyi's *Creativity* on systems affecting creativity.
Population: Students and educators from preK–12 to postsecondary grades.
Context: Topical relevance and quality sources bearing on transnational educational contexts (China, Canada, and Australia).
Evidence-based criteria: Reference point, cross-cultural, knowledge building, pedagogic application, impactful forces, and disciplinary crossovers. (Researcher Mullen derived these criteria from her literature review analysis, as Chap. 4 explains.)
RESEARCH STRATEGIES
Keywords: Accountability, creative economy, creativity, dynamic creativity, glocal(ity), Hidden-c, culture, social justice, Four C Model of Creativity, etc.
Preselected sources and authors (sample only)
Journals
Action in Teacher Education
Creativity Research Journal
Creativity: Theories–research–applications
International Journal of Leadership in Education
International Journal of Psychology
New Ideas in Psychology
Psychology of Aesthetics Creativity and the Arts
Review of General Psychology
Teaching and Teacher Education
The Educational Forum
Books
Creative contradictions in education (Beghetto & Sriraman, 2017)
Creativity (Csikszentmihalyi, 1996)
Creativity in theatre
Creativity, talent, and excellence (Tan, 2013)
Creativity under duress in education?
Dynamic perspectives on creativity (Beghetto & Corazza, 2019)
International handbook of educational leadership and social [in]justice
Survival of the fittest (Li & Gerstl-Pepin, 2014)
The Cambridge handbook of creativity
The creative self
The Palgrave handbook of creativity and culture research (Glăveanu, 2016)
The pedagogy of standardized testing (Kempf, 2016)

(continued)

Table 4.1 (continued)

Who's afraid of the big bad dragon? (Zhao, 2014)
Reports
PISA
Report of the Royal Commission on aboriginal peoples
State of the world's Indigenous peoples: Education
Authors and models
Primarily, Kaufman and Beghetto's (2009, 2013) Four C Model of Creativity and their related publications
Databases
ERIC from WorldCat and Education Research Complete from EBSCOhost; also, Google Scholar for accessing literature
Reporting categories
Empirical studies, articles, books, chapters, theoretical frameworks, conceptual essays, documents, reports, news stories

aspects in each case are a contextualized research design, methodology, and data collection process, and modified creative tool and activities. Details of participants, programs, and places are extended with thematic results that "story" perspectives through which voices (and values) are enlivened. (Following on the heels of these cases is a synthesis [Chap. 8] that establishes data-based themes.)

4.3.2   Participants, Procedures, and Approvals

Participants in this longitudinal glocal study constituted three groups of university educators: students, faculty, and leaders (student participants only in China). The participant number ($N = 152$) encompasses this numerical breakdown: $n = 34$ (Chongqing, China); $n = 80$ (Toronto, Canada); and $n = 38$ (Sydney, Australia). Those contributing across the three research sites were mostly currently enrolled students who produced artifacts during their class session. In China and Australia, they were at the undergraduate level whereas in Toronto they were at the graduate level (in masters and doctoral programs). While these populations were in educational degree programs within the Chongqing and Toronto locations, in Sydney, they were in humanities programs with a cultural–educational emphasis. Demographics that include ethnicity, gender, and international status are reported in the case study chapters, tailored to each classroom setting. Variability of demographics is reported in the Canada and Australia cases, and homogeneousness in the China case. In the glocalities, all participants were studying or working in a leading university located in an urban metropolis. Additional participants (in Canada and Australia) were faculty and leader interviewees who, as a whole, were heterogeneous (in race, ethnicity, gender, age, sexual preference, background, status, expertise, etc.).

Before the study was conducted at the three research sites, participants were given an information sheet and a consent form in person. The forms were verbally covered by me in Canada and Australia, always in the presence of a host representative, and by my bilingual translator and a dean's delegate in China. All of this information was written and spoken in the English language. For the Chongqing location, it was also translated in Mandarin, the native language, and presented in both languages. As the researcher, I used culturally specific and appropriate language in the study protocols. The paperwork was reviewed in advance by various entities: the Institutional Review Board (IRB) and compliance officers at my U.S.-based university; a Chinese bilingual translator; and representatives of the host institution (the unit head overseeing my visit or a program coordinator and the professors interested in having their class engage in my creativity workshop and, optionally, the research aspects). For all participating groups in classes and at seminars, at least one host representative was present when the study was explained and research procedures were covered. Constituting the groups were students and their professors in university courses, and educators in my sponsored seminars, all of whom are considered educators in this book.

In the deliberation of my roles as researcher, course instructor, and guest lecturer (in courses and seminars), I separated the research process from the pedagogic activity. Over the 4-year study, I was responsible for teaching only one course, an elective in China that was held during a summer term. In the more frequent instances where I conducted a workshop in professors' classes and lectured in a seminar series, occurring exclusively in Canada and Australia, I addressed key points on the research protocols at the outset of each data collection session. Present in the space was at least one host representative who had reviewed my materials in advance and invited me to do the workshop or lecture. However, to ensure that students and other university inhabitants did not feel pressured to sign the consent form, the consent form was managed by a representative who returned the printed consent forms (signed and unsigned) to me after the workshop or lecture.

Thus, in keeping with my ethical responsibilities as researcher, all participants were informed and gave written consent for use of their 4-C artifacts (i.e., completed activities—posters, activity sheets, essays, scripts, and assessments). Non-identifiers are consistently used for them, so identifiable names do not appear on the artifact renderings (figures/graphics), in the case study chapters, or anywhere else in this text. Universities' names and titles of units, programs, and courses are also withheld, along with insignia/mottos and identifying landmarks. All measures taken satisfy the terms of non-disclosure of participant names approved by the Institutional Review Board (IRB) at my home institution where I am a tenured full professor in the Educational Leadership Program.

To expound on the handling of research procedures in Chongqing, bicultural strategies were utilized to make certain that human rights were protected and that the pedagogic scope, procedures, and privacy were all clearly conveyed. Not knowing Mandarin, I hired a Chinese bilingual translator (with university teaching experience in China) to translate my approved IRB protocols (and the course syllabus) into Mandarin, thereby ensuring research transparency, clear expression, and cultural appropriateness. Prospective participants each received the Mandarin and English versions of the documents. This translator, along with a Chinese mediator (the dean's delegate) from the host university in China, co-led an ethics discussion in Mandarin and English while I was out of the room. Goals were to check for understanding of the pedagogically-conceived research and informed consent, and, importantly, the voluntary nature of participation. To protect student privacy, students were informed verbally and in writing that study participation was noncompulsory, and that lack of participation would not impact their course grade (and, conversely, that participation in the research would not result in payment or extra credit). The precautions taken were directed at monitoring researcher power, privilege, and authority by separating my roles as teacher and researcher, and participants' roles as student and research participant.

Regarding the IRB process, my home institution approved the research methods as described. The ethics committee reviewed the procedures proposed for research, ensuring that they were ethical and complied with research regulations. For each application, all materials were uploaded to IRB Protocol Management, a web-based system. A separate IRB application for the research sites was required for review, which included a consent letter and site-specific protocols for the 4-C activities and interviews. (While the group-based activities took place in all sites, as mentioned, the interviews with leaders and faculty were accommodated in Canada and Australia only.) Because the approval received in 2015 for the research in China did not extend to the subsequent data collection phases, new IRB applications were submitted, and approvals granted, for the Canada and Australia phases. For each biennial website upload (in 2015, 2017, and 2019), a compliance officer was on hand to help clarify procedures and ensure the safeguarding of participants. Periodically, I underwent human subject protection training and attained completion status from the Collaborative Institutional Training Initiative Program, a requirement of the approval process. Letters of approval resulted for the three IRB applications that underwent full review in accordance with my university's scholarly integrity and research compliance division.

A final point about research procedures concerns electronics and technologies. Technology was permitted for sharing my PPT slides and photographing task-specific creative artifacts. Artifacts were returned by me to participants via a host representative. I asked that participants not put their names on materials they intended to submit; when this did occur, I removed their identifiers. Another point concerns laptop computers. Because these commonly have an integrated camera/webcam, they can be perceived as a threat. Considering this possibility, I used a paper notepad in the presence of participants for documenting observations, exchanges, and interviews. I did not want to chance anyone feeling unnecessarily wary, self-conscious, or awkward when my creativity prompts and exercises were meant to trigger free thinking and creative expression. Openly penning my notes during encounters, I left the majority of time for participants to reflect on, and respond to, the activity prompts. Research protocols, distributed in paper copy, were shared for the first time once sessions commenced. Navigating unknown interpersonal and cultural waters called for vigilant compliance with the approved procedures.

4.3.3 Germane Data Sources

Besides the broad and tailored literature reviews that were conducted, other methodology components consisted of six postsecondary data sources. Collected onsite in China, Canada, and Australia, these were coded and analyzed as text-based documents (see Table 4.2).

Common across the cases are six discrete but overlapping data sources:

1. 4-C Classroom Activity and Conversation Protocol for Glocal Adaptation
2. 4-C creative activities with classes and groups (introduced with creative tools—Fig. 4.1 and Appendixes 4.1 and 4.2—with a message inviting participation [Appendix 4.3])
3. 4-C interviews with individuals and groups (also introduced with Fig. 4.1 and Appendixes 4.1 and 4.2)
4. Local and onsite documents
5. Photographic archive of artifacts and materials
6. Researcher's field notes (including PD)

At the outset of all sessions with groups and individuals, I shared Fig. 4.1, my illustration of the 4-C Model of Creativity. This figure's relevance to data collection with groups and individuals alike is described in sections of the present chapter, along with Appendixes 4.1 and 4.2. My 4-C PowerPoint (PPT) delivery of these 4-C research materials directed participants' attention to the 4-C theory and an application of it (i.e., Appendix 4.1 with classes and groups). This singular exposure to my

Table 4.2 Methodology components and postsecondary data collected (C. A. Mullen)

Methodology components and data sources	Chongqing, China–2015) Chapter 5	Toronto, Canada– 2017) Chapter 6	Sydney, Australia–2019) Chapter 7
Broad literature review methods used to locate relevant creativity sources in global economies	✓	✓	✓
Tailored literature review for identifying creativity sources in the nation studied	✓	✓	✓
4-c research protocol for glocal adaptation	✓	✓	✓
4-c creative activities with classes	✓	✓	✓
4-c interviews with individuals and/or groups	✓	✓	✓
Local and onsite documents	✓	✓	✓
Photographic archive of artifacts and documents	✓	✓	✓
Researcher's field notes (including PD)	✓	✓	✓

Note. Data sources (six in all) are identified in italic letters
Also, 4-C interviews in China occurred, but in preK–12 schools

Fig. 4.1 Graphical
interpretation of the Four C
Model of Creativity
(C. A. Mullen)

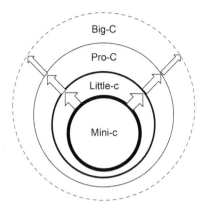

4-C creativity activities with graduate students in Canada contrasted with a fuller exposure at the undergraduate level in China. In three instances, undergraduates in China and Australia were immersed in the creativity program. Exposure occurred through my in-person teacher education course in China, and implementation of engagement activities in Australia in two classes in Indigenous and gender studies.

All data sources were collected live through my face-to-face encounters and these vary structurally, temporally, and in other ways. The three case studies share the methodological processes and strategies explained in this chapter. Methods were modified to fit the needs, demands, interests, preferences, expectations, opportunities, and constraints of each situation.

Understandably it was necessary to develop a highly flexible, responsive approach. For example, my creative activity could not be accommodated within the closely managed educational classrooms I visited as a peer observer in Chongqing. However, I was granted the opportunity to teach an undergraduate course of my own, a credit-earning elective, although it was constrained by a short timeframe and may have been monitored (a professor on staff would show up periodically, sit at the back, and observe). Also, bilingual English–Mandarin strategies proved indispensable for teaching my course, engaging the learners, and collecting data. As Chap. 5 details, due to the Chinese students' responsiveness to my creative intervention, it turned out to be dynamic and rewarding, yielding insights not otherwise attainable.

An inverse of this situation emerged in Toronto and Sydney, where there was no prospect of teaching a course or leading a workshop. So, I met with faculty and administrators, negotiating the implementation of my creative curriculum, in expedited and selective forms. (In Canada, my public talks were organized and publicized, generating opportunities for creative engagement and data collection). Being flexible and persistent with my research plan, methods, and activities meant that I could adjust to differing expectations and interest of receptive "gatekeepers." The exposure and challenging circumstances benefitted my 4-C creativity program "forcing" its delivery and fit across variable contexts, and my adaptability.

4.3.4   4-C Classroom Activity and Conversation Protocol (Data Source 1)

The research-informed creativity instrument I developed is named the 4-C Classroom Activity and Conversation Protocol (Appendix 4.1). Used for data collection purposes, this tool was implemented at the three research sites with groups and individuals, specifically with undergraduate and graduate classes, and mixed educator groups, in addition to interviewees. Using the 4-C question prompts, I drew out contextual and cultural perspectives on creativity and accountability in education. The protocol was adapted to the country local/regional/national context of interest (with the applicable place-bound words inserted into the tool).

Follow-up questions evoked spontaneous associations with this theme. Active and genuine sense-making around each of the 4-Cs was sought; participants wrestled with the creative challenge at hand, providing, to varying degrees of thoroughness, descriptions and examples of creativity and accountability as situated within context and culture.

4.3.5   4-C Creative Activities with Classes and Groups (Data Source 2)

Postsecondary classes and groups served as activity-based venues for stimulating creativity. Through my creative intervention, the challenge was to authentically interpret, represent, and describe the 4-Cs. Hopefully, this process supported participants' creative self-confidence (Hidden-c) and development, which it did in China where ideas were also sparked for transferability of the new learning to other contexts (e.g., future classes). Considering the project as a whole, across the three research sites the 4-C creative intervention took three forms: classes I visited once, immersive workshops I facilitated, and a scheduled course I taught.

1. *Classes I visited once.* In Canada and Australia, I facilitated from 60 to 120 minutes, in the lecturers' presence, part or all of five class sessions. First, I presented live on the 4-C creativity model and global (creativity and accountability) trends. As handouts, students received three of the PPT slides—focused on the study's data collection aspects—Fig. 4.1, and Appendixes 4.1 and 4.2. Information generated from the class visits consisted of (a) each team's written responses recorded on the 4-C activity sheet, (b) my summation of the teams' verbal sharing of their results with the class, (c) my pre- and postsessions with the professors (as explained in the researcher's field notes later on), (d) my write-up of contextual statements drawn from pertinent local documents (e.g., course syllabus), and (e) my field note record consisting of these four components for each class session.

2. *Immersive workshops/seminars I facilitated.* In Canada only, I facilitated three 60- to 75-minute public workshops dealing directly with my creativity program. Participants ranged from students, faculty, and visiting professors to alumni.
3. *A scheduled course I taught.* In China I taught a scheduled course for which I was formally assigned as the professor of record. Teaching face-to-face for the duration, I was responsible for all aspects (syllabus, lectures, project-based activities, office hours, grading, and assessment). These students did not view/receive Fig. 4.1 and the two protocol appendixes—they were exposed to the same concepts and information but more generally; on PPT slides presented live, the 4-C theory was succinctly described, including all 4-Cs, with examples; also provided at the outset was a summary of the classic 4-C framework and 4-Cs (i.e., Kaufman & Beghetto, 2009). After reading this article, my students embarked on activities addressing educational creativity and accountability within the Chinese culture, transitioning from personal to group creativity. Creative modalities were ignited with a solo essay on an experience of personal creativity from their early years, moving to collaboratively creating a 3D paper poster incorporating the 4-Cs and "performing" it, and ending with student assessment of the experiences.

In this larger category (of data sources), 4-C creative activities with classes, undergraduate and graduate students alike (e.g., preservice and inservice teachers; undergraduate students in the humanities) generated creative and informative responses. They penned their perspectives on creativity and accountability (sometimes with pictorial accompaniment), without using technologies/devices or the Internet, in accordance with my directions (submitting one copy per team). (In Australia, several students did consult the Internet.) Consequently, what they reflected on, discussed, and wrote (and designed) signaled active engagement and genuine sense-making of the 4-C prompts. This semistructured, open-ended tool contains high abstractions of *creativity, accountability*, and *context* that I anchored with general and specific examples of each of the Cs. This pedagogic process guided initial thinking and stimulated reflection, steering creators in grappling with the key concepts and collaboratively making meaning of them. The tool (Appendix 4.1) was piloted in China, then refined and adapted to the Canadian and Australian contexts, with the addition of Appendix 4.2 (a development of my PPT slides containing the 4-C examples); the two appendixes worked hand-in-glove.

The creative activities unfolded as shorter and longer PD workshops held with classes in which students earned course credit in their programs of study. In academic buildings on the campus, I had the classes pre-organized into groups at roundtables, converting the rows in China.

To clarify, for all classes visited and the course I taught, the data collection steps were as follows. Planning sessions with key gatekeepers launched this process; at the start of sessions, my mini-lecture was delivered to the groups via PPT, complete with time reserved for whole-group dialogue and questions. On the slides were my overview of creativity and accountability as global trends (with the nation of interest highlighted; e.g., Canada); my visual illustration of the 4-C model (Fig. 4.1); the research protocol (Appendix 4.1); and synopsis of the 4-C creativity model and examples (Appendix 4.2). The three-page handout mirrored this sequence. (In China, this information was presented, but in more general terms.) Thus, before undertaking the activity, participants were exposed, verbally and visually, to essential highlights and an interchange.

When reporting the amount of time spent in classes, I have stuck to the data collection frame, omitting any additional time spent on add-on lectures. In two of my visitations to preservice courses in Toronto, the professor requested a topical presentation in an area of my expertise that would connect a theme in the course, before turning to my 4-C creative intervention. During these planning sessions, I provided choices as to what I could "lecture" on; one talk given was on creativity in a science and engineering context (see Mullen, 2017).

Following my PPT presentation on the 4-C creative intervention, teams were asked to assign roles (e.g., facilitator, recorder, time keeper). Peers worked interactively, turning the abstractions with examples into culturally and contextually relatable, illustrative ideas and specifics, connecting to the country of interest where applicable. (Group recorders penned highlights to accompany the seven main prompts [Appendix 4.1]). Directly following the creative conversations was a synthesizing activity with the whole class; teams took turns as speakers shared aloud while I took notes and asked clarifying questions. Students' verbal reports to the class put me in an ideal position of actively listening while crafting a rough summation in my field notes. I was able to both verify that targeted learning was occurring and ensure that I would be able to make sense of teams' written activity sheets. In my classroom record I also noted any areas of confusion that could benefit from clarification. Consistently, during the sharing in class, the lecturers spontaneously made comments, also captured in my field notes.

Collecting data from teams was also a strategy I consider productive in my own teaching in the United States, and it's efficient for brainstorming ideas. Temporal constraints on my creative intervention meant that my PPT setup had to be crisp and brief while conveying the open-ended nature of the activity. In my long career of teaching in colleges and universities in two countries, I've found that most students prefer to process ideas with their peers, even when not guided to or encouraged. In China, students were eager to try the team approach to learning, despite it being new to them. While Canada-based students were sitting in groups, they had not yet worked as teams because the semester had recently begun; thus, the discussion of creativity and the 4-C model posed challenges on two levels (i.e., collaboration and content). Similarly, students in the Australian context, having only met once, had not yet engaged in activity. Thus, my creative intervention—lecture and team project—may have paid dividends for future classes.

Engaging as small teams can propel creative focus and immersion in compositional tasks, which is conducive to experiencing "flow" (Csikszentmihalyi, 1996; Mullen, 2017, 2018). I went into every data collection session believing that despite constraints (particularly the restriction on time), students could apply a creativity model that was unfamiliar to them and even become absorbed (lost) in the task, deriving both value and meaning. Csikszentmihalyi's (1996) take on peak engagement that transcends restraints in creative situations emboldened my creative risk-taking. This meant that time limits, newness of creativity (especially theory-informed models), unfamiliarity with peers, lack of creative confidence, poor motivation, fear of the unknown, and so forth were barriers that could be surmounted in the experience of flow.

4.3.6   4-C Interviews with Individuals and Groups (Data Source 3)

For category 2, interviews with individuals and groups, 4-C interviews generally took two forms. One-on-one interviews were conducted with faculty and leaders, and group-based interviews were held with available stakeholders in various professional roles, typically faculty, leader, and student. (There was also minor representation from alumni and visiting professors in Canada.)

Individual interviews, approximately 30–40 minutes, took place in faculty/leader offices. Sessions began with my visual depiction of the 4-C theory in which each C exists as a domain and in relation to the others; just like the participating groups, interviewees were given the creativity handouts. For a few minutes, individuals silently read the printed materials. I wrote their responses in my researcher notebook, documenting key points and verbally checking for understanding. (Interviewees verbalized ideas, but did not prepare, write, or produce anything.)

Group interviews were organized to occur concurrently with a seminar of mine in a workshop series. Attendees of my public talks (unknown in advance) could respond to the activity prompts with others or alone. Typically, they opted for the latter arrangement, so more time was allotted for sharing by individuals. Listeners picked up on a particular point of interest and elaborated, without addressing all of the prompts, an efficient tactic proving informative and inclusive. While listening to individual responses, I produced a draft research summary, later verified for accuracy and completeness by consulting attendees' written activity sheets, in addition to the video/audiotape that one institution automatically recorded for public events. Thus, written, verbal, and, in one instance, visual data were obtained from group interviews, supporting the triangulation of results.

4.3.7   Local and Onsite Documents (Data Source 4)

Local and onsite documents were collected when they contained relevant contextual information. Examples are reports citing demographics and trends, course syllabi and outlines, program bulletins with course descriptions, biographies of lecturers, topical publications, mission statements, academic and cultural events, talks and workshops, global education programs, etc.

4.3.8   *Photographic Archive of Artifacts and Materials (Data Source 5)*

A photographic archive of artifacts and materials was accompanied by descriptions. Containing dozens of snapshots taken at each site, this archive served as an invaluable visual record. Certain photographs were selected for possible reference and/or display in this book, especially the case studies. Using my camera, pictures taken were of task-specific creative artifacts (with non-identifying information), including my own PD and creative learning. While building the archive for myself, I matched photographs with contextual detail. In research terms, certain field-based photographs and descriptions jogged my memory of critical moments. This documentation clarified details and nuances in my field notes by way of a visual reminder.

4.3.9   *Researcher's Field Notes (Data Source 6)*

Researcher's field notes (including PD) is the last major classification of data collection. These site-based records developed into a substantial, lengthy document. Like my other handwritten data sources, I spoke aloud written notepads into a recording device, turning it into a Word document, subdivided to match each glocality and timeframe. My field notes encompassed three themes and numerous study elements.

4.4   Technology Decision-Making and Usages

I refrained from using electronics and technologies (with the exception of my PPT presentation and photographs). Because laptop computers commonly have an integrated camera/webcam, they can be perceived as a threat. For the duration of the study, I used an old-fashioned paper notepad for documenting conversations and occurrences. I didn't want to chance anyone feeling unnecessarily wary, self-conscious, or awkward when my creativity exercise was meant to trigger free thinking and creative expression.

Another point is that research materials/handouts were not shared before my visitations with groups. Because I was navigating unknown interpersonal and cultural waters, I was vigilant about complying with the approved research procedures from my home institution. While openly penning my notes during data collection encounters, I constantly made eye contact, leaving the majority of time for participants to reflect and respond to my prompts and impromptu questions.

4.5   Stakeholder Buy-in and Participation

For this study, buy-in was solicited in a few ways. Higher educational institutions were my sponsors. Before and after my visit, the Fulbright Commission directly made contact with the two research sites (China and Canada) it sponsored. For all three sites, buy-in came through connections, whether it was the Fulbright Commission communicating with my institutional host (after I had secured the official invitation) or a colleague who conveyed my interest.

Having a "Fulbright" is respected, worldwide, which was the main criterion for acceptance in China and Canada. Being a senior J. William Fulbright alumnus facilitated my entry into Australia. In all of these cases, my visit was financially supported by grants and matching contributions from the host institutions. During my negotiations with the university host in the foreign country, agreements covered voluntary services I would perform. (These included giving public talks, holding topical seminars, giving feedback on manuscripts, tutoring students, and advising faculty in their research). In all three locations, I gained entry because of my willingness to perform voluntary tasks helpful to the institution and because of my expertise and reputation. Along these lines, in addition to carrying out my research agenda, which included doing the 4-C lecture in classrooms, in China and Canada I gave talks and conducted seminars in mutual areas of interest (e.g., creativity and science). In China, I even facilitated a synchronously delivered conference (organized while in the US) on teaching and leadership (see Mullen, 2017).

Once on location at the three sites, it was up to me to secure the commitments for my research plan, specifically data collection. I relied on seven basic strategies while trying to be visible, flexible, adaptive, and persistent while expressing appreciation for others' kind efforts:

1. Developing two-way familiarity with institutional host and staff in advance of the visit.
2. Organizing what was possible prior to the visit (public talks, seminars, conferences).
3. Working on managing communications and details with the host's executive assistant.
4. Posting authorized messages with a self-introduction and brief description of my study, extending an invitation to participate in it, and offering to do the 4-C activity in classes.
5. Attending events/gatherings/functions/workshops/public talks to meet insiders and invite participation in my project.
6. Accepting invitations to interact more casually and initiating them; spending time getting to know stakeholders; and visiting faculty in different spaces.
7. Distributing a personalized flyer, bookmark, and/or business card with my information.

4.6   Researcher's PD and Creative Learning

Accounts of PD and creative learning undertaken by researchers in foreign environments are not typically shared. In educational research, PD is typically aimed at others' learning, reflection, and performance, often preservice and inservice teachers, not at the researcher's own PD (An academic journal devoted to educators' PD is Routledge's *Teacher Development*.) My PD as a researcher–pedagogue proved an enriching facet of experience that better prepared me for doing my study and reporting results. The creative learning I describe centers on my cultural-historical-political appreciation and immersion that was sponsored by the institutional hosts, evolved serendipitously onsite through invitations, or was self-enacted. Descriptions of my PD are restricted to this chapter, for which I draw upon my field notes and photographic archive.

4.7   China and Researcher PD

PD options, presented upon my arrival in Chongqing, were to be selected and added to my schedule. Delighted, I chose opportunities that might propel my knowledge about creativity in the Chinese culture: papercutting, musical instruments, calligraphy, music, tai chi, and hiking.

Participating in these PD sessions were Chinese stakeholders from the faculty of education, in addition to myself. Lacking a basic grasp of Mandarin, I felt self-conscious initially and was at a disadvantage because everyone at the Chinese research site spoke English, but with variable competency. The chance to interact in a pleasurable way did add naturally to the few Mandarin words I knew, but the important, unexpected result was that our language differences, and even my foreigner status, did not seem to matter in any of the PD contexts. Differences were less stark with the synergy of creating with others.

Because the paper design seminar turned out to be the most relevant to my pedagogic research in China, I focus on my creative breakthrough while papercutting. But first, I'll set the scene. Participating in the seminar were students (not enrolled in my course) and faculty. We were luxuriating in the company of an internationally acclaimed, prize-winning artist. Our teacher opened with background information on the art of paper design, explaining that papercutting is a famous Chinese innovation that continues to this day. Evolving uniquely all over the world, it's been adapted to different cultural styles. Viewable from both sides, papercutting is "hollow art"; belonging to the "mother arts," it has an "intangible cultural heritage." After Cai Lun (a Chinese official) invented paper in 105 AD, the cultural practice of "paper cut art appeared during the Han dynasty in 4th century AD; the oldest surviving paper cut out is a symmetrical circle from the 6th century found in Xinjiang China" ("Papercutting," 2020).

While directing us to create designs on a single piece of paper, our teacher refer-enced papercutting as using few resources (only simple tools—scissors, pencil, glue, wax, and other types of paper, etc.). As I worked on my designs, everyone seemed relaxed and familiar with the art form. Shaping some of their designs into modern calligraphic lettering, they were combining this Chinese visual art form of writing with paper art, a kind of impressionistic linguistic–visual code. Learning became apparent at various levels: working with one sheet of paper in a continuous fashion; utilizing basic resources; observing visual symbolism and imagery emerge across an entire group; and being in a non-judgmental space where all were encour-aged to express ourselves. The teacher expressed confidence in our ability to do papercutting, and she did not hold up her well-known artwork until the end.

Absorbed in the moment with scissors and paper in hand, it struck me that what I had in store for my preservice class in Chongqing (soon to begin) could be thought as "papercutting," but in an academic sense with the support of creativity theory in action. My students would be using one sheet of paper for their poster activity, as planned, but now I knew that I could make this assignment culturally relevant—as a modern-day twist on Chinese papercutting. This thought process influenced how I introduced the activity to my undergraduate class, thereby bringing cultural reso-nance to the 4-C model and creativity project.

A few days later, I introduced to my own class the culminating paper poster proj-ect as an educational take on papercutting. The creative challenge set before them was to modernize the ancient art form by creatively rendering the 4-Cs in a uniquely personal and cultural way. I also enacted, with the reinforcement of my well-liked Chinese translator, an invitational, non-judgmental tone for our course, backed by the support of explicit instructions to be creative in a relaxed atmosphere within a small theater in the education building.

With few resources at their disposal, students had the golden opportunity to turn inward. They were encouraged to trust the creative process, make meaning, and feel confident, problem-solving the constraints and welcoming the unknown. Manifesting as one continuous artwork, the paper poster project was fashioned by every team, despite restraints, through a series of interconnected activities. To get to this point, the class interpreted and applied the 4-Cs to a large sheet of paper after mining their personal essays for images to use. Then the teams extended the 4-Cs with a unifying image for integrating the Cs on their poster, which was designed to have dimension-ality and depth and reflect joint decision-making. Working collaboratively, students absorbed theory-informed creativity with my guidance while navigating educa-tional constraints.

Returning to the PD papercutting session, as it drew to a close, the student cre-ators spontaneously arranged their paper designs on the floor to make a collage (Fig. 4.2).

The collage kept changing form and expression in the hands of the young female students who seemed earnest about conveying "coded" messages. A central image of each shape was "double happiness," a ligature composed of 囍, meaning joy. Viewable numerous times in the photograph, this red symbol denotes marriage and wedding ceremonies in the Chinese culture. The butterfly image was also duplicated

Fig. 4.2 Paper designs being arranged into a collage by student creators (C. A. Mullen)

across the artwork, symbolizing marital bliss and immortality. As is characteristic of Chinese symbols, they often overlap and their meanings become layered. The meanings changed with each new formation, especially as images were differently grouped. In Chinese culture, the butterfly represents a young love's heart. The double happiness symbol next to the butterfly implies many possible storylines or moments (such as the happiness felt by, and wished for, a young couple taking a vow). Also repeated in the picture, the panda, like double happiness, was cast as a twinned image. Perhaps the panda triggers happiness when paired or grouped with the symbols of double happiness and/or the butterfly. Pandas symbolize peace and friendship, echoing the wedding motif or wish for a happy marriage.

I managed fleeting bits of storylines as creators moved around their designs. Their eager (and crowded) photographing made me think that delightful messages had been inferred from the changing collage. I was left wondering what dynamic creative processes might be in store with my own class and if I could usefully capitalize on what I had witnessed that day. Once alone, I created a 4-C poster (not shown here or to anyone) divided into four *unequal* parts in which I applied the 4-C theory: Big-C—China/Cai Lun's invention of paper; Pro-C—our Chinese teacher known for her papercutting expertise; Little-c—the Mini-c artifacts she showed us, thereby honoring a few previous participants; and Mini-c—the act of papercutting and creation of meaningful art/ifacts. Mini-c occupied the center of the poster, taking up the most space, with Little-c close in size and overlapping. Moving footprints were sketched, integrating the 4-Cs.

4.8 Canada and Researcher PD

In contrast, in Canada, I created my own PD opportunities for exploring creativity, which introduced me to deeper aspects of contemporaneous Canadian culture. Inspiration came from two sources: the Canadian literature and life around me. What may have seemed unrelated or recreational at the time helped me better understand the data being collected.

My select Canadian PD creative activities ranged considerably. I documented compelling collections in art galleries and museums, and live performances, including educators' talks. One was a creative performance by a multicultural class—the subject, asbestos poisoning and cost to humanity. Australia was used as an example, given its asbestos legacy and the vulnerability of Aboriginal people to asbestos-related cancers (Asbestos Safety and Eradication Agency, Australian Government, 2017). Graduate students interactively "read" the script that drew upon their papers. Under the participatory guidance of their professor and an Australian environmental activist, they educated their audience about the facts and "protested" asbestos as socially unjust.

Canada had changed so much since having completed my education there decades earlier, so I immersed myself in learning anew. Particular cultural phenomena that struck me revolved around its booming immigrant population and rapidly changing diversity, Indigenous invisibility and protests, and the related anniversary celebration of the nation. Canada's claim of its birth date in 2017—and 150 symbol of its anniversary—showed up in my data. Graduate student participants had cited the anniversary as a Big-C Canadian creative product. Without an explanation of what this meant to them (their comments were vague), I investigated the symbol.

This led me to an Indigenous protest exhibition organized around nationhood and identity, and this message: Canada was celebrating its 150th anniversary, even though the First Peoples of Canada had inhabited the old world for hundreds of years before European settlers arrived. To override the originating creation story with its own, the nation blatantly denied the existence of the original inhabitants, in effect obliterating Canadian history while perpetuating colonialism's living legacy. The omission of Indigenous history and, indeed, existence invoked modern-day colonial racism. Paradoxically, Canada was an immigrant safe haven.

In fact, a Big-C experience of creativity most Canadian participants mentioned was Canada's unique social justice mindset: "Canada, as a model of diversity and tolerance, has a creative culture; absorbs immigrants and refugees, offering asylum." This viewpoint was shared by some graduate students engaged in creative activity and interviewed in mixed demographic groups. Offering contrast, some faculty criticized colonizing dynamics in Canada (and elsewhere) that subjugate visible minorities, particularly Aboriginal people. Canadian Indigenous pupils have been deprived of racially honed creative cultural curriculum. While Canada-based published academics were urging societal change through decolonized policies and practices in North America and worldwide, Canadian Aboriginal artists were asserting their own agency.

My creative PD experiences in Canada, then, materialized differently than in China. Creative learning at the Canadian research site was sparked, in part, around data that were at times too stark, even cryptic, to decipher. (My interpretations of Canadian Indigenous literature and art have been published [e.g., Mullen, 2019c].)

4.9   Australia and Researcher PD

Two of my PD-related creative experiences stood out in Australia: self-guided excursions to Aboriginal heritage sites, and a conference implicitly recognizing issues critical to creativity.

Visiting Aboriginal heritage sites, such as rock engraving locations, propelled my creative PD learning. In 2019, I returned to several places of Aboriginal significance in Sydney that I had once visited as a tourist with my partner. This time, though, I was mindfully consulting Indigenous cultural heritage guidebooks, with the understanding that while not all sacred historic sites can be "seen," the stories can and should be told. An archetypal example is the iconic Sydney Opera House, a famous performing arts center that sits on the harbor. Standing before the distinctive innovative structure, I imagined what had once been—Bennelong Point, where, in 1790, a British governor "had a hut built for Bennelong, the most renowned Aboriginal mediator of the early colonial period" (p. 26); in 1788, during the first British settlement in Australia, he served as an interlocutor between the Eora and the British (Hinkson & Harris, 2015). In this place, Aboriginal people gathered—presumably to learn of governmental views. Despite the significance of this event and excavation of the site before 1959 that uncovered remains, the opera building was constructed on the same spot. One is hard pressed to find traces of the activity or anything that honors him in the vicinity. Land rich in Indigenous and colonial heritage is conspicuously celebrated for the Opera House only.

Broader in scope, Sydney's "heritage landscapes" celebrate the "architectures" of "British settlement"; the Opera House is presumably emblematic of not only the "invention" of British "settlement as heritage" but also "an associated capacity to forget." Ongoing "dispossession and poverty," explained Shaw (2007), manifests in the denial of "Aboriginal entitlement to land" and inherent tribal rights and reparations (pp. 82–84). One can "see" from "touring" Sydney that environments are built and artifacts erected to signify what is valued.

Additionally, I attended a conference focused on psychology in medical education where I learned of exciting creativity ideas and alternative techniques being used in Sydney to cultivate medical students specializing in cancer treatment. Referred to as arts and theatre (not creativity per se), an intervention for resocializing health professionals involves role play (simulation) of case dynamics. Scripts composed of verbatim conversations between actual health professionals and cancer patients are prepared in advance. Then, among observers (e.g., medical students), a "patient" (intern) shares with the "doctor" (another intern) feelings like vulnerability and fear of the unknown (about cancer treatment). The words always originated in real-world settings, teaching health care professionals sensitivity to each person's trauma (Lim, 2019).

Grace Under Pressure, a public theatrical production in the making, is, as Lim (2019) presented, a reflection of transformative work at her university-based medical school. According to her, a medical doctor and trained actress, the production is meant to provoke social change—it weaves together health professionals' experiences and the words of patients. The work is about cultivating caring professionals who do not exercise dynamics of bullying, harassment, and "teaching by humiliation." Fostering "healthcare worker resilience in the face of [an] adverse health culture" is a motivation for this endeavor. A "voice" is being given to taboo health issues.

4.10   PD Experience for Participants

Participants were exposed to PD and learning through my 4-C creativity program. My interest around educators' (students and faculty) increased awareness of creativity led me to deliver the 4-C activities in ways that accommodated varying circumstances and requests. As part of the PD experience, planning and debriefing sessions were held for my workshops in Canada and Australia. I engaged (and was engaged by) lecturers, with attention on continuity in student learning and the fit of my program. One institutional host acknowledged the effort behind my collaborative planning efforts with staff, writing, "Your 4-C activities have been designed with collaboration and input from the lecturers and align with the learning outcomes of each course."

4.11   Graphical Representation of the 4-C Creativity Model

I now compare my image (Fig. 4.1) to Beghetto's (2019) 4-C visual rendering. To clarify, participants were exposed only to my graphical version of the 4-C model. (Beghetto's version was not published until 2019.)

As mentioned earlier, Fig. 4.1 served as my lead-in for communicating aspects of the 4-C theory and establishing the purposes of the session. Use of this slide helped to ensure consistency in my (verbal and visual) explanations about the model and creative task(s) ahead.

For Fig. 4.1, while in data collection mode, key points were that (1) Mini-c is the focal point of this framework, which affirms and even "privileges" creators' everyday creativity in the learning process (Kaufman & Beghetto, 2009); and (2) the activity being undertaken in the educative space reflects this philosophy. A personal and sometimes private experience of creativity, Mini-c involves being creative on one's own terms, and not subject to the judgment of an external source. By definition, Mini-c is at the center of creative existence; corresponding with this theorizing, it is the centerpiece of the image (Fig. 4.1), denoted by the thickest and boldest line of a circle. Deserving emphasis, Mini-c and Little-c can be empowered within teaching and learning contexts. Should the organic act of creativity be recognized (such as for its novelty and usefulness), it becomes Little-c. Suggesting this transition are the arrows moving from Mini-c to Little-c on the figure.

In turn, Little-c becomes Pro-C when the professional/expert individual or collective is acknowledged, such as by peer evaluators, for making a creative contribution of some distinction. (The arrows pointing from Little-c to Pro-C denote this.) Rarely do Pro-C educators make a Big-C splash, so the leap from Pro-C to Big-C is not considered particularly realistic, unlike the Mini-c to Little-c movement. Big-C, which as "eminent" and "legendary" creativity (Beghetto & Kaufman 2007), is recognition of greatness or something great—importantly, it emerges from the other creativity types (as the directional arrows suggest).

Note, in my illustration, that the thickness of the circles changes, as the eye moves from Mini-c to the other Cs. Being signaled is Kaufman and Beghetto's (2009) special contribution to creativity theory, which addresses a gap in the literature that biased Big-C creativity in empirical studies of creativity. (Eminent creativity, having dominated creativity theory, closed off possibilities for identifying everyday creativity, and theorizing and studying it.) Over a decade ago, the 4-C theory advanced Mini-c as "a new category of creativity" for "creativity theory and research" (p. 73). Mini-c gives space and credibility to creativity in forms other than its most celebrated that, paradoxically, depend on the incubation and potential for something greater. With the Mini-c type, not only did Kaufman and Beghetto (2009) add a new category of creativity to research, but they also conceptualized a relatable type that is inclusive: "Mini-c creativity differs from Little-c (everyday) or Big-C (eminent) creativity as it refers to the creative processes involved in the construction of personal knowledge and understanding" (p. 73).

Besides Mini-c, the creativity duo also introduced Pro-C—professional creativity—"the developmental and effortful progression beyond Little-c that represents professional-level expertise in any creative area" (Kaufman & Beghetto, 2009, p. 1). While publishing an article, performing a play, or exhibiting a painting are all examples of Pro-C accomplishments, the Pro-C creator with in-depth domain expertise who is especially productive, well recognized, and impactful reflects Pro-C at an entirely different level. A pattern of achievements, solidified with major awards of distinction and acknowledgment from other Pro-C creators, adds value and significance to this category. "Creative impact" in "disciplines, domain, or practice" is striking, as is having reached "creative acumen" in a field (Kaufman & Beghetto, pp. 5, 32).

Worth noting, perhaps, Fig. 4.1 shows the 4-Cs somewhat differently than Beghetto's (2019) graphical representation (p. 30). In his chapter, influential elements stand out in a creator's transition, notably the "time" involved in moving from Pro-C to Big-C (for a discussion of time and its significance in the creator's life and death, see Kaufman and Beghetto [2009]). The illustration by Beghetto also denotes a shift for creators from the "internal" to the "external" world, with the small cs reflecting a more internal experience of creativity than the large Cs, which bring forth an external dimension (e.g., recognition from content experts in a field).

Additionally, Beghetto's (2019) figure depicts each of the progressive Cs in a larger font, with Big-C denoted as the largest of the 4-Cs and Mini-c as the smallest. His staircase-like diagram contains the 4-Cs positioned increasingly higher with each step (Mini-c is at the bottom and Big-C at the top). In my illustration, a series of interdependent circles with arrows links domains of creativity, suggesting degrees of time and creative impact. Mini-c is center stage, commanding the viewer's attention, with its disproportionately bolder line, and with Little-c also "forcing" itself within the line of vision. Pro-C, of definite significance, is reachable; in fact, countless professionals attain Pro-C recognition, thus its circle is denoted with a solid line. Differing from Pro-C, Big-C's circle is a dotted line. Achievable to very few, Big-C, a grand challenge, is practically unreachable in the worlds of education and academe.

Might my graphic and explanation add to the discourse that acknowledges Kaufman and Beghetto's (2009, 2013) unique perspective on creativity and contribution to educational knowledge? Owing to their creative conceptualization of creativities otherwise unrecognized and likely undervalued (i.e., Mini-c and Pro-C), the 4-C creativity model has attracted support for its viability, value, and impact. Many peer experts, some highly accomplished Pro-C contributors themselves, cite, describe, and reference the 4-C theory. It invites new ideas and proposed spinoff Cs, in my case Hidden-c (see Chap. 8). Such "playful" intellectual thought is, I think, a response to the generative space this model invites, and the re-theorizing and ongoing investigations and applications it inspires.

4.12 Analysis of All Project Data

In this final section, I discuss how I managed, coded, organized, and analyzed the data. Processes used for validating data are included in this description, as well as both established and unconventional methodologies for coding and interpreting data.

4.12.1 Managing Data

NVivo 12® (QSR International, n.d.) qualitative software allowed for the systematic management and organization of all data sources. Providing assistance with these tasks was a skilled doctoral assistant. In addition to the data being coded independently in NVivo, I manually coded all data sets using the keywords list. Because my early years training in qualitative research involved hard copy data organization and analysis rooted in a close read of raw data, I also organized the data sets in Microsoft Word and Excel. This way, any similarities and differences in coding might be more readily discerned. Interrater reliability was established for primary keywords/codes arrived at deductively and, in the second round of analysis, inductively. These procedures, proving fruitful early on, were refined in later phases.

Other technologies (e.g., smart phone, camera, software) were also utilized for recording handwritten field notes and participant activity response sheets. Technological activities involved creating a photographic archive of visual artifacts; converting my photographs of original artifacts into figures (using Photoshop), complete with descriptions tagged to pictures; and managing and analyzing data.

Speech-recognition software proved essential. After each onsite data session with a group or interviewee, I recorded my research field notes. While material was fresh, I used a handheld device (i.e., smart phone) to speak aloud my handwritten notes, thereby initiating a detailed transcription. After emailing myself the notes, I downloaded them to a protected laptop computer. Then I corrected the Word-formatted notes, checking for accuracy, after which the transcriptions were coded and analyzed. Collecting raw data and highlighting themes and participants' voices in storied accounts put "flesh" on the "bones" of this qualitative process.

Through a web portal, administrators in Canada provided access to the audio portion of my public talks. While listening to the tapes, I typed the relevant parts into Microsoft Notepad, a simple text editor enabling me to create documents that were later coded and analyzed.

4.12.2 Coding Data

Processes used to code, analyze, report, and display data adhered to an established convention of qualitative coding (e.g., Miles, Huberman, & Saldaña, 2020). Search terms—derived from my main research question and initial literature review findings—were used for identifying and coding educational concepts. Pre-existing keywords, subjected to deductive coding, included those previously listed herein. These first-level codes helped narrow my provisional start codes.

A document analysis (Miles et al., 2020; Stage & Manning, 2016) of the data was performed after all pertinent data sources were turned into searchable electronic files. (The thick pile of local sources, such as course syllabi, was reduced to applicable phrases and passages, and the hand-picked material was scanned, tracked, and coded.) To arrive at predetermined and emergent patterns, a basic coding and frequency count of codes ensued.

Following this cursory step, I performed "in vivo coding" (Miles et al.) of words and phrases surrounding keywords (e.g., *creativity*) in a sentence(s). This data analysis process attended to the context and nuances of each code while tracking participants' actual word usage (in the original, either written or spoken). Accounting for contextual associations with keywords, this effort yielded subcodes. My coding of words in context (i.e., short phrases, including quotes and citations) allowed for systematic documentation of participant statements about creativity, accountability, and context within the place/culture of interest. Coding context clues extended and deepened the process of counting primary keywords.

For each initial and emergent keyword, a corresponding colored highlighter/font was used, encompassing all data (e.g., interview transcriptions and artifacts), and eventually tentative themes. Afterward, for each glocality I created results-based graphics of topical information using Excel and Microsoft Word, serving to condense and clarify the data. The most informative of these displays are shown in this book.

As additional keywords were identified for the three nations, more codes resulted, expanding the initial precodes. The 4-Cs, appearing constantly, contributed significant weight to the keyword *creativity* and its pre-existing subcodes—*Mini-c, Little-c, Pro-C,* and *Big-C*. Besides occurring deductively, the data analysis process unraveled inductively; each case study profited from the starter and elaborated keywords, with customization of usages benefitting emergent themes and eventually meaning-making illustrated in the three cases that follow.

4.12.3   Organizing Data

Kaufman and Beghetto's (2009) creativity model served as an advanced organizer for eliciting information relative to the 4-Cs in the live encounters. Table 4.3 shows my 4-C shell for identifying select Mini-c, Little-c, Pro-C, and Big-C examples from the Chinese, Canadian, and Australian settings. In each glocal case study, there's a chart with data-based highlights around these 4-C dimensions: scope of creativity, example of creative product, example of creative person and collective, creative curriculum and assessment, and experience of creativity.

Participants were not asked to provide examples of the dimensions (e.g., creative product) on this chart for any of the C's (like Mini-c). Indeed, they were not even aware of my table and categories on it; rather, this was the analytic structure I developed for both organizing the data on a more discrete level and identifying as precisely as possible what individuals, groups, and teams were thinking (and not thinking) relative to the C's in their responses.

With this conceptual tool, I was able to both discern and differentiate types of creativity in the glocality and corresponding nation, in addition to crucial dimensions (e.g., Mini-c creative product, etc.). Not only this, the organization of data using displays clarifies my process of analysis, facilitating readers' own interpretations and conclusions.

Table 4.3 Shell for Mini-c, Little-c, Pro-C, and Big-C examples in participant data (C. A. Mullen)

	Mini-c	Little-c	Pro-C	Big-C
Scope of creativity				
Example of creative products				
Example of creative people				
Creative curriculum and assessment				
Experience of creativity				

4.12.4   Analyzing Data

For coding, analyzing, and displaying data, I used conventional guides (i.e., Miles et al., 2020). I manually created keyword-in-context charts, along with frequency distributions of keywords and phrases (in addition to code counts).

Also, I analyzed my photographs of creativity/cultural phenomena (e.g., creative artifacts), attributing contextual and cultural meanings. Stage and Manning's (2016) content analytic approach to documents extended to my descriptions tagged to pictures (organized by location and data session). These researchers affirmed my exploratory approach to the research, noting that "visual artifacts" are still the most "under-utilized technique." As such, my approaches to analysis were inevitably open ended and discovery oriented yet rooted in conventional social science techniques.

Another unconventional stance adopted in the data analysis process involves transparency around researcher biases, assumptions, and judgments. Data do not speak for themselves; sociopolitical observations, including opinions on contentious issues, shape interpretations and results. Methodologist Charmaz used a social justice lens in concert with this methodological standpoint, thereby openly refuting the notion that any methodology is neutral or unaltered by psychological, sociocultural, and political forces, including researcher and participant biases (e.g., Charmaz, Thornberg, & Keane, 2018). She viewed social justice ideology as a legitimate standpoint for interpreting data (inevitably) shaped by dynamics of justice and injustice (e.g., equality and inequality, power and powerlessness). Seeing the task of data analysis this way sensitized me to perspectives of social (in)justice, often implicit, extending to Western and Eastern worldviews. Simple binaries were also complicated in the analysis (e.g., the notion that creativity is automatically just and ethical, and accountability unjust and unethical).

Data were validated by triangulation at different levels. Creswell and Poth's (2018) recommendations were among validation strategies used to help illuminate findings:

1. Multiple data sources at different locations were incorporated to ensure rigor of the results and increase their richness. Divergences were allowed in what data were collected, from whom, and how to accommodate varying dynamics and different opportunities for collecting information at the three sites.
2. Meaning was triangulated across sources (see Craft [1997]); using keyword searches to locate contextually germane statements in texts, the pivotal concepts of creativity, accountability, and culture from the literature reviewed were triangulated. The keywords/codes (listed in Table 4.1) were cross-referenced by participants in numerous ways (e.g., the intersection of *creativity* with *accountability* and *education*).

3. Patterns were identified and data triangulated by cross-verifying multiple sources, with an experienced pedagogue from the glocalities analyzing a sample set of field notes (while addressing my marked omissions and ambiguities). An information graphics expert confirmed the accuracy and effectiveness of my data displays.
4. Interrater reliability was established for the entire data set and coding differences resolved. Moreover, different experts were involved in the longitudinal process.
5. The entire data set was independently managed, coded, and analyzed by a skilled doctoral assistant and myself who used NVivo 12. In addition to guiding this process, I analyzed and coded data in Microsoft Word and Excel. Comparisons were made in person, focusing on codes/subcodes, emergent themes, and displays. Before data-based results were determined, we compared the various yields for the analysts. The detailed in vivo coding occurred through my manual categorization of data.
6. Recognized qualitative guides/texts, such as those cited herein, were consulted to ensure rigor and thoroughness.
7. Ronald Beghetto, co-originator of the 4-C theory, offered feedback on my methodological plan in 2016. Encouraging a lively approach to my creative technique, he did not think it would be difficult for college students to tackle the activity after hearing about his theory for the first time: "Creative thought and action are dynamic phenomena." Acting on this logic, students immediately engaged in the activity following their exposure to the 4-C model, which I succinctly described on slides and handouts, with examples (see Appendix 4.2). These strategies helped foster creative thought and action.

4.13 Summary

The focus of discussion was my methodological translation and application of the 4-C creativity model in colleges within transnational cultures. Relative to my creative intervention, I described dynamic case study strategies for eliciting educators' cultural views of educational creativity and accountability in China, Canada, and Australia. Three facets of the qualitative methodology were covered, in addition to six data sources. Readers are welcome to adapt my creativity strategies and approaches. Each reader will be the judge as to whether the case applications that follow express dynamic creativity in select glocalities, and the extent to which creativity is being released and revealed under constraint and within competitive global cultures. Chapter 5 follows with the account of creativity and accountability in China, the first case study.

Appendices

Appendix 4.1: 4-C Classroom Activity and Conversation Protocol for Glocal Adaptation (C. A. Mullen)

1. What does creativity look like in [your country's local/regional/national/global context] from your perspective?
2. What examples spring to mind for each component of the 4-C creativity framework?

    (a) Mini-c (creativity)?
    (b) Little-c (creativity)?
    (c) Pro-C (creativity)?
    (d) Big-C (creativity)?

3. In each example, what does accountability look like, or what forms does it take?
4. When you think about creativity and accountability on a global scale, how might the nation being considered compare with other nations' (testing) cultures?

Appendix 4.2: Synopsis of the 4-C Creativity Model and Examples (C. A. Mullen)

Mini-c. Mini-c is a transformative creative learning experience, action, or event that is novel and meaningful to creators of any age, anywhere; discoveries bring forth something new and useful.

- *General examples*: Writing a story, drawing an illustration, performing a history event, making a robot, discovering Earth's size, and solving a problem.
- *Specific examples*: Learning our planet is small in a vast solar system—discovering that Earth is smaller than other planets in our solar system, that the planets are small relative to the sun, and that the sun is a small star in our galaxy.

Little-c. When Mini-c is recognized by someone (e.g., a teacher), it transforms into Little-c within that context (classroom or elsewhere); feedback is key.

- *General examples*: Being acknowledged for writing a story, drawing an illustration, performing a history event, making a robot, discovering Earth's size, and solving a problem.
- *Specific examples*: Recognition for making a Mini-c discovery—discovering that Earth is smaller than other planets in our solar system, that the planets are small relative to the sun, and that the sun is a small star in our galaxy.

Pro-C. Pro-C belongs to a creative professional (not famous) recognized for contributing something of merit, achieving distinction (the seeds being Mini-c and Little-c discoveries).

- *General examples*: Improving a product, offering a fresh solution to a problem, clarifying another's innovation or finding, moving a field or discipline to a new place, rethinking a structure of knowledge, developing a new pedagogic approach or framework, etc.
- *Specific examples*: An astronomer discovered that a galaxy's stars do not always rotate in the same direction. She proved to be professionally creative, and her accomplishment was validated by experts (Csikszentmihalyi, 1996).

Big-C. Big-C is creativity of great magnitude reserved for famous achievements that transform cultures or societies, even the world. Mini-c and Little-c are seeds leading to creativity that makes a big splash and is celebrated (like an innovation that changes thought or behavior).

- *General examples*: Making a new discovery, creating something that stands on the shoulders of everything before it, accomplishing something never achieved or seen as impossible, finding a solution to a profound problem (e.g., societal), launching a breakthrough innovation or finding, moving a field or discipline to a new place, rethinking a structure of knowledge, offering a new way of thinking (idea, framework, or model) that goes "viral."
- *Specific examples*: The first moon landing—Australia's signal from the Parkes radio telescope transmitted live images of the Apollo 11 moonwalk on TV.

Appendix 4.3: Message Inviting 4-C Participation from Educators (C. A. Mullen)

Hello. I am writing to invite your participation as an educator in creative activities. These are theory-informed and provide insight into creativity in relation to accountability and culture. Creativity is an important twenty-first-century skill and capacity that we are expected to demonstrate in the global economy. In this PD seminar, we will first talk about creativity theory and then apply the 4-C Model of Creativity from educational psychology (Kaufman & Beghetto, 2009). To do this, we will draw upon four types of creativity (the 4-Cs) to identify examples in your cultural contexts. This activity will occur within peer groups so we can compare results. Time permitting, we will also produce a paper poster representing the 4-Cs: Mini-c, Little-c, Pro-C, and Big-C.

What you can expect to gain from this experience is to be able to discuss and apply a major educational theory of creativity. You'll also develop a greater appreciation of your own creativity and how to express it using a popular framework of creativity. Because creativity is under duress with constraints like testing and accountability, we must intentionally develop our creativity and apply it in meaningful ways. All that is produced within our time together will be returned so you can retain your original work. Carol Mullen, facilitator, designed this program to turn the 4-C theory into a method for authentically and creatively engaging educators.

References

Asbestos Safety and Eradication Agency (Australian Government). (2017). *National asbestos profile for Australia* (pp. 1–40). Retrieved from https://www.asbestossafety.gov.au/sites/asea/files/documents/201712/ASEA_National_Asbestos_Profile_interactive_Nov17.pdf

Au, W. (2011). Teaching under the new Taylorism: High-stakes testing and the standardization of the 21st century curriculum. *Journal of Curriculum Studies, 43*(1), 25–45.

Beghetto, R. A. (2019). Structured uncertainty: How creativity thrives under constraints and uncertainty. In C. A. Mullen (Ed.), *Creativity under duress in education? Resistive theories, practices, and actions* (pp. 27–40). Cham, Switzerland: Springer.

Beghetto, R. A., & Corazza, G. E. (Eds.). (2019). *Dynamic perspectives on creativity: New directions for theory, research, and practice in education* (pp. 137–164). Cham, Switzerland: Springer.

Beghetto, R. A., & Kaufman, J. C. (2007). Toward a broader conception of creativity: A case for "mini-c" creativity. *Psychology of Aesthetics, Creativity, and the Arts, 1*, 73–79.

Beghetto, R. A., & Sriraman, B. (2017). *Creative contradictions in education: Cross disciplinary paradoxes and perspectives*. Cham, Switzerland: Springer.

Burnett, C., & Smith, S. (2019). Reaching for the star: A model for integrating creativity in education. In C. A. Mullen (Ed.), *Creativity under duress in education? Resistive theories, practices, and actions* (pp. 179–199). Cham, Switzerland: Springer.

Cancienne, M. B. (2019). Embodying *Macbeth*: Incantation, visualization, improvisation, and characterization. In C. A. Mullen (Ed.), *Creativity under duress in education? Resistive theories, practices, and actions* (pp. 361–381). Cham, Switzerland: Springer.

Charmaz, K., Thornberg, R., & Keane, E. (2018). Evolving grounded theory and social justice inquiry. In N. K. Denzin & Y. S. Lincoln (Eds.), *The Sage handbook of qualitative research* (5th ed., pp. 411–440). Thousand Oaks, CA: Sage.

Ciuffetelli Parker, D., & Craig, C. J. (2015). An international inquiry: Stories of poverty–poverty stories. *Urban Education, 52*(1), 120–151.

Craft, A. (1997). Identity and creativity: Educating teachers for postmodernism? *Teacher Development, 1*(1), 83–96.

Craft, A., Cremin, T., Burnard, P., Dragovic, T., & Chappell, K. (2012). Possibility thinking: Culminative studies of an evidence-based concept driving creativity? *International Journal of Primary, Elementary and Early Years Education, 41*(5), 538–556.

Craft, A., McConnon, L., & Matthews, A. (2012). Creativity and child-initiated play: Fostering possibility thinking in four-year-olds. *Thinking Skills and Creativity, 7*(1), 48–61.

Creswell, J. W., & Poth, C. N. (2018). *Qualitative inquiry and research design: Choosing among five approaches* (4th ed.). Thousand Oaks, CA: Sage.

Cropley, D. H., & Patston, T. J. (2019). Supporting creative teaching and learning in the classroom: Myths, models, and measures. In C. A. Mullen (Ed.), *Creativity under duress in education? Resistive theories, practices, and actions* (pp. 267–288). Cham, Switzerland: Springer.

Csikszentmihalyi, M. (1996). *Creativity: The psychology of discovery and invention*. London, UK: HarperPerennial.

Csikszentmihalyi, M. (1999). Implications of a systems perspective for the study of creativity. In R. Sternberg (Ed.), *Handbook of creativity* (pp. 313–335). Cambridge, UK: Cambridge University Press.

G20. (2020). *Wikipedia.* Retrieved from https://en.wikipedia.org/wiki/G20

Glăveanu, V. P. (Ed.). (2016). *The Palgrave handbook of creativity and culture research.* London, UK: Palgrave Macmillan.

Henriksen, D., Creely, E., & Henderson, M. (2019). Failing in creativity: The problem of policy and practice in Australia and the United States. *Kappa Delta Pi Record, 55*(1), 4–10.

Hinkson, M., & Harris, A. (2015). *Aboriginal Sydney: A guide to important places of the past and present* (2nd ed.). Canberra, Australia: Aboriginal Studies Press.

Kaufman, J. C., & Beghetto, R. A. (2009). Beyond big and little: The Four C Model of Creativity. *Review of General Psychology, 13*(1), 1–12.

Kaufman, J. C., & Beghetto, R. A. (2013). Do people recognize the four Cs? Examining layperson conceptions of creativity. *Psychology of Aesthetics, Creativity, and the Arts, 7*, 229–236.

Kauper, K., & Jacobs, M. M. (2019). The case for slow curriculum: Creative subversion and the curriculum mind. In C. A. Mullen (Ed.), *Creativity under duress in education? Resistive theories, practices, and actions* (pp. 339–360). Cham, Switzerland: Springer.

Kempf, A. (2016). *The pedagogy of standardized testing: The radical impacts of educational standardization in the US and Canada.* New York, NY: Palgrave Macmillan.

Kim, K. H. (2011). The creativity crisis: The decrease in creative thinking scores on the Torrance tests of creative thinking. *Creativity Research Journal, 23*(4), 285–295.

Kim, K. H., & Chae, N. (2019). Recapturing American innovation through education: The creativity challenge for schools. In C. A. Mullen (Ed.), *Creativity under duress in education? Resistive theories, practices, and actions* (pp. 215–233). Cham, Switzerland: Springer.

Li, Q., & Gerstl-Pepin, C. (Eds.). (2014). *Survival of the fittest: The shifting contours of higher education in China and the United States.* Heidelberg, Baden-Württemberg: Springer.

Lim, R. (2019, September). *Grace under pressure: Healthcare worker resilience in the face of adverse health culture.* Presented at the Inaugural Psychology in Medical Education symposium, Sydney, Australia.

Miles, M. B., Huberman, A. M., & Saldaña, J. (2020). *Qualitative data analysis: A methods sourcebook* (4th ed.). Thousand Oaks, CA: Sage.

Mullen, C. A. (2017). *Creativity and education in China: Paradox and possibilities for an era of accountability.* New York, NY: Routledge & Kappa Delta Pi.

Mullen, C. A. (2018). Creative learning: Paradox or possibility in China's restrictive preservice teacher classrooms? *Action in Teacher Education, 40*(2), 186–202.

Mullen, C. A. (Ed.). (2019a). *Creativity under duress in education? Resistive theories, practices, and actions.* Cham, Switzerland: Springer.

Mullen, C. A. (2019b). Global leadership: Competitiveness, tolerance, and creativity – A Canadian provincial example. *International Journal of Leadership in Education, 22*(5), 629–643.

Mullen, C. A. (2019c). De/colonization: Perspectives on/by Indigenous populations in global Canadian contexts. *International Journal of Leadership in Education,* 1–20. https://doi.org/1 0.1080/13603124.2019.1631986

Mullen, C. A. (2019d). Dynamic creativity: Influential theory, public discourse, and generative possibility. In R. A. Beghetto & G. E. Corazza (Eds.), *Dynamic perspectives on creativity: New directions for theory, research, and practice in education* (pp. 137–164). Cham, Switzerland: Springer.

Mullet, D. R., Willerson, A., Lamb, K. N., & Kettler, T. (2016). Examining teacher perceptions of creativity: A systematic review of the literature. *Thinking Skills and Creativity, 21*, 9–30.

Narey, M. J. (2019). Who stands for what is right? Teachers' creative capacity and change agency in the struggle for educational quality. In C. A. Mullen (Ed.), *Creativity under duress in education? Resistive theories, practices, and actions* (pp. 313–337). Cham, Switzerland: Springer.

Papercutting. (2020). Retrieve from https://en.wikipedia.org/wiki/papercutting

QSR International. (n.d.). *Nvivo 12 for Windows.* Retrieved from https://www.qsrinternational.com/nvivo/nvivo-products/nvivo-12-windows

Sawyer, K. R. (2017). Creativity research and cultural context: Past, present, and future. *Journal of Creative Behavior, 51*(4), 352–354.

Shaw, W. S. (2007). *Cities of whiteness*. Carlton, Australia: Blackwell.

Stage, F. K., & Manning, K. (Eds.). (2016). *Research in the college context: Approaches and methods* (2nd ed.). New York, NY: Routledge.

Sternberg, R. J. (2006). Introduction. In J. C. Kaufman & R. J. Sternberg (Eds.), *The international handbook of creativity* (pp. 1–9). Cambridge, UK: Cambridge University Press.

Tan, A.-G. (Ed.). (2013). *Creativity, talent, and excellence*. London, UK: Springer.

Tienken, C. H., & Mullen, C. A. (Eds.). (2016). *Education policy perils: Tackling the tough issues*. New York, NY: Routledge & Kappa Delta Pi.

Yin, R. K. (2018). *Case study research and applications: Design and methods* (6th ed.). Thousand Oaks, CA: Sage.

Zhao, Y. (2012). *World class learners: Educating creative and entrepreneurial students*. Thousand Oaks, CA: Corwin Press.

Zhao, Y. (2014). *Who's afraid of the big bad dragon?* Thousand Oaks, CA: Jossey-Bass.

Part II
Applying the 4-C Creativity Model in Three Glocal Cultures

Chapter 5
China Case: Revealing Creativity and 4-C Responses

China compass Shutterstock

5.1 Questions and Purposes

"I'm not creative. I don't have much creativity and it's a born gift. The question is, can creativity be dug out?" wrote one Chinese preservice teacher participant. A widely held myth or misconception about creativity is that it's reserved for the talented and gifted when, in reality, "creativity is for everyone" and can be cultivated (Burnett & Smith, 2019, p. 183; Kaufman & Beghetto, 2009). Not long ago, creative pedagogical interventions overseas would have been highly unusual, at least as

© Springer Nature Switzerland AG 2020
C. A. Mullen, *Revealing Creativity*, Creativity Theory and Action in Education 5, https://doi.org/10.1007/978-3-030-48165-0_5

reported in the literature. However, the importance of globalization—and its benefits and detriments within learning environments—is gaining traction at last. Still,
"research on globalization in teacher education is in its early stages of development" (Brown, Lycke, Crumpler, Handsfield, & Lucey, 2014, p. 261), even though
creativity is recognized as an important skill in the twenty-first century (e.g.,
Cropley & Patston, 2019; Tienken & Mullen, 2016).

This case study describes a pedagogical innovation in China despite problematic
beliefs about creativity and globalization pressures. Together, these limit creativity
as a capacity for the arts (Burnett & Smith, 2019), derail creativity as something that
cannot be taught (Cropley & Patston, 2019), and restrict curriculum's content and
formats to tests and international measures of comparison (Brown et al., 2014;
Staats, 2011; Tienken & Mullen, 2016; Zhao, 2014).

A White American female professor awarded a Fulbright, my impetus as a
researcher was to see if Chinese candidates could demonstrate creativity and collaboration within a rule-bound testing environment. Could they show creativity
alone and in groups on educational activities when given explicit instructions to be
creative and guidance? Framing the creative intervention was the pedagogic research
question, Can preservice students within a college course in China discover creativity when encouraged under educational constraint? If student-centered curriculum
does have the potential to foster creativity in this nation's undergraduate programs,
I wondered what conceptions and examples of creativity students might identify
when prompted.

A conceptual and methodological focus was Kaufman and Beghetto's (2009)
four classifications of creativity: personal meaning-making (Mini-c), problem-
solving (Little-c), professional value (Pro-C), and cultural innovation (Big-C). The
4-Cs constitute their Four C Creativity Model (also, 4-C model). Creativity was
paired with active learning (AL) in this creative intervention. AL is countercultural
to the traditional lecture style and methods that dominate some university classrooms, subjecting students to only listening and receiving information (Bonwell &
Eisen, 1991). In their influential report on turning classrooms into dynamic places
of learning, Bonwell and Eisen ventured to define *AL* as instruction that "involves
students in doing things and thinking about the things they are doing" (p. 2). This
struck me as a starting point for defining AL, although they also identified five "general characteristics" of strategies that encourage AL in classrooms:

1. Students are involved in more than listening.
2. Less emphasis is placed on transmitting information and more on developing
   students' skills.
3. Students are involved in higher-order thinking (analysis, synthesis, evaluation).
4. Students are engaged in activities (e.g., reading, discussing, [and] writing).
5. Greater emphasis is placed on students exploring their own attitudes and values. (p. 2)

AL has become a recognized framework for generating dynamic engagement and
new knowledge in classrooms, and for moving students from simple to complex
tasks (e.g., Bean, 2011; Bonwell & Eisen; Creekmore & Deaton, 2015; Mullen,

2018). Drawn to AL for its strong fit that I see with dynamic creativity (Mullen, 2019b), I utilized it for clarifying pedagogic goals and activities and facilitating creative teaching and learning. In my role as a visiting professor and "Fulbrighter" in China, I was assigned to teach a class of undergraduate preservice students who had only known, up to that point, rote-based learning in their university preparation.

5.2 Background: Trends and Constraints

Contemporary world influences offer direction for researching teacher education in global contexts. The World Economic Forum (2013) identified creativity as a global competency needed for career success. Despite the forum's call to world leaders to shape agendas that prepare citizens for the creative economy, in mainstream China constraints such as rote-based testing goals overshadow creative teaching and learning (Staats, 2011; Starr, 2010; Zhao, 2014).

China's test-centric culture is said to greatly strain its citizens' creativity. Around the world and across the disciplines, China attracts strong criticism for negating creativity in favor of high test scores and respect for teacher authority (Mullen, 2017a; Staats, 2011). While at the forefront of enforced test-centric schooling around the globe, China's culture is nonetheless widely seen as impeding creativity and innovation (e.g., Niu & Sternberg, 2001; Niu, Zhang, & Yang, 2007; Zhao, 2014). The narrowly conceived test-driven culture not only limits expansion of new courses but also perpetuates a conformist environment that impinges on creative curricula (Mullen, 2017a). Because learning in China occurs within a rigid system of exams and accountability measures, an untested, commonly espoused belief is that Chinese students lack a creative capacity.

Given that my account of creativity unfolded in China, it makes sense to reference Sternberg's (2006) arguably controversial cross-cultural findings. In a study carried out in Hong Kong, creativity was compared in different countries. It was found that Asians tend to have a collective orientation and Westerners an individualistic orientation. Also, China's culture is broadly described as "collectivist," wherein "a greater emphasis [is placed on] the needs and goals of the group, social norms and duty, shared beliefs, and cooperation with group members" (Cox, Lobel, & McLeod, 1991, p. 828).

Nonetheless, a prevailing view of modern-day China is that its domination by a competitive mindset does not support its collectivist strengths (Zhao, 2014). Obviously, AL activities could be developed to capitalize upon its deeply-rooted cultural orientation.

On the educational front, the United States and China—generalized in the literature as a liberal democracy and a communist regime, respectively (e.g., Dimitrov, 2013)—are vigorous competitors. China, looking to the United States and its long history of creative inventions, has been yearning for world recognition in creativity and innovation; the United States, bedazzled by Shanghai's lead, has ironically shifted from its stronghold on creativity and innovation to relentlessly pursue accountability for American public schools (Lee & Pang, 2011; Zhao, 2014).

Scores from science, math, and reading measure and rank countries: China—labeled a developing country despite being predicted to have the world's largest economy before 2030—has been topping the charts, with the United States at/near the bottom.

In general, scholars from the West and the East may think that Chinese students are not ready for the new world. Notably, they have seen as bereft of "creativity and the ability to engage in unstructured decision making, which is the basis for innovation and creativity," despite their "extremely strong math and basic science skills" (Li & Gerstl-Pepin, 2014, p. 7). Assumptions worldwide about Chinese people engender a negative mindset about their very capacity to be creative and, by way of implication, fully capable. Yet developmental models of creativity, dynamically applied to educational settings in Chinese universities, while rare and emergent, have revealed otherwise—for example, observations undertaken in preK–12 schools affirm that culturally embedded creativity exists (e.g., Mullen, 2017a, 2017b, 2019a).

However, the negative bias, both explicit and implicit, that creativity is a rare gift unfortunately characterized the outlook of my undergraduate Chinese students. In fact, their sense of themselves as creatively impoverished (and hopelessly so) introduced a weighty psychological barrier in our classroom. It surprised me how relatively openly and persistently they expressed, through their self-introductions and personal essays, apprehensions and self-doubt about having any creativity. They also suspected that they would not be ready for employment requiring creativity, given the rising global demand for entrepreneurship, innovation, and creativity (Cropley & Patston, 2019; Tienken & Mullen, 2016; Zhao, 2014).

Compounding the belief that Chinese learners cannot create is the literature on China and the global news. A popularized image of Chinese students as rigid, uncreative beings within a nation that emphasizes and rewards recalling facts is commonplace and even reinforced by China itself (Mullen, 2019a). The problem is attributed largely to China's ancestral reproductions, hierarchical society, and narrow schooling (Niu et al., 2007). Evidence also suggests that the Communist Party imposes grave constraints on creativity in education by enforcing a test-based system across grade levels, upholding authoritarian-centered teaching and learning and separating winning from losing schools (Zhao, 2014).

My creative pedagogic intervention aimed to discover if there really is no creativity in China. Could China, a country requiring conformity and assessment through high-stakes standardized tests, for example, evidence any educational creativity in its university system? My search was for an understanding of possibilities for creativity in teaching and learning within the world's leading test-centric schooling culture.

5.3 Literature Review

An intellectual challenge for this study was to find a theory of creativity for informing it and a pedagogic strategy for engaging students in the innovation. Selected for
the Chinese preservice setting was the 4-C creativity typology—Kaufman and
Beghetto's (2009) validated psychology framework. To bring process-based enrichment to the classroom, the AL approach was utilized. Before describing the theory
and approach undergirding this article, creativity is defined, then AL more fully, and
each is anchored to the study context.

5.3.1 Creativity and AL

For this case study (like the two chapters that follow), creativity is operationalized
as something that is personally meaningful, involves problem-solving, stimulates
reflection on professional creativity, and creates space for pondering significant discoveries. Translated pedagogically, methodologically, and contextually as a brainstorming activity in my classroom in Chongqing, China, students were encouraged
to become immersed in (inter)personal meaning-making, problem-solve, animate
professional creativity, and identify breakthrough creativity or innovation in their
world, past or present. Of critical importance, they were guided to actively learn
alone and as teams in an open-ended, facilitated growth-oriented climate. Other
creative actions included expectations for asking questions with no single answer or
solution (Eisner, 2004) and thoughtfully appraising knowledge considered creative
(as per Robinson, 2015).

Put in the position of having to think and create on their own terms, with explicit
instructions to be creative but without a formula or access to any technology, they
became active learners. Emphasizing inquiry, learning, and teamwork, AL is pedagogically driven, educationally focused, and classroom based. Foci are skills-
building and higher-order thinking (Bean, 2011). AL being context dependent is
enriched by teacher or student goals and expectations, subject-matter content, grade
level, student population, and learning strategies (Creekmore & Deaton, 2015).

5.3.2 4-C Creativity Model

The 4-C Creativity Model is described more thoroughly in Chap. 3. To recap, its
four types/levels of creativity are "Mini-c," "Little-c," "Pro-C," and "Big-C."

5.3.3 AL Approach

AL, a guide for process-oriented pedagogy, is conductive to dynamic creativity (Mullen, 2019b). Within AL environments, students engage in meaningful activity, are absorbed in concepts and problems, and reflectively assess their understandings (Collins & O'Brien, 2011).

Actively learning across grades and subjects is beneficial. Working in groups helps with retaining ideas more than when the same content is delivered as a lecture (Kurczek & Johnson, 2014). Conversation, negotiation, and debates cultivate meaning-making and a disciplined but spontaneous setting. Hong's (2014) study involving 93 teacher education students in a Taiwanese university found that learner-centered environments can be effective. Interestingly, satisfaction with school life increases with group projects (Collins & O'Brien, 2011).

AL pedagogies also support learning and development, as well as reflective and improved practice (Collins & O'Brien, 2011; Johnson, Johnson, & Smith, 2006). King (2016) described teachers' learning as a complex system that furthers or limits changes in practice. Glocal settings can offer new challenges and opportunities for AL-oriented pedagogues.

Classroom teachers are expected to design environments that foster all students' learning (Creekmore & Deaton, 2015). Johnson and colleagues' (2006) influential report (originating in the 1990s) made known AL's popularity in college classrooms. AL strategies, primarily cooperative learning, guide content and skills development. A meta-analysis of cooperative learning studies confirmed that the skills acquired cultivate learning that is social, psychological, and academic (Kurczek & Johnson, 2014).

Within grades subjected to high-stakes testing, AL-oriented interactive classrooms connect learning, engagement, and achievement. In these, teachers target the processing of ideas and information, identifying and resolving problems, and performing meaningful tasks. Nondirective pedagogies propel higher-order critical and creative skills while purposefully interacting with peers (Johnson et al., 2006). Bean (2011) used AL writing strategies so college students' critical and creative capacities will develop. A transformative outcome of his classes is the ability to work with big ideas while discovering new ways of thinking, seeing, and being.

5.4 Creative Pedagogic Methods in Chongqing, China

This description of pedagogic methods addresses the details of the research exploration. Also explained is the handling of issues particular to cross-cultural study.

5.4.1   Case Study Research Design

Probing Chinese preservice teachers' creative and collaborative learning fit with a case study research design (as explained in Chap. 4). Knowing that I would guide the creative challenge with my bilingual translator's assistance, I developed learning strategies and activities for this educational setting. My curriculum was improved based on my translator's feedback. All materials were translated into Mandarin. In order to propel students' development of creative and collaborative capacities, AL goals, content, strategies, and exercises directed the learning.

The research design was supported by theory-building from psychology and education. Kaufman and Beghetto's (2009) 4-C theory was translated for the targeted context and applied within the classroom.

5.4.2   Syllabus, Materials, and Activities

With my translator, I worked around the clock to prepare the course I titled Creativity and Accountability in Education. (Arriving in China, there was a sudden decision not to offer the graduate course I had been asked to teach in advance and instead have me teach an undergraduate course.) Producing the syllabus and materials in both English and Mandarin, we nailed down procedural details.

My pedagogic goal was to have the class consider creativity in relation to accountability in education (see Appendix) using a variety of creative methods. With regard to the learning process, the class would read Kaufman and Beghetto's 2009 article and hear/receive my synopsis of the 4-Cs, complete with general and specific examples. The idea was for the students to imaginatively apply the 4-Cs by working creatively and collaboratively in groups. They were challenged to produce three-dimensional (3D) poster interpretations of the 4-Cs.

Students would be encouraged to identify specific images for each of the four creativities from individual essays on personal and professional creativity in their early lives. The only examples supplied for each of the four categories of the Cs would come from their personal writing, a creative challenge they might find appealing although probably unprecedented in their adult education. In small peer-based mentoring groups, they would collectively (1) draw upon their archive of essays; (2) select ideas, images, and symbols from their individual creative writing and integrate these with a symbol; (3) and share results with the entire class.

For the cooperative poster activity, the eight preservice teams would be guided to:

Together create a 3D paper poster of the 4-C creativity model: Selectively use the content from your essays to create personal and cultural visual images. Represent all 4-Cs and integrate your ideas creatively with a unifying symbol, image, or theme. Collaborate using the large sheet of paper, without electronic devices or consulting the Internet. Be resourceful. Utilize the basic tools at your disposal (e.g., scissors, markers, pencils). Think of the single paper as Chinese papercutting; working with it in a thoughtful manner, shape your paper into a meaningful design of something (e.g., a person, place, or thing). Be ready to perform on our stage using a script, which you'll create after your poster. Then your team will prepare a postreflection report in response to these questions:

- What example of Mini-c did you select for your poster and why? *Repeat this step for Little-c, Pro-C, and Big-C.*
- What was the integrative symbol your team incorporated into the poster? Why did you choose it?
- Did you experience any accountability constraints and/or cultural barriers while trying to identify a Mini-c example? *Repeat this step for Little-c, Pro-C, and Big-C.*
- What did your team learn from applying the 4-Cs from the 4-C creativity model?
- As collaborators, what did you feel after completing the project? Did anything change? If so, what and why?
- In what ways might this activity be improved for future classes?

Students were eager to know if they could use "Chinglish" (Chinese English) for creative activities, including the stage performance. Thus, for all generative work language became a source of creativity, with Mandarin used instead of English for words and phrases known or preferred in their first language. Mandarin-infused English permits slang and ungrammatical and nonsensical English—it's a friendly broken mix of languages ("Chinglish," 2020). (However, Chinglish can also be used or received in a pejorative way.) The exercises did not preclude creative languages because they would be graded holistically for the quality of cognitive and creative self-expression in relation to the 4-Cs, not language aptitude or artistic skill. Sentence structure (e.g., grammar) and artistic measures (e.g., technical skill) did not appear on my assessment rubrics. In fact, written feedback was even provided in English and Mandarin. Blending the languages in speaking and writing was welcome in our judgment-free workshop.

Facing what appeared to be poor self-confidence in their creative abilities—a widespread plight that Zhao (2014) underscored about Chinese students in mainland China—I became resourceful. Turning to the associate dean, I negotiated use of a small renovated theater with round tables to hold my classes (conveniently located in the education building). Besides drinks and snacks, without prompting he also used budgetary dollars to cover a master's student's assistance with basic tasks and classroom translation. In that theatrical sociocultural space, teams would be guided to cooperatively create a 3D paper poster of the 4-C model and dramatize their work using microphones, props, and music. A PowerPoint slide would be projected of each team's poster, with close-up shots of the components. (I photographed the artifacts.)

5.4.3 Participants, Program, and Place

Undergraduate education majors ($N = 34$) completed this intensive one-credit generic course, meeting twice weekly for 4 weeks. The course had just been titled; the syllabus and specifics were not shared until the first class session, so these sophomores intending to teach after graduation could not have prepared in advance or consulted with anyone.

The class was 82% female, an imbalance found in China's teacher education programs (Hernandez, 2016), just like the United States (U.S. Department of Education, 2013). Participating students were Han Chinese (90% of China's population; Wasserstrom, 2013), with varying English skills. Like other preservice programs in mainstream China, the ministry-set general education curriculum excludes the liberal arts (Starr, 2010), but an elective was accommodated for my visit. This classroom otherwise reflected the generic, underresourced, 4-year teacher education program being offered in an agriculturally historic university. While Chongqing is a large (but poor) city with over 30 million, the institution was physically located in a low-income, mountainous borough of an urban metropolis (Mullen, 2017a).

5.4.4 Bilingual Strategies

The bilingual translator translated my approved Institutional Review Board protocols written in English into Mandarin. Both versions were circulated, with students preferring the Mandarin documents. The Chinese translator (from China, where he taught college before pursuing a doctorate in the United States), along with a mediator (the master's student) from the host university, led the ethics discussion. Goals were to elicit questions and protect student privacy.

China and North America are depicted as an authoritarian monarchy and liberal democracy, respectively (Dimitrov, 2013). Knowing this profound cultural difference, I used bilingual strategies (e.g., Chinese translator, English–Mandarin translation, peer mediation) to help bridge the cultures while monitoring my American mindset. Researchers He and van de Vijver (2012) concur that investigator bias in cross-cultural research can be addressed.

5.4.5 Data Collection and Analysis

Data collection, during the month of the course (June 2015), reflected four completed activities:

1. Personal experience of creativity essay (individual)
2. 3D paper poster of the 4-C Creativity Model (group)
3. 4-Cs script and presentation (group)
4. Summative course assessment (individual)

Operationalized as AL activities, these were presented to the class as a needing a Chinese take on the 4-Cs. A reading-based discussion of the 4-C theory tied to education launched the workshop.

Data sources (i.e., the activities) were qualitatively coded and analyzed using keywords like *Mini-c*, *Little-c*, *Pro-C*, and *Big-C*. I created keyword-in-context charts, along with frequency distributions of such words. My teaching assistant (the translator) independently coded the information generated. During our data sessions, we made constant comparisons. We compared our results on sample sets of the data using the keywords; then we expanded and collapsed the keyword list, refining it; next we compared outcomes on the complete data sets, finalizing the codes; and also we identified emergent themes. Initial results were cross-checked with the peer mediator. A methodologist read a sample of the raw data. After inter-rater reliability was confirmed among parties, I generated the results-based displays (Table 5.1 and Fig. 5.4).

Table 5.1 Select Chinese usages of Mini-c, Little-c, Pro-C, and Big-C (C. A. Mullen)

	Mini-c	Little-c	Pro-C	Big-C
Scope of creativity	Creativity that is personally meaningful in learning and life	Creative problem-solving in everyday life that may have value or benefit	Notable accomplishment by a professional that contributes to a field	Groundbreaking creativity that redefines or reforms a field or domain
Example of creative product	Essays on personal creative experiences for which students chose a range of activities; 3D paper posters; group reflection on posters	Problem-solving through creative learning (e.g., inventing something out of found objects; using observation in the artistic process)	Preservice teacher validation of 4-C Creativity Model; transformation in understanding of creativity as within self and culture	China's great inventions (e.g., compass, hybrid rice); building feats (e.g., Great Wall, hydraulic engineering)
Example of creative person and collective	Generation of categories of Mini-c (e.g., "building new objects") for the 4-C Creativity Model	Generation of categories of Little-c (e.g., "inventing" and "creating") for the Creativity Model	Treatment of Pro-C as major professional teaching and learning activities with a social purpose	China's teacher, renowned worldwide (Confucius); generation of categories of Big-C
Creative curriculum and assessment	Introspective writing on creativity from childhood or youth by preservice class conveying values (e.g., nature, family)	Creation of 3D images of symbols and words on group posters representing everyday creative problem solving	Creation of 3D images of symbols and words on group posters representing major professional creativity	Creation of 3D images of symbols and words on group posters representing groundbreaking cultural creativity
Experience of creativity	Experiencing creative learning using a model and discovering different levels of creativity	Using explicit problem solving in relation to creativity in the personal essays and groups	Understanding creativity as a vast professional undertaking by schools and cultures	Importance of proactively supporting China in becoming creative and entrepreneurial

5.5 Thematic Results-Based Discussion

Across all sources three salient themes formed: creativity model, cooperative learning, and balanced curriculum. With its prevailing importance, description begins with the first theme and incorporates a breakout analysis of three teams' posters relative to the 4-Cs. Mini-c and Little-c are intertwined at times in the treatment of the themes and sometimes they are differentiated; Pro-C and Big-C are included in the analyses. (Reflection on cultural issues follows.)

5.5.1 Valuing the 4-C Creativity Model (Theme 1)

Valuing the 4-C creativity model is the primary data-based theme. In response to having approached this framework as an instrument of creative engagement, the Chinese students expressed worth and significance. Individually and collectively, they gave more attention to the Mini-c and Little-c elements of creativity in their work and within the classroom (just as Kaufman and Beghetto [2009] seem to do). While treating these as the sources of creative generativity, they also offered an expressive take on Pro-C and Big-C (see Table 5.1).

Successfully applying the 4-C typology across their activities, these preservice teachers consistently favored personal creativity in meaning-making and problem-solving while struggling more with its professional and cultural forms. China, their homeland, was intentionally credited with Pro-C and especially Big-C innovations and inventions. Assessing their learning experiences in this course, they expressed strong value for the 4-C model, anticipating transfer of the new learning into their future classrooms. Indeed, based on the enthusiasm, engagement, and originality of the students, their 4-C–informed 3D projects turned out to be the heart of the curriculum. About my research question, the student-centered creative curriculum was met with a high level of responsiveness, supporting not only the pedagogic intervention but also the experience of creativity within an undergraduate classroom in China.

Hence, value for the 4-C model was demonstrated in all of the AL activities, including the initiating exercise. To illustrate, take the personal essay for which the AL prompt was: "Describe a personal experience of creativity from your childhood. What have you experienced that helped you to find meaning through creativity in your everyday life (Mini-c)? Has your creativity ever been recognized by someone, such as how you made meaning of something or approached or solved a problem (Little-c)?"

In their essays on childhood creativity, interactive learning situations involving influential figures loomed. Value for being discovery-oriented—a creative process—and collaborating—an AL component—was stated or implied. Acceptance of creativity mostly came from primary teachers and friends. Friction was relayed in the perceived rejection of personal creativity by most parents and teachers of secondary and college grades, as well as society. With AL being context dependent, the preservice students whose influence was positive or negative from an early age felt that such forces had facilitated or hindered their experience of creativity.

Analyses of the essay data led to four subthemes in which Mini-c and Little-c overlapped where recognition of one's personal creativity (Mini-c) was sometimes recognized by at least one other person, thereby transforming into Little-c:

1. *Building new objects*, materials, or items out of ordinary things or natural resources, in effect utilizing things found at home and especially in nature, such as bamboo and clay
2. *Transforming objects* by discovering a new or unintended function, perhaps resulting in small inventions, such as carts made out of found objects
3. *Role-playing* teachers, family members, characters (e.g., film and cartoon characters), and others; playing games; singing, dancing, and performing (e.g., in school dramas)
4. *Creating new languages* by trying out unfamiliar words in English and Mandarin; discovering and perpetuating an unofficial language, specifically Chinglish

These subthemes arose from students' examples of personal meaning-making and creative problem-solving. For this exercise, they had all individually generated something new and valuable that is tangible (a typed story in essay form using Chinglish) and intangible (recall of positive and negative influences on their creativity from childhood). As these four abstractions of creative activity indicate, from the outset the class was showing itself to be budding creatively and potentially discovery oriented. This group had even identified enough examples of transforming things into something new that a category (number 2) was devoted to this.

To illustrate, in the first Mini-c/Little-c category, as a child the preservice teacher had built new objects out of ordinary things. Her creative response to a primary teacher's lesson involved observation and documentation of "shapes" (e.g., of nature, home, and life) in the children's worlds. Completing her first "life study," the girl had created an intricate collection: "My models were of frogs, birds, boats, flags, clothes, etc., out of folded paper, and how it all came together surprised me." The early experiential research project transcended arts and crafts.

This undergraduate was tacitly describing an open-ended, complex problem. As a girl, she was faced with the creative challenge of conducting a life study for which there was no single representation or solution. Just as she demonstrated creativity in childhood, as an adult she rendered her experience in yet another form, the personal essay in which this early memory was captured. In turn, her team thoughtfully appraised the creative experiences and knowledge reflected by each member's essay before selecting which ideas to put to the test. They felt moved to extract the idea of life study by turning their poster into a three-dimensional life object (a chrysalis). Conveying the self as a chrysalis and self-transformation as metamorphosis with this product, they engaged in more paper shaping to capture each of the 4-Cs. The originating student's AL creative process was enriched through engagement, skills-building, and higher-order thinking within her group. Shared inquiry, learning, and teamwork were all demonstrated components of the AL experience.

Another example from the same category details the story of a classmate who, as a boy, had brought together his pals after reading about "three-wheel carts." Roaming the countryside, they found discarded objects like broken machines. Out of the array something emerged—a working vehicle with a handle. Fondly recollected, he wrote, "I remember how excited we were when we finished—it must have been the first creative idea in my life that my friends admired." The preservice collaborative production transformed paper into a 3D cart with a handle that you could actually take hold of and move—and the project was 4-C inspired (Fig. 5.1).

The third category classifies role-playing. In high school, a preservice candidate had put on the drama *Feast at Hong Gate* with friends for the annual art festival. They did not want to simply "play a famous story in history for this competition— [they decided] to be creative so that [they could] make it more attractive." They identified a "historical fact that could not be revised" and yet altered the story line to enrich "body language and script." They "watched movies and read books," puzzling over how to make the "essence" their own. (They won the competition.)

Category four, creating new languages, was multifaceted and germane to the essays. Ironically, while some of the students could not remember a creative experience in their youth, they wrote creatively about language. One touched upon creative vocabularies from her past, largely extinguished by society's strict observance of grammar and pronunciation in learning English: "Chinese students are usually afraid to speak English in public places, although most of us are used to remembering English words every day for tests. We don't dare to face mistake." She added, "Singaporean English mixes languages—Singlish is a new and creative thing."

Fig. 5.1 Miracle Geniuses' 3D paper poster rendering of the 4-Cs (Chinese student team)

Yet she proposed a creative solution: "Why fear making mistakes? Why not make new rules and something unique, such as Chinglish?" It was this very storying of her recent exposure to creative uses of language and communication in Singapore that made her wonder if Chinglish could be innovative, as opposed to rebellious. The Mini-c and Little-c breakthroughs were something that she had hoped to claim for herself. Moreover, the hybrid communication system was becoming a collective Mini-c and Little-c phenomenon within our AL classroom.

5.5.1.1   Miracle Geniuses Team

Mini-c

Miracle Geniuses' poster (see Fig. 5.1) has a 3D paper construction of a three-wheel cart (previously mentioned). The Mini-c category was signified with the "little wooden car" that was invented in childhood. Thus featured by the team for this category of personal meaningfulness was the building of new objects out of ordinary ones and making something user-friendly.

Little-c

Little-c was a "hot-pot" (see lower right-hand quadrant of Fig. 5.1); after making this paper object, they added potato chip crumbs and foil from chip bags (denoting hot pot food). This iconic image proved attractive with its cultural, legendary status of having creatively solved everyday problems of cold and survival: "In the beginning days of China, sailors invented hot pot to get rid of the chill." Little-c was attributed to the recognition sailors would have received (from other sailors) for their innovation. (Hot pot is a popular way to dine in Chongqing.)

Pro-C

In the upper-left quadrant of the creative poster (Fig. 5.1), 3D IMAX films are associated with Pro-C (and subcategory Little-c). The explanation is that this art form, presumably only discovered in 2008 in China, could alter classrooms of the future, with the new generation—including young educators—entranced with media and blockbusters like *Harry Potter*.

Big-C

Struggling with which famous creation to depict, the Miracle Geniuses shifted their thinking from historical landmarks like the pyramids to celebrating their homeland. They chose a hydraulic engineering project of the Qin dynasty, an irrigation infrastructure (lower left-hand corner, Fig. 5.1), reasoning, "It's on China's world heritage list and even though it was built 2200 years ago it can prevent floods and irrigate fields." Captivated by the ingenuity involved, they added, "We can't imagine how the people could have built such a great thing in that time, with no machines, so this is definitely our Big-C."

Integration

To integrate the four Cs in their poster, this team had a creative spark. After identifying the places of their births, they drew a map of China (shown at the center of Fig. 5.1). This image effectively linked their four areas of origin to which they attributed the special meaning of being destined to be teachers with creative ideas. On their map they named each of the Big-C famous places that had emerged from their brainstorming, including Dujiangyan, thereby giving a "home" to the Big-C category within their holistic design. Like the other teams, the Miracle Geniuses presented their project on stage in our theater space—microphone in hand while describing their poster (projected on the screen)—as the other teams observed attentively. They all presented that same day. Team members manipulated their creative poster project, "showing off" its 3D aspect.

5.5.1.2   Step-by-Step Team

Mini-c

In this view of Step-by-Step's poster (see Fig. 5.2), three of the four flaps are open to reveal the information and images underneath. This 3D paper model actually has four moveable flaps, as exhibited by the single flap in the bottom right-hand corner, which conceals a chrysalis. Appearing in the other three quadrants as stages of metamorphosis and eventually a butterfly (upper left-hand quadrant), the entire poster is suggestive of movement and change.

As a folded image, the poster actually evokes a different metaphor, the wrapped Zongzi it holds. To explain, on the poster (lower left-hand side, Fig. 5.2), labeled "Mini-c" on the exterior of the flap that faces outward (not shown) are drawings of leaves and mud alongside hands making a Zongzi (exemplifying "making crafts and using natural materials"). Inside, as shown in the lower left-hand corner, is the emerging chrysalis that carries the words, "Use the mud to model a cup, use the leaves and mud to make a Zongzi." Made of glutinous rice in reality, it's usually wrapped in bamboo, just like the poster itself, both literally and metaphorically a wrapping with all four flaps folded.

The team (and entire class) hinted at the significance of Zongzi as a plant (rice) native to China, a country built on agriculture: Rice is prepared daily and used in festivals. The Zongzi-like poster is a tribute to its role in human survival. Like the

Fig. 5.2 Step-by-Step's 3D paper poster rendering of the 4-Cs (Chinese student team)

deep-rooted significance of Zongzi, the poster may be personifying beloved family, custom, and culture, as well as homeland.

Little-c

"Inventing and designing something new out of found objects" merged creativity and problem-solving (subcategory of Little-c). Student creators' chrysalis of "different shapes of bowls, bottles, and cups that make songs" was marked "Little-c" on the outside flap. The problem students had in mind was how to make music, arriving at the solution of transforming ordinary household utensils into musical instruments. Even the utensils they drew and wrote about were made of clay found in nature (e.g., river beds). These clay sculptures were quite literally seen as the basis of musical instruments, with clay a resource holding potential for making music. (Perhaps students were trying to circumvent the problem of making guardians angry by using household objects, conveyed in a personal essay from this team.) Presenting to the rest of us, they played a Chinese song referenced in one of their essays.

Pro-C

In the upper right-hand quadrant of the poster, the creators wrote, "In order to encourage our classmates from the past to donate money, we composed a play about it. To our delight, it really worked." To arrive at this statement, Step-by-Step had pulled from the empowering story of a theatrical production authored by one of them. The teammate who had written the essay talked glowingly at her roundtable about this experience of creativity in her schooling years. With her primary teacher's support, she and her friends had managed to turn what would have been an ordinary school event into a successful community fundraiser for a sick child who benefitted.

Meaningful learning and professional teaching can coalesce, for example, through school productions that have a social and educational purpose, such as helping vulnerable people in need. The subcategory of role-playing teachers, family members, and characters had professional merit for this team, given that the school event was purposeful and community oriented.

Big-C

"An irrigation system of wells connected by underground channels used in Xinjiang" symbolized the mature butterfly (upper left-hand quadrant of Fig. 5.2). The Turpan water system contains dug wells and underground water canals from mountain runoff. This water system was an oasis stopover for travelers in Turpan's historic development; it had been prosperous, owing to the water from the well system.

Integration

For the team, "the process of the caterpillar turning into a butterfly represents the different levels of creativity depicted on the outside and inside paper flaps." As shown in Fig. 5.2, metamorphosis was portrayed on the inside base of the poster to suggest China's survival owing to innovations in agriculture and infrastructure. The butterfly and cocoon images stretch across the poster, as though to imply the inevitability in a nation's story of becoming.

5.5.1.3   Cardinal Direction Team

Mini-c

Cardinal Direction got creative using the expressive game they once played that translates into "all directions"—north, east, west, and south (N, E, W, and S on the poster [see Fig. 5.3]).

Fig. 5.3 Cardinal Direction's 3D paper poster rendering of the 4-Cs (Chinese student team)

Little-c

Another invention, a source of national pride, helps fill stomachs, and it came at a time when the booming population craved low-cost nutrition: "Hybrid rice was engineered by 'Father of Hybrid Rice' and it's eaten at a rotating table." In the 1970s, Chinese inventor Longping produced high-yield crops by crossbreeding rice, which helps combat world food crises (Hybrid Rice, 2016). On Fig. 5.3, the hybrid rice image (upper left-hand corner) has a plate and chopsticks next to it.

Pro-C

The category associated with professional teaching was a sketch of Confucius, China's legendary teacher, depicted with his fabled white beard (bottom of the poster; to the left of this photograph is a mentee). With Pro-C and Big-C creativity, the mythic teachings have permeated Chinese culture. Confucius envisioned the family as a basis for ideal government. The Cardinal Direction Team depicted him on a flap next to a family table with hybrid rice. With the placement of these symbols, this figure of morality and government as family was connected.

Big-C

With the flaps turned outward, as shown, images of direction include the compass, an invention of ancient China (although controversial in European history). Finding direction in China was resolved with the "precursor of the compass—a piece of magnetized iron that looks like a spoon and tray" (on the right-hand side, Fig. 5.3, accompanied by the affirmation "great!"). Little-c creativity was traced as a compass in the hand of the imagined Chinese inventor.

Integration

The compass image, and its four directions, was the unifying theme, allowing the epic creative achievement of the compass, and its transformational effect on life on this planet, to be felt.

5.5.1.4   All Poster Projects and Presentations

The other five teams also moved from the smaller to the larger kinds of creativity. There were widely varying creative results across all teams with respect to the examples given in each category and the overall statement of integration.

Relative to the Little-c themes and topics, I generated two classifications: inventing and designing something new, and creating artistic works out of observations.

The three posters featured here stood out: Postreflection reports referenced debating, planning, and designing, and the presenters explained key poster elements, including their theme of integration. Images (such as symbols) and written descriptions (such as captions) were thought out. Like the other teams, on stage, Step-by-Step presented its 4-C influenced poster, actually physically demonstrating the unifying (metaphysical) image of the chrysalis (self-transformation). The poster was being manipulated in the hands of its makers, as it "moved" with fluency from one "C" to another. For this team, the self grows through meaning-making, problem-solving, developing professionally, and profoundly contributing to society. Highlights from their notetaking (the postreflection report) were captured on a long scroll, from which they read, triggering, in my mind, hanging scrolls—an art in the Chinese culture.

5.5.2   Favoring Cooperative-Based Learning (Theme 2)

A second theme is cooperative-based learning as a preferred approach to creative experiences. Judging from students' appraisal of all activities, learning at the level of the group resulted. Strongly favored, in fact, was cooperative-based learning and group projects over individual learning and solo exercises. *Values* and preferences of the entire class showed a tendency toward collaboration for such benefits as social bonding, cognitive cohesion, and creative performance.

All students proved more creative in teams than alone. They brought to the teamwork experiences of novelty and discovery and got lost in time when doing the activities. Despite time constraints and the demands of using the 4-C model, they enjoyed being peer collaborators on creative projects. The teams enacted characteristics and descriptions of creativity as an "optimal" flow experience arising from a creative contextual challenge (Csikszentmihalyi, 1996). Reflected in their individual assessments of the activities and their learning, the class expressed strong value for contextually and culturally interpreting the 4-Cs as a team (see Fig. 5.4). Importantly, cooperative project-based activities were considered far more valuable than individual activities, which paled in comparison. Writing individually about childhood creativity as groundwork for working generatively with others was not recognized or perhaps valued in light of the team synergies experienced. Dynamic creativity (Mullen, 2019b) was enlivened for them through each other's stories; the negotiation of "best" or "ideal" experiences to represent for each of the 4-C classifications; and the chance to see other teams' creative artifacts also explained and performed.

Ironically, the personal essay—comparatively rated much lower on creativity and transference as an individual endeavor—was the catalyst for the poster project and creative performance (stage presentation). Without having taken the time to reflect on creativity, students would have lacked this vital frame of reference for working progressively on the poster exercise. Mini-c and Little-c stories from personal recollections (the essays) were deconstructed in the making of a collective poster in order to decide how to portray each small c, and through continued dialogue the search persisted for Pro-C and Big-C representations. Teams would discuss, sometimes robustly, which images to choose for each type of creativity and what integrative pattern made sense for the poster. Collaboration was identified as a learning strategy to use in their own teaching, embodied through creative action before stated in their assessments.

The results-based display (Fig. 5.4) provides a view of the course curriculum as a whole, according to these education students (Chinese preservice teachers) and their assessment of the 4-C learning activities. The descriptive results from this learning unit are derived from my inferential, numerical interpretation of the results. Represented by this display is the classroom learning performance relative to the four creative tasks.

Based on the frequency of learning activities considered of greatest value and interest, the cooperative activities (B, C, D, and E), particularly the 3D paper posters (B), were clearly the class favorite. Activity D had the next highest value or interest, followed by C, E, A, and F. The two individual activities (A and particularly F) were categorically and comparatively lower in value and interest. Thus, activity F had the least amount of creativity and transference for the class. Unlike activity A, which served as the basis of the 3D poster project, activity F was not associated with teamwork or embedded in the creativity unit.

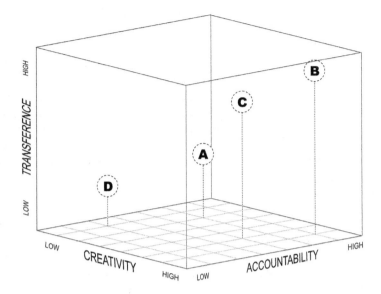

Legend of Activities:
A Personal Experience of Creativity Essay (individual)
B 3D Paper Poster Representation of the 4-C Creativity Model (group)
C Postreflection Report on 3D Poster and Presentation (group)
D Summative Course Assessment (individual)

Note. Activity B was deemed to have the greatest merit, with C close behind.
Ironically, Activity A, the personal essay upon which B and C were dependent,
had less merit. Collaborative activities (B & C) were strongly preferred over
individual activities (A & D).

The figure depicts the Creativity and Accountability in Education course.
Bold letters represent student judgments on the value of classroom activities.

Fig. 5.4 Chinese preservice students' assessment of the 4-C activities (C. A. Mullen)

Analyzed results of this course suggest that the class had developed an appreciation of transferability in teaching and learning for the cooperative group activities.
In their individual assessments, students wrote that while teamwork was new to
them in practice, it was invaluable as developing teachers interested in the creative
engagement of children and youth using pedagogical techniques (e.g., team- and
skills-building, and brainstorming, negotiating, debating, and representing ideas).
They made linkages among creativity, collaboration, and context. Also, together
they accomplished challenging creative work with minimal resources, making
remarkable gains in real time through cooperative AL.

As communicated by the students, the educational team experience was novel
and worthwhile; further, the experiential learning involved in interpreting and
applying the 4-C model had merit. High transference as lifelong learners and future
teachers resulted from the cooperative activities performed by and across teams. As

such, performance exercises enabling novelty, discovery, and adaptability and fostering intrinsic motivation best served the curriculum on creativity, in which reflections on high-stakes accountability were incorporated (see Theme 3).

Such creative productivity potentially debunks generalizations about Chinese students as uncreative, even when, contradictorily, they themselves hold this view. When working individually, the students conveyed a lack of creative confidence. In their essays of creative genesis, some struggled to identify a personally meaningful example of creativity and creative problem-solving. Some spent more time writing about the struggle of recall or intercepted creative activity (e.g., parental disapproval over the child's conversion of household utensils into musical instruments) than describing a salient creative experience. However, writing about the repression or clash of forces—and using storytelling devices (e.g., vivid imagery, dialogic exchanges)—ironically channeled their creativity. On works of this nature, my written feedback affirmed that they were being creative in the process of describing blocked or failed creativity.

Family, nature, friendship, and culture were overriding themes from the poster data. Examples of 4-C creativity with respect to symbols and captions on these artifacts included:

- Family: family life and customs, such as making Zongzi and sitting at the household table; designing clothing; depicting family members interactively using objects (e.g., household utensils) (Mini-c)
- Nature: nature and landscapes involving insects, animals, plants, and flowers used in artwork and inventions; utilizing found objects, such as clay, to make musical instruments; creating a habitat by turning a family pool into an aquarium (Little-c)
- Friendship: friends, Confucius, and primary teachers at the center of the child's world; phonetically trying out new linguistic sounds (Chinglish); making new things (e.g., musical instruments); contributing to communities (e.g., fundraising) (Pro-C)
- Culture: crediting China with Big-C cultural breakthroughs; Confucius as legendary teacher and the basis of family and government; the compass invention; heritage landmarks (e.g., a functioning hydraulic project from the Qin dynasty) (Big-C)

Team members negotiated conceptions and representations, moving from the intrapersonal (Mini-c and Little-c) to the professional/cultural (Pro-C), to the societal/global (Big-C), articulating Pro-C and Big-C creativity. Brainstorming beyond essays, they produced drawings, captions, and integrative images of the 4-Cs. Poster designs connoted practical value as 3D folded renderings of cocoons (Fig. 5.2), compasses (Fig. 5.3), maps, books, and clothes.

In their postreflection reports, teams outlined decision-making steps. Creatively problem-solving, they discussed pertinent images from their essays and gave reasons for their selections. Thinking went beyond the single snapshots of each of the 4-Cs to integrating them. Interpretations of the 4-C model connected the self to the world. Teams prepared a script for performance, reflectively appraising their work afterwards—demonstrating creativity in action.

5.5.3 Supporting a Balanced Curriculum (Theme 3)

Supporting a balanced curriculum is a noteworthy theme. Balance and harmony, contradiction and integration, were prevalent concepts in the data. Regarding the assessment feedback, in sometimes nuanced, often abstract ways, students expressed the need for balancing creativity and accountability in education. Integrating the contrary educational goals of creativity and accountability, it was argued, could support holistic human development. This general vision of integrated curriculum transcended otherwise disconnected aims of education. To this class, teachers of all grades need to approximate a more balanced and humane curriculum.

Unlike teachers in China today, these college students do not want to have to succumb to high-stakes accountability and its imbalances that, they implied, are unjust. The either/or forced choices upheld in exam-centric curricula speak to how the educational system is lopsided and unfair. The ideal of curricular balance integrates the best creative learning pedagogies and practices from the West to benefit Chinese education.

With the pervasiveness of Confucianism in China, it's probably not surprising that concepts of balance, harmony, and integration bubbled up in students' sense-making about accountability and creativity. Accountability and creativity were described individually using culturally specific language—*wisdom* and *teacher* in relation to *balance* and *harmony* were unifying refrains. These concepts, even the words, are central to Confucianism (Li, 2014). Thus, Confucianism may very well have influenced the preservice mindset.

Advocacy stances permeated the preservice feedback involving teacher capability, responsibility, and control in education reform: "Teachers should have the ability to balance the test and the fun of teaching." "A teacher can spend some time on creative teaching and balance the time with accountability." "Teachers must strive to balance the test and teach students as a relationship." Creativity invoked relationships, then, as well as inspiration and fun. As such, these undergraduates considered ways that creative curricula can enhance teaching and learning.

Within the data set, there was no clear evidence that creativity was viewed as a source of AL relative to such capabilities as higher-order thinking. Creativity also was not associated with content-based knowledge, as socially constructed knowledge (such as during collaborative learning), or as a tool for student advocacy and voice. However, unlike testing, creativity did not carry associations with curricular and relational fragmentation or inhumanity.

Regarding the harmony construct they introduced and used interchangeably with *balance*, a typical sentiment was, "Creativity and accountability can have a harmonious coexistence, but we still need more creativity in our lives and we must improve the way of accountability." Thus, it appears that both creativity and accountability were subsumed by this organizing construct (balance). From the perspective of Confucian harmony and balance, accountability and creativity would not be inherently contradictory or oppositional. Rather, the teacher has the authority and power to combine these in such a way as to propel student development and dynamic learning.

In the search for balance, harmony, and integration, a Confucian paradox could be glimpsed in student writing as "accountability is not the opposite of creativity." This begs the question, if these educational goals are not opposites, what are they relationally? Perhaps the Confucian logic subtly expressed was that "accountability needs balance with creativity" and that "deep problem-solving" "opens up the imagination"; socially constructed knowledge is just as natural as change is constant from this viewpoint. With accountability and creativity being dominated by a high-stakes takeover in the Chinese education system, test-centric curricula are unfaithful to this vision of the creative imagination and, by way of extension, Confucianism.

Confucian philosophy is about creative conflict, not only balance (Li, 2014). In fact, balance without conflict is undesirable—in many life situations, movement, growth, and change occur. For example, conflict and change can come from education reforms that introduce liberal arts thinking within a testing regime, as in the presumed effects of Hong Kong's policy changes on mainstream China. This idea of conflict was not in the data.

Yet as a group, the preservice teachers revealed something akin to an emerging advocacy mindset—take their stance that testing can have merit without the high stakes. Consider as well their affirmation of the value and need for creativity in the accountable curriculum. Having conceptualized accountability bereft of its survival of the fittest mentality and thus problematic associations with competition, penalty, and consequence, they saw a clearing for the role of testing in education. In this new world, they set conditions, such as testing is only appropriate when reasonable and respectful of students, and when creativity is used to balance the learning from testing. A guiding ethic seems to be that when accountability is not enacted suitably or is misused, it is unreasonable and can be disrespectful and "harmful."

As such, they identified widespread imbalance in education systems and within humans. While one "can't escape accountability in China," as some students declared, it is ironic that for others, "accountability is essential in education." All agreed, though, that accountability should be "moderate" and balanced with creativity. Hence, accountability is "not the opposite of creativity," except when high stakes are attached.

Creativity, they implored, is not a frill—teachers and students must practice it to bring a sense of balance to the curriculum. With creativity as a liberating dynamic, constructive associations are relaxation, independence, and bravery, but self-expression and freedom are endemic. For them, creative learning as such can work powerfully in the reimagined curriculum.

5.6   Cultural Issues of Creativity

Supporting a balanced curriculum demonstrated critical thinking, which likely disrupted the Chinese students' known world. With the stimulus provided by the reflective activity to generate their own beliefs, students took three positions: curriculum must be balanced by removing the high stakes attached to testing, the accountable curriculum should coexist with creative teaching and learning, and the imagination must be cultivated to bolster freedom of expression. Having removed the stakes from accountability and merged its new form with creativity, they made the Mini-c and Little-c discovery that testing can coincide with creativity in a democratic accountable model of education.

A contradiction, then, was that while my curriculum in China encouraged new thinking, it was steeped in a hierarchy of values. Conspicuously favored were creative and cooperative learning, as well as critical thinking and democratic education. Ironically, just as high-stakes testing has implied value, such as formal knowledge tied to privileged content areas (e.g., math) and global competitiveness, cooperative learning has value. Among the latter are the expectation for collaboration within relationship-building contexts and discovery-oriented learning within open knowledge systems (Kurczek & Johnson, 2014). Is the new world these students hinted at simply a revision of the status quo, or was their imagination sparked?

Also inherited by the preservice teacher was China's collectivist culture (see Sternberg, 2006). Dynamic classroom synergies around creativity and collaboration may have tapped into it. Students selected their own teams wherein creative ideas were cognitively processed and applied. Embrace of the 4-Cs in a geospatial location of disadvantage, while a preliminary exploration, raises the question about the potential for engagement within cultures stigmatized as uncreative. While a small intervention, this study may have broader implications. Might other students in different glocalities excel with few resources (e.g., time, equipment, and materials) and gain from creative pedagogies practiced in classrooms? Might they also anticipate experimenting dynamically with creative strategies as new teachers or other professionals?

Patience and persistence can be rewarded the collaborative pursuit of creative discovery. At first, preservice teams struggled with differentiating the Little-c concept of creativity, confusing it with Mini-c until they grasped *recognition* (in the move from Mini-c to Little-c) as a main distinction (see Kaufman & Beghetto, 2009). Focusing on daily problem-solving and examples also helped them to solidify possibilities for both Mini-c and Little-c. In one team, someone shared her creative childhood challenge (from her essay) of trying to work out the physiology of pronouncing words in different languages. Back then, when using the Internet, she discovered how to engage the speech organs, which led her to create an intricate map (Mini-c) recognized by her homeroom teacher as a clever endeavor (Little-c).

By collaborating, brainstorming, problem-solving, debating, negotiating, and organizing, student thinking skills more quickly develop and improve (Bean, 2011). Cooperative group work, while new in the Chinese context, proved indispensable for learning in fresh ways. Team members inspired ideas and traded strategies to empower themselves as future teachers, taking notes within groups to support dynamic project learning, with one activity building upon another. (However, I am left with questions from the summative assessment for which less value was assigned for the individual activities that initiated and concluded the course.)

Inventive productivity in the preservice classroom cannot help but debunk generalizations about Chinese students as mechanized, unoriginal thinkers. As I see it, at least three significant factors account for the (over-) generalizations of Chinese students as rote learners. First, the imperial exam, administered by the *keju* system across dynasties (until abolished in 1905), tested memorization and the Confucian classics. Norms of standardization honor ancestral lineage; however, the legacy of rote-based education readily allows for teaching to the test (Zhao, 2014).

Besides China's living past, a second factor contributing to the negative stereotype is political. The Communist Party's public stance on creative innovation and policy-based reforms of education systems is contradicted by its single-minded test-based system. Transmissive learning is perpetuated within a closed knowledge system driven to attain high student achievement scores (Starr, 2010; Zhao, 2014). This competitive mindset exacerbates paradoxical aspirations for global-minded entrepreneurial citizenship.

Byproducts of the test-centric culture are tight restrictions on freedoms that drain creative energies. The suicide rate has been escalating for failing students who feel shame for having disgraced their families (Mullen, 2017a). Consequently, China has the dubious honor of top international rankings in tested subjects. Flocking to overseas universities, students question their homeland's quality of education while Beijing tries to change China's education system by instilling creative thinking in an economy wherein invention is tied to healthy labor markets (Woetzel & Towson, 2013).

Finally, a third factor compounding the belief that Chinese learners cannot create, only memorize, is the existing literature on China. Writing on creativity from respected scholars across countries and disciplines has reinforced the image of a rigid, uncreative Chinese learner within a nation that stresses and rewards recalling facts. The problem is attributed to China's hierarchical society and static educational system. Chinese educators use memorization and recitation as instructional methods; graduates have strong memory, math, and science skills but "weak creative and analytical skills" (Starr, 2010, p. 270). Because China's "pedagogy lends itself best to teaching to the test," as Li and Gerstl-Pepin (2014) stated, "teaching institutions" have "little flexibility" (p. 7). Consequently, students lack opportunities to develop creative, critical, and analytical thinking, as well as take risks (Zhao, 2014). Preservice teachers have an "[impoverished] ability to engage in unstructured decision making" (Li & Gerstl-Pepin, p. 7).

Niu and Sternberg (2001) shed light on influences from Chinese learning environments as forces limiting student creativity. Evaluators rated Chinese and American college students' artwork, finding the latter to be "more creative." It was concluded that Chinese students' creativity was likely reduced due to "restrictive task constraints" or "the absence of explicit instructions to be creative" (p. 225). Niu et al.'s (2007) outcomes were the same. Since Niu's two studies, there is more reporting of creative education in Asia with younger students. Darling-Hammond (2010) observed unexpected creativity, writing that "Asian systems" surprisingly "engage in more collaborative learning activities, and require applications of knowledge to more complex problems" (p. 185). She was comparing these systems to "under-resourced American districts" where "harried, underprepared teachers dominate instruction" (p. 185).

Darling-Hammond (2010), like myself (Mullen, 2017a), lend credibility to Chinese people as capable of being creative and generating creative learning environments. This perspective resonates with Biggs's (n.d.) pushback against the deficit Asian stereotype. To him, Chinese learners' stellar success, worldwide, cannot be strictly attributed to rote memorization. As evidence, he referred to Chinese students' academic achievement on international testing and in universities that surpasses Western students, especially in math and science. Besides, learning any complex subject inevitably involves reflective or "deep memorization" in that one memorizes a symphony before understanding it. With these ideas as a base, Biggs (n.d.) mounted the "paradox of the Chinese learner" (para. 2), perpetuated by mistaken beliefs about neo-Confucian cultures and learning.

Given all such weighty issues, China is poised as a case of extremes, engendering debate. In this nation's competitive culture, change has been reported where education sectors or individuals have moved toward dynamic learning to stimulate inventiveness, confidence, creativity, and critical–analytical thinking. President Xi Jinping's dream for the People's Republic of China's rejuvenation sets the tone for innovation, although inventiveness is largely prized for its capacity to generate profits in manufacturing (Wasserstrom, 2013).

Expecting college graduates to improve the world demands that education students learn to reflect, create, collaborate, and assess. In their essays of creative genesis, many of the Chinese preservice teachers struggled to identify a personally meaningful example of creativity and creative problem-solving. A few spent more time on the struggle of recall and describing themselves as uncreative than sharing a salient experience. Just as the act of writing about the repression sparked their capacity for inventiveness, so too did the collaboration with peers.

Helping students see their vital role in the future also demands that educators model new techniques or established ones dynamically. For instance, in the classroom I welcomed the creation of a global language hybrid. Breaking from outmoded norms is part of becoming a global-minded, dynamic creative educator. The entrepreneur, an activist dreamer, turns ideas into creative action. The Chinese students had this inner quality and the courage to reveal it. Communicating about creative learning with one another, they did not hold back from storying the impact of oppressive pedagogies and societal norms on how teacher and parent educate.

Mini-c classroom creativities were spurred on by individual and collective sense-making of lives, despite the apprehension about communicating in English. Using a hybrid lexicon to speak, write, illustrate, perform, and assess, students experimented with turning languages (Chinese and English) into a creative hybrid shared beyond their educational circles, albeit informally (Pro-C). Symbolically, they were bridging the East and West, transforming official languages, otherwise unbridgeable (Big-C). Fusing expressions—unconventional and surprising—transpired as a solution for managing glocal barriers (Little-c). Tam's (2016) Hong Kong study found that language-rich contexts facilitate linguistic advances and positive learning.

5.7   Reflections and Implications

At the first class, I was struck by creative language uses in students' self-introductions. As stated earlier, I read their work holistically for meaning and welcomed Chinglish—efficiency was at a premium in a short, fast-paced course. If I had been strict about requiring proper English, it's unlikely the class could have been as creative. I would have missed the Mini-c creativity around me, and failed to acknowledge it. Having a safe, relaxing environment was essential to this AL intervention. Nurturing creativities relies on surprises and unexpected turns.

As I pen this chapter, these students would have entered the teaching profession in their homeland. Likely, they are navigating an exam-centric society that yearns to become inventive and prolific. Are they encountering contradictions in creativity? Apparently, ambitious creators are vigorously competing to prove their merit in a hierarchy that, according to Zhao (2014), suddenly placed a premium on originality. In a world of profound paradoxes, one can look to changing education reforms in Asia to speculate on what might come. Might there be support for a brand of liberal education that the Communist Party of China would filter and organize based on democratic centralism? Policy mandates such as *Learning for Life, Learning Through Life*, with requirements for comprehensive learner-centered education systems, suggest support for quality education and lifelong learning (Draper, 2012). Such curriculum and teacher development reforms have liberal components ostensibly benefitting new teachers.

Final points now address 4-C and AL complementary outcomes, and lessons and explanations. Hidden-c, the personal power of creativity, is an implication emerging from this writing, lightly touched upon herein. In Chap. 8, the Hidden-c concept is unpacked.

5.7.1   4-C and AL Complementary Outcomes

Through cultural immersion, the 4-C creative AL program I designed invoked the curious, unexpected, and unknown, owing to active engagement. The 4-C model, translated into a creative pedagogy to which undergraduates were exposed, was conceptually framed and problem based, as well as activity generated and reflective oriented (also, Mullen, 2018). This intervention yielded meaningful and informative results and thus has merit. Productive student responses were elicited in creativity and creative endeavor within a Chinese context, not at arm's length (as in through a survey instrument) but rather close up and personal.

5.7.2 Lessons and Explanations

Chinese students utilized the 4-C creativity model I imported from educational psychology for interpretative and cultural response. However, the creative curriculum and learning explored do not guarantee results with any education population, anywhere. Custom designed, this study utilized a creativity model and an AL approach in a glocality with one preservice class. The 4-Cs were applied to individual and team-based creativity with personal, problem-solving, professional, and cultural dimensions. The psychology lens proved indispensable to the creative learning and this pedagogic research. While the curriculum and results could not be further tested to make adjustments at the China location, the students productively assessed them, indicating overall satisfaction with the creative intervention. Reported outcomes are displayed.

For teachers navigating test-centric cultures worldwide, challenging the imagination and providing conditions for inventiveness is a struggle. Imitation and literal comprehension, a nineteenth-century focus, cannot advance global education (World Economic Forum, 2013). An international calling is to prepare future-minded global educators, but even the best of schools tend not to work with the creativity and entrepreneurship proficiencies (Zhao, 2014).

Moving in this direction, global-ready preservice candidates will have developed Hidden-c and their capacity as creative collaborators. Such globally literate teachers face the challenge of a twenty-first-century curriculum that advances creativity as a global competency, some within regimes requiring pedagogical fidelity to rote-based testing. Might Hidden-c be in service of Hidden-C, for which collective creative self-beliefs are a real force of change in schools and life?

But how can we be developing our global competencies as professionals when stereotypes about entire races and countries exist? When we pierce the veil of generalizations as site-based educators, what might we learn and teach, and what do we leave behind? While I cannot make general statements about the creative capacity of Chinese students due to the limitation of my exposure, I can say that the group I worked with was in no way preselected. Beyond this, they had to work under pressure and without preparation and samples or devices and supplies. By relying on themselves and each other, they creatively and cooperatively interpreted an American framework (i.e., Kaufman & Beghetto's 2009 theory), thereby satisfying an AL challenge that depended on their capacity to teach and learn as peers.

Preconceived notions that Chinese students and teachers cannot think or perform creatively are a problem for everyone in a global world. While China's rote-based, mechanized educational system in the upper grades is surely repressive, it cannot be stamping out creativity altogether. Indeed, China is actually highly adaptive, capable of rapid change (Dimitrov, 2013). Paradoxically, in 2019, the central government of the People's Republic of China continues to exert control, igniting Hong Kong's unprecedented widespread protests in the struggle for autonomy and human rights, which has been a reality for decades (Richardson, 2019).

Against a repressive political backdrop that permeates education, while showing themselves to be creative, the undergraduate Chinese students in my course reclaimed their creativity from childhood, forging a creative teacher identity. Yearning to work collaboratively on exciting creative and cognitive challenges, these preservice teachers embraced the 4-Cs, stimulated by their creative learning. But questions also come to mind that concern me and should concern educators everywhere.

Importantly, can college students in tyrannical cultures be sparked to do creative, cooperative, and collaborative work? For all who are denied dynamic opportunities for learning and success, what might be the effects over time? What mechanisms and preventions can be put in place? If entire cultures are being stigmatized as lacking in creativity and collaboration, and thus the collaborative capacity for novelty and utility, what can be done to socialize students to become global-minded in these ways? How might cultures be penetrated using AL creative strategies? What new knowledge can be disseminated about the capacity to learn, guide, create, and innovate? All such questions strike me as worthy of fine-grained investigations.

A lesson taken from a page of Dewey (1934) is that the human condition through which creativity manifests must not be lost or buried—everyday creativity born out of circumstance and conflict should be part of cultural stories. For Dewey (1934) and Eisner (2004), creativity is the soul of the humanity—schools, if transformed, can enable human development in service of creative societies. Kaufman and Beghetto's (2009) model, once translated, put this vision in motion.

Most of the dynamics that unfolded in this project-based journey to China were not self-evident at the time. Still others required my re-evaluation of the agreed-upon plan so I could adjust and find a new direction. All of this speaks to the capacity for being creative, not just teaching and learning about creativity. Thus creatively adapting my activities, negotiating with key personnel, working closely with my translators, and inventing an international support system all contribute to the deeper, more soulful story. What has stayed with me is just how creative and cooperative the Chinese students were and how their receptivity made the creative challenge possible. What also has staying power is the capacity to meaningfully engage in creativity when guided explicitly, even when socialized narrowly in order to succeed.

5.8 A Final Word

Finally, dynamic creativity (Mullen, 2019b) can prove remarkable where least expected. I hope this creative innovation in learning within a perplexing glocality adds something new to the conversation in education, and creativity specifically. Curricular interventions can cultivate dynamic creativity and capitalize on being creative and collaborative. Educators worldwide can possibly benefit from the stimulus for reflexive action and transferability of new learning to their own platforms.

Readers can adapt any of the ideas to assist with their own teaching or research. Anyone interested in preK–12 schools may wish to consult my other study of creativity within China that encompasses underresourced and privileged sites (see Mullen, 2017a, 2017b, 2019a).

Acknowledgments and Notes Project funding in 2015 was from The J. William Fulbright Foreign Scholarship Board, U.S. Department of State's Bureau of Education & Cultural Affairs, and Council for International Exchange of Scholars (grant #6219). Also providing grant support was Virginia Tech's Institute for Society, Culture, and Environment, Global Issues Initiative Research Support Program.

I wish to thank the Chinese university that generously hosted me as a Fulbright Scholar and visiting professor. Institutional Review Board approval was granted in 2015 from my home institution. This chapter is an update and revision of Mullen (2018; see References).

Appendix: 4-C preservice classroom activity protocol for China (C. A. Mullen)

1. What does creativity look like in China's local/regional/national/global context from your perspective?
2. What examples spring to mind for each component of the 4-C creativity framework?

   (a) Mini-c (creativity)?
   (b) Little-c (creativity)?
   (c) Pro-C (creativity)?
   (d) Big-C (creativity)?

3. In each example, what does accountability look like or what forms does it take?
4. When you think about creativity and accountability on a global scale, how might China compare with other nations' (testing) cultures?

References

Bean, J. C. (2011). *Engaging ideas: The professor's guide to integrating writing, critical thinking, and active learning in the classroom* (2nd ed.). San Francisco, CA: Jossey-Bass.

Biggs, J. (n.d.). *The paradox of the Chinese learner.* Retrieved from http://www.johnbiggs.com.au/academic/the-paradox-of-the-chinese-learner

Bonwell, C. C., & Eisen, J. A. (1991). Active learning: Creating excitement in the classroom. In *ASHE-ERIC Higher Education Report No. 1.* Washington, DC: The George Washington University. Retrieved from https://files.eric.ed.gov/fulltext/ED336049.pdf

Brown, R. A., Lycke, K. L., Crumpler, T. P., Handsfield, L. J., & Lucey, T. A. (2014). Editors' notes. *Action in Teacher Education, 36*(4), 261–263.

Burnett, C., & Smith, S. (2019). Reaching for the star: A model for integrating creativity in education. In C. A. Mullen (Ed.), *Creativity under duress in education? Resistive theories, practices,
and actions* (pp. 179–199). Cham, Switzerland: Springer.

Chinglish. (2020). *Wikipedia*. Retrieved from https://en.wikipedia.org/wiki/Chinglish

Collins, J. W., & O'Brien, N. P. (Eds.). (2011). *The Greenwood dictionary of education* (2nd ed.).
Santa Barbara, CA: Greenwood.

Cox, T. H., Lobel, S. A., & McLeod, P. L. (1991). Effects of ethnic group cultural differences
on cooperative and competitive behavior on a group task. *Academy of Management Journal,
34*(4), 827–847.

Creekmore, J., & Deaton, S. (2015). *The active learning classroom: Strategies for practical educators*. Stillwater, OK: New Forums Press.

Cropley, D. H., & Patston, T. J. (2019). Supporting creative teaching and learning in the classroom:
Myths, models, and measures. In C. A. Mullen (Ed.), *Creativity under duress in education?
Resistive theories, practices, and actions* (pp. 267–288). Cham, Switzerland: Springer.

Csikszentmihalyi, M. (1996). *Creativity: The psychology of discovery and invention*. London, UK:
HarperPerennial.

Darling-Hammond, L. (2010). *The flat world and education: How America's commitment to equity
will determine our future*. New York, NY: Teachers College Press.

Dewey, J. (1934). *Art as experience*. New York, NY: Perigee Books.

Dimitrov, M. K. (2013). Understanding communist collapse and resilience. In M. K. Dimitrov
(Ed.), *Why communism did not collapse: Understanding authoritarian regime resilience in
Asia and Europe* (pp. 3–39). New York, NY: Cambridge University Press.

Draper, J. (2012). Hong Kong: Professional preparation and development of teachers in a market economy. In L. Darling-Hammond & A. Lieberman (Eds.), *Teacher education around the
world: Changing policies and practices* (pp. 81–97). New York, NY: Routledge.

Eisner, E. W. (2004). What does it mean to say that a school is doing well? In D. J. Flinders &
S. J. Thornton (Eds.), *The curriculum studies reader* (2nd ed., pp. 297–305). New York, NY:
Routledge.

He, J., & van de Vijver, F. (2012). Bias and equivalence in cross-cultural research. *Online Readings
in Psychology and Culture, 2*(2), 1–19.

Hernandez, J. C. (2016, February 6). Wanted in China: More male teachers, to make boys men.
New York Times. Retrieved from http://www.nytimes.com/2016/02/07/world/asia/wanted-in-
china-more-male-teachers-to-make-boys-men.html?emc=eta1&_r=0

Hong, H. (2014). Exploring college students' perceptions of learning and online performance in a
knowledge building environment. *Asia-Pacific Education Researcher, 23*(3), 511–522.

Johnson, D. W., Johnson, R. T., & Smith, K. A. (2006). *Active learning: Cooperation in the college
classroom* (3rd ed.). Edina, MI: Interaction Book Company.

Kaufman, J. C., & Beghetto, R. A. (2009). Beyond big and little: The Four C Model of creativity.
Review of General Psychology, 13(1), 1–12.

King, F. (2016). Teacher professional development to support teacher professional learning:
Systemic factors from Irish case studies. *Teacher Development, 20*(4), 574–594.

Kurczek, J., & Johnson, J. (2014). The student as teacher: Reflections on collaborative learning in
a senior seminar. *Journal of Undergraduate Neuroscience Education, 12*(2), A93–A99.

Lee, J. C. K., & Pang, N. S. K. (2011). Educational leadership in China: Contexts and issues.
Frontier of Education in China, 6(3), 331–241.

Li, C. (2014). *The Confucian philosophy of harmony*. New York, NY: Routledge.

Li, Q., & Gerstl-Pepin, C. (Eds.). (2014). *Survival of the fittest: The shifting contours of higher
education in China and the United States*. Heidelberg, Germany: Springer.

Mullen, C. A. (2017a). *Creativity and education in China: Paradox and possibilities for an era of
accountability*. New York, NY: Routledge & Kappa Delta Pi.

Mullen, C. A. (2017b). Creativity in Chinese schools: Perspectival frames of paradox and possibility. *International Journal of Chinese Education, 6*(1), 27–56.

Mullen, C. A. (2018). Creative learning: Paradox or possibility in China's restrictive preservice teacher classrooms? *Action in Teacher Education, 40*(2), 186–202.

Mullen, C. A. (2019a). Do Chinese learners have a creativity deficit? *Kappa Delta Pi Record, 55*(1), 100–105.

Mullen, C. A. (2019b). Dynamic creativity: Influential theory, public discourse, and generative possibility. In R. A. Beghetto & G. E. Corazza (Eds.), *Dynamic perspectives on creativity: New directions for theory, research, and practice in education* (pp. 137–164). Cham, Switzerland: Springer.

Niu, W., & Sternberg, R. J. (2001). Cultural influences on artistic creativity and its evaluation. *International Journal of Psychology, 36*(4), 225–241.

Niu, W., Zhang, J. X., & Yang, Y. (2007). Deductive reasoning and creativity: A cross-cultural study. *Psychological Reports, 100*(2), 509–519.

Richardson, S. (2019). Hong Kong protests broaden despite police crackdown. *Human Rights Watch.* Retrieved from https://www.hrw.org/news/2019/08/05/hong-kong-protests-broaden-despite-police-crackdown?gclid=eaiaiqobchmi7zsrwfrh5qivarbich0jtwuoeaayasaa egjbjpd_bwe#

Robinson, K. (2015). *Creative schools: The grassroots revolution that's transforming education.* New York, NY: Viking.

Staats, L. K. (2011). The cultivation of creativity in the Chinese culture—Past, present, and future. *Journal of Strategic Leadership, 3*(1), 45–53.

Starr, J. B. (2010). *Understanding China: A guide to China's economy, history, and political culture* (3rd ed.). New York, NY: Farrar, Straus and Giroux.

Sternberg, R. J. (2006). Introduction. In J. C. Kaufman & R. J. Sternberg (Eds.), *The international handbook of creativity* (pp. 1–9). Cambridge, UK: Cambridge University Press.

Tam, A. C. F. (2016). The romance and the reality between pre-service teachers' beliefs about the potential benefits of a short-term study abroad programme and their practices. *Teachers and Teaching: Theory and Practice, 22*(7), 765–781.

Tienken, C. H., & Mullen, C. A. (Eds.). (2016). *Education policy perils: Tackling the tough issues.* New York, NY: Routledge & Kappa Delta Pi.

U.S. Department of Education. (2013, August). *Characteristics of public and private elementary and secondary school teachers in the United States: Results from the 2011–12 Schools and Staffing Survey.* Retrieved from http://nces.ed.gov/pubs2013/2013314.pdf

Wasserstrom, J. N. (2013). *China in the 21st century: What everyone needs to know.* New York, NY: Oxford University Press.

Woetzel, J., & Towson, J. (2013). *The 1 hour China book.* Cayman Islands, UK: Towson Group LLC.

World Economic Forum. (2013). *The global competitiveness report: 2013–2014.* Geneva, Switzerland: Author.

Zhao, Y. (2014). *Who's afraid of the big bad dragon?* Thousand Oaks, CA: Jossey-Bass.

Chapter 6
Canada Case: Revealing Creativity and 4-C Responses

Canada refugee

6.1 Overview: Questions and Purposes

"Toronto education culture focuses more on fostering creativity in classrooms than testing," expressed a preservice participant. Offering contrast, a faculty member claimed, "Creativity is no longer associated with liberty, freedom, and choice—creative innovation is serving neoliberal motives." Worldwide, teachers and other

© Springer Nature Switzerland AG 2020
C. A. Mullen, *Revealing Creativity*, Creativity Theory and Action in Education 5, https://doi.org/10.1007/978-3-030-48165-0_6

educators must navigate the policy reform milieu that casts creativity in new ways, which begs the question, what are they thinking?

We know that teaching demands creativity from teachers and learners in changing contexts (Baker, 2013; Craft, 1997) and that creativity is under duress in testing cultures (Mullen, 2018, 2019a; Tienken, & Mullen, 2016; Triplett, 2017). We know, too, that creativity has value in social and cultural contexts (e.g., Gardner, 1991; Tan, 2013) and education reform (e.g., Collard & Looney, 2014). Research coming out of North America on teacher/educator conceptions of creativity in relation to accountability within policy reform contexts is under development (exceptions include Ciuffetelli Parker & Craig, 2015).

In response, this chapter probes developing teachers and associated educators' understandings of creativity in the context of a global trend toward increased performance-based accountability in education. I sought Toronto-based educators' thoughts about creativity and accountability in Canada and how they align or conflict with policy reforms' accountability-based view of creativity. Framing the creative intervention was the pedagogic research question: Can diverse graduate students and educators in Canada discover creativity when encouraged under educational constraint? In the process of exploring seemingly opposing phenomena— creativity and accountability—within a Canadian milieu, I uncover lay conceptions and examples of creativity from diverse urban educators.

A related purpose of this qualitative case study is to describe dynamics of creativity, competitiveness, and multiculturalism with regard to Canadian policy. These are influential global trends that resulted from my literature review and data analysis. Of interest is the interplay of public and government discourse on reform initiatives and policy changes impacting education in Canada. This problem context concerns the inadequate representation of educators' perspectives and real-life issues in policymaking. Tackling this problem, Ciuffetelli Parker and Craig (2015) used "'small stories" to give shape to experiences that exist on the periphery of public policy. At the preK–12 level, they targeted Toronto-based public school educators and pupils' invisibility in the policy reform domain. Policies' "meganarratives," they wrote, do not account for human difference and diversity in schools and hasten the "standardization of education" (p. 121). Said to negate educators' voices, this conflict led me to wonder what developing teachers (preservice candidates and novice inservice teachers) and associated educators (e.g., their professors) perceive as "the dance" of creativity and accountability in their world. I analyze the same broad policy problem as Ciuffetelli Parker and Craig who pursued small stories as dynamic accounts of creativity and accountability in a public school context, but within a public university setting.

The term *small stories* is being used here in the same way as these narrative researchers—that is, as educator perspectives worth storying within the contemporary policy milieu that are not typically heard or valued (i.e., Ciuffetelli Parker & Craig, 2015). To clarify, I am not following sociolinguists' usage of the term that also appears in the narrative literature. Notably, De Fina and Georgakopoulou (2012) offered a sociolinguistic perspective on *small story*, which is more common than my public policy orientation. Briefly, they view small story as a "linguistic structure of narrative" and stories as interactions that potentially convey "complex communicative practices" within "participation structures"; analysis of these conversations focuses on tellers and/or "tellership" (p. xi).

Background information follows, then the literature-oriented framework. After it, I address my methods and results. The discussion is rooted in my analysis of the perceptions and judgments of urban educators on accountability-steeped creativity within their contexts.

6.2   Theoretical Background: Trends and Contexts

An American–Canadian citizen who has resided in the United States for decades, I conducted this study in Canada during an unprecedented time of immigration influx and explosive diversity (see Edmonston, 2016). To capitalize on these urban trends and reform initiatives, I situated my study in Toronto, a dynamic center of cultural diversity and "immigrant newcomer gateway" (Tucker-Raymond & Rosario, 2017, p. 33). Toronto, Ontario's capital, is a global "megacity" (Toronto, 2020). Reflecting aspects of twenty-first-century immigration and diversity trends in Canada is a Toronto-based faculty of education that sponsored my research in 2017.

A "'federal parliamentary democracy' and 'constitutional monarchy'" ("Politics of Canada," 2017), Canada aspired to become a creative economy with strong multiculturalism *and* a first-rate global reputation (Canadian Heritage, 2017). Canada does not have a national education system, thus Ontario is not a mirror of the nation. Elsewhere, Saskatchewan's government eliminated standardized testing in favor of evaluating student success with teacher involvement (Stinson, 2014). Promoting student learning inclusive of creativity, Alberta uses its own computer-based exams, which has the effect of reducing the weight of secondary-level standardized tests (Mertz, 2013). While high-stakes international testing via the Organisation for Economic Co-operation and Development's (OECD, 2019) Programme for International Student Assessment (PISA) has taken hold in Canada (Kempf, 2016), nuances differentiate the 12 provinces and territories. I contextualize my discussion of Toronto and Ontario accordingly.

6.3   Frames: Creativity, Competitiveness, and Multiculturalism

As a road map for navigating this framework, I identify primary lenses for conceptualizing pertinent research and public policy discourse. For this purpose, I obtained empirical studies on my topic. Documents were accessed via Google Scholar and a university library database. ERIC from WorldCat and Education Research Complete from EBSCO host located academic sources. Search terms, derived from the research question and literature findings, included *accountability*, *Canada*, and *creativity*.

Creativity, competitiveness, and multiculturalism resulted from the search process as primary concepts and intermingled in the sources. Regarding policy discourse, for example, a governmental scripting of "creativity" as "creative economy" makes creativity the conduit of competitiveness. Such melding reinforces the value and interdependence of the terms, at times signaling a co-opting of language from public education. Next, I distinguish the three frames to set up their study treatment.

6.3.1 Creativity Frame

Creativity and dynamic creativity have already been defined, so I highlight a few of the ideas and add several. As commonly understood, novelty and usefulness are creativity's chief criteria (e.g., Corazza, 2016; Plucker, Beghetto, & Dow, 2004). As such, creativity involves "the interaction among aptitude, process, and environment by which an individual or group produces a perceptible product that is both novel and useful as defined within a social context" (Plucker et al., p. 90). Arguably, the creativity research enlivens this concept with dimensions that are humanistic, developmental, values oriented, dynamic, exploratory, aesthetic, behavioral, intellectual, and social. Amenable to these lenses is the Four C (4-C) Model of creativity (Kaufman & Beghetto, 2009). Deemed a highly influential contemporary creativity theory, it has been authenticated within educational psychology and outside (e.g., Mullen, 2019b).

Creativity takes a different direction in the Canadian public policy discourse. Notably, it has value for its commercial potential for innovation through bolstering markets, strengthening global competitiveness, and preparing pupils for employment in market economies (Tienken & Mullen, 2016). Underlying these directions are economic biases and globalization drivers. One such prevalent economic driver in education around the world, including Canada, is the OECD's (2019) PISA campaign. According to many academics, these forces of globalization are *not* sensitive to the needs of public education or equity, diversity, and cultural difference (e.g., Ball, 2012; Kempf, 2016; Ravitch, 2014; Triplett, 2017).

Fallen to the wayside are creativity's humanistic associations with growth, discovery, and contributions valued for originality and usefulness (e.g., Tienken & Mullen, 2016). Critics at universities, schools, and organizations from different nations—among them Oliveira Andreotti (Canada), Stephen Ball (Great Britain), and Diane Ravitch (United States)—penned an open letter to the OECD director. They relayed their concerns about the damages PISA inflicts on public education and its destruction of the public good through the erosion of humanitarian values, such as safeguarding equitable opportunities for education and success.

Preparing young men and women for gainful employment is not the only, and not even the main goal of public education, which has to prepare students for participation in democratic self-government, moral action and a life of personal development, growth, and wellbeing. (excerpt of letter, as cited in *The Guardian*, 2014)

As the "Results" section reveals, most of the faculty also found the neoliberal direction of public education troubling, with creativity's humanistic values and agendas being co-opted.

Pitted against educators' "small stories," public and governmental policy discourse casts creativity as "innovation," with the assigned role of spurring global stature and national prosperity. Consequently, in Canada, "innovation is a key driver of productivity" (Boily et al., 2014, p. 1). Market expansion to the education sector, with the turning of education into a marketplace, is a boost for "creative industries," according to the Government of Canada (Canadian Heritage, 2017). "Creative Canada," a national policy document, rescripts education as a "market" and pupils as entrepreneurial agents for the global market. Canadian educators whose creative works are expressions of advocacy for social justice and equity via reform of public education invalidate this direction (e.g., Goldstein, 2013).

Within the marketplace milieu, pedagogy has been altered, with the engulfing of "new pedagogies" by creative innovation and its commercialism. Pedagogy—the jurisdiction of teaching—leverages entrepreneurial gain (Fullan & Langworthy, 2013). A pathway for growing Canada's creative economy (Canadian Heritage, 2017), pedagogy is the access point for tying classrooms and schools to commercial investment and privatization (Ball, 2012). While debatable, Canadian change theorist Fullan's innovation New Pedagogies for Deep Learning (NPDL; Fullan & Langworthy) arguably supports a neoliberal course for public school reform. The model spearheads "deep learning" around six proficiencies, including "creativity and innovation," characterized as "economic and social entrepreneurialism, considering and pursing novel ideas, and leadership for action" (p. 3). Conglomerate sponsored, the model partners teachers with pupils in technology-rich spaces led by global partnerships. Who these "education stakeholders" are, and how they will guide teachers and in what kinds of spaces, is not stated (Mullen, 2017). A global partnership endorses the NPDL model, including the OECD—all powerful influencers of public education that concern critics (e.g., Ball, 2012; Ravitch, 2014).

6.3.2   Competitiveness Frame

Competitiveness is the drive to outperform other nations' productivity and achieve "rising prosperity" (World Economic Forum, 2019). Creativity—and its counterpart *innovation*—is an economic measure of transnational and global competitiveness. To foster competitiveness and strengthen a struggling economy, the Canadian government has targeted creative product manufacturing (Canadian Heritage, 2017). A national crisis attributed to an innovatively struggling Canadian economy has blamed "competitors in innovation and productivity," particularly competition from the United States (Boily et al., 2014, p. 1).

The OECD (2019), a powerful economic body that measures and ranks nations' productivity, sparks governments' new goals and policies. Its PISA accountability benchmark has severe consequences for poorly performing testing cultures (Triplett, 2017). Despite being global competencies for workers, creativity, innovation, and entrepreneurship all became peripheral in much of schooling tied to market economies (Tienken & Mullen, 2016). In 2016, when PISA testing was executed within 80 nations' better and poorer resourced educational systems (OECD, 2019), Canada rose to the "top 10 for math, science, and reading" (BBC, 2017). A belief is that profit spawns a culture of winners and losers, diminishing equitable outcomes for high-poverty schools (Triplett, 2017). In Ontario, independent testing programs preceded PISA testing; mandated testing took hold with the Education Quality and Accountability Office legislation (EQAO Act, 1996). EQAO's standardized tests, administered in grades 3, 6, 9, and 10, measure reading, writing, and math skills (People for Education, 2017, para. 1).

Policy-driven change, apparent in Ontario's education system, has been confirmed on a larger scale. Kempf's (2016) international study of teachers identified an increase in high-stakes standardized testing across K–12 education in Canada, with a negative impact on teaching and learning. Special-needs populations, racial minorities, and poor pupils were especially affected. Compared with U.S. schooling, he explained, such changes occur "to a lesser but nonetheless significant degree in Canada"—"the key driver of current education reform is a radical new blanket call for standardization and data-driven accountability" (p. 2). Earlier, Goldstein (2013) observed that standardized testing sacrifices creative processes in Canadian public schools.

But variability exists in Ontario's pace of high-stakes testing. For one thing, teaching is a unionized profession with some autonomy over pedagogy and instructional decision-making. For another thing, education in Canadian curriculum and assessment practices is provincial, not federal. In fact, some Canadian jurisdictions eliminated standardized testing amid a growing consensus within testing cultures that pupils gain little from such tests (Hart & Kempf, 2018).

6.3.3 Multiculturalism Frame

At the heart of multiculturalism, *tolerance* is a fair attitude toward others who are different from oneself ("Tolerance," 2020). In creativity research, tolerance, or "social tolerance," is associated with "greater societal creativity" (e.g., Van de Vliert & Murray, 2018, p. 18). Economic concepts of creativity and human potentialities for being creative and innovative run parallel. As such, governmental sources (e.g., "Creative Canada") consider diversity the nation's "greatest resource" making Canada a global leader in innovation; national policies call for unity from the economic perspective of "federal initiatives" that can "unite" stakeholders in making

Canada "more competitive and creative" (Boily et al., 2014, p. 1). Commercially viable innovative products are expected to arise from diversity and metric-driven creativity and collaboration.

Immigrants may have an overall positive impact on economic growth, and acceptance of diversity seems endemic in Canada, according to public sources (e.g., Ibbitson, 2014). Yet empirical research reveals areas of marginalization and injustice. For example, while visible minorities have more postgraduate education (than nonminorities), their employment rate is lower (Hasmath, 2010). With workplace discrimination against "foreign" employees, ethnic minorities are not fairly represented in labor markets. The economy, especially unemployment, spawns bigotry in Canada (Edmonston, 2016), even though Canada absorbs droves of migrants and refugees, despite backlash from anti-immigrationists. Immigrants' contribution to the health of the economy demystifies Toronto's reputation as an "immigrant-receptive city," wrote Hasmath. However, a rigorous process and uncertainty await immigrants, making receptivity conditional (Edmonston, 2016). Such contradictions inform this chapter's conceptual frames.

6.4 Linkages Among Three Frames

The theoretical background presented ideas, trends, and contexts specific to creativity, competitiveness, and multiculturalism in global Canada. What are some of the critical linkages (and tensions) between and among the three frames? Unlike competitiveness within global societies, creativity, as understood in educational disciplines, is steeped in humanism and values of human development, growth, and change; beyond this, creativity, a social process, involves interaction with the environment through which original products considered useful can transpire. Creativity is also appreciated for its everyday value—personally meaningful creativity does not require an external referent, assessment process, or judge to establish its worth (Mini-c), the logic of which applies to daily problem-solving (Little-c).

Global competitiveness changes this terrain. It abides by a different set of values, subjugating public education to the global marketplace and corporate goals and needs. Nations are pitted against nations. "Winners" and "losers" are declared nationally and within nations where high-poverty, poorly resourced school communities are usually left behind. Creativity and innovation are sought in policy and reform contexts for building competitive and economic capacity, with schools part of this mix (e.g., Canadian Heritage, 2017). As one prevailing problem, schools burdened by standardized testing face serious barriers to creative and inclusive learning environments (Bogotch & Waite, 2017). Paradoxically, standardized testing (and the standardization of teaching) arises from competitive economies seeking superpower status in the world of education. The narrowing of the official curriculum to reading, writing, and math on the PISA tests minimizes the time teachers can give to creative expression and intellectual growth. Labor priorities compromise teachers and schools' capacity to mindfully attend to inequities, such as by incorporating culturally responsive creative curriculum. Advocates of tribal justice (e.g., Castagno & Brayboy, 2008; Mullen, 2020) urge culturally oriented creative interventions for fairly educating Indigenous pupils.

Nations' test-centrism within educational cultures is pervasive. Commonly, content areas (e.g., the arts) and electives that foster creativity are eliminated—judged as outside the scope of what pupils need to know to be prepared for testing, in favor of performance-driven "goal structures" that narrow curricula to the content on standardized and high-stakes tests (Frick, 2013; also, Tienken & Mullen, 2016). Established findings from the 1980s of creativity researcher Ruth Butler indicate that assigning grades to student work does not excite interest or inspire creativity: "Grades may encourage an emphasis on quantitative aspects of learning, depress creativity, foster fear of failure, and undermine interest" (Butler & Nissan, 1986, p. 215). Yet, global societies have furthered this path by investing in testing measures. If the rationale for evaluating pupils in the first place is to encourage them to learn and perform better, including on creative tasks, this is a particularly ironic result, especially where scores carry consequences.

More high stakes than grades, scores on standardized tests quash creativity, stifle curiosity, and arouse fear. With schools' focus on test scores through the elementary and secondary levels, pupils' liberal knowledge, democratic capital, and opportunities to secure "progressive" positions in the workforce diminish. Standards-based accountability reform movements have gained ground in some nations, but many academics argue that these trends arguably demoralize, not improve, the educational enterprise (e.g., Bogotch & Waite, 2017; Ravitch, 2014; Tienken & Mullen, 2016; Triplett, 2017). Alternative pedagogic approaches pay attention to intrinsic motivation and ways to productively and creatively encourage learning.

Along these lines, even multiculturalism has come to mean something different in our neoliberal world. The end game seems to be about channeling ethnic pluralism to make economies vigorously competitive, creative, and prosperous through metric-driven, commercially innovative products. A glaring social justice problem is that visible minorities and immigrant populations experience workplace discrimination. Labor markets spawn bigotry, even in Canada, where immigration trends and patterns have been studied. Edmonston's (2016) analysis reveals marginalization and injustice against non-White populations and immigrant workers. Educated visible minorities struggle to secure jobs that go to less educated White people. Canada's labor discrimination is not widely known, unlike its receptivity to immigrants.

6.5   Creative Research Methods in Toronto, Canada

With the lenses of creativity and accountability, I approached the Canadian culture in Toronto. I tailored my 4-Cs creative methods and research design to the specific academic setting in an urban landscape, applying the 4-C model (Kaufman & Beghetto, 2009). The "China–2015" application occurred before this one

("Canada–2017"). Kaufman and Beghetto's (2013) publication based on the preliminary testing of their model predated the initiating year (i.e., 2015) by 2 years. What they found from investigating college students' responses to the 4-Cs has relevance for my Canadian study results. (The explanation appears in the "Discussion" section.)

6.5.1 Case Study Research Design

Case study is addressed elsewhere (Chap. 4), with my reasons for choosing this research design. In the bounded context of my inquiry, student diversity had significantly increased within a few years at the Toronto education building (research site). Reflecting Canada's recent immigration trends (see Edmonston, 2016), the demographics of this institution's multicultural and higher education programs were heterogeneous. Public workshops/seminars also attracted cultural diversity. All of these realities were reflected in the data amassed.

6.5.2 Data Collection

Preceding this Canadian study, I piloted the data collection instrument and procedures in China, also with preservice candidates, faculty, and leaders (Chap. 5; also, Mullen, 2018). The 4-C Classroom Activity and Interview Protocol for Canada (Appendix 6.1) is a contextualized version of the generic protocol that appears in Chap. 4.

Onsite Canadian data sources emerged from these sources: the 4-C workshop and interview (individual and group) that was organized around my theory-informed creativity instrument (Appendix 6.1); participant feedback (oral and written), including my group summaries; field notes; and local materials. The brainstorming activity with three graduate classes generated written team responses to the 4-C prompts on the protocol and verbal results shared with the class. (Time restrictions in classrooms did not allow for the poster activity.)

6.5.2.1 Planning Sessions and Cycles

Procedural steps taken with groups and individuals for the study in Canada, with respect to planning sessions and cycles, are described here graphically and narratively. A table encapsulates what occurred before, during, and after. The workshop facilitator and interviewer roles were carried out by me, the researcher; professors, students, and leaders embodied the participant role. Faculty and administrator participants functioned as institutional host representatives (Table 6.1).

Table 6.1 Procedural steps taken with groups and individuals in Canada. (C. A. Mullen)

Participant classification		Before	During	After
	Classes (groups)	1-hour planning for three courses with two professors Explained 4-C model and creativity activities Reviewed the research protocols and activities 4-C lesson aims, contexts, roles, and responsibilities Expectations and ideas for contextualizing workshops Student demographics and changes in population Changes in education programs and response to international dynamics Invited professor to interject ideas during class	Facilitator and creativity topic introduced Workshop purpose and focus conveyed by facilitator Research procedures and consent form/ voluntary participation covered PPT slides on 4-C theory and original graphic of 4-C model presented, with examples 4-C classroom activity and Interview protocol for Canada interactively addressed Small groups at roundtables brainstormed activity, penning responses to protocol Groups verbally shared results with whole class (conversational highlights stated) Facilitator listened, took notes, and asked clarifying questions; brief exchanges ensued Professor drew workshop activity to a close 90- to 120-minute workshop conducted	Signed (and unsigned) consent forms given to facilitator/researcher Brief postreflection sessions with both professors They addressed gaps on completed activity sheets Facilitator checked for understanding; fixed notes Unstructured reflection on experience and activity occurred Two-way sharing of new learning and takeaways A professor contributed to data analysis and case
	Public seminars (groups)	Information flyer circulated by host university inviting attendance Time and place established for the research presentation and group interview	Facilitator and creativity topic introduced by series coordinator Workshop purpose and focus conveyed by facilitator Review of research procedures and consent form/voluntary participation covered PPT slides on 4-C theory and original graphic of 4-C model presented, with examples 4-C classroom activity and Interview protocol for Canada interactively addressed Attendees chose how to complete task, typically individually Volunteers verbally shared results with attendees in session Facilitator listened, took notes, and asked clarifying questions; brief exchanges ensued Coordinator drew workshop to a close 90- to 120-minute seminar conducted	Signed (and unsigned) consent forms given to facilitator Host university posted recordings of the talks, complete with PPT slides

| Faculty (individuals) | Information sheet about the research circulated
Follow up by researcher via email to faculty listserve
Time and place established for individual interviews | Research topic and interview purpose conveyed by researcher
Review of research procedures and consent form/voluntary participation covered
Handout of 4-C theory delineating types provided, with original graphic of 4-C model
Interviewee silently studied the information
Responded to prompt, "What does creativity in Canada look like?"
Verbal responses to single, open-ended prompt recorded in notes by researcher
Clarifying questions asked by researcher to elicit details and confirm meanings
30-minute interview conducted | Signed consent forms given to researcher
Interview summary provided for confirmation to interviewee
Feedback on summary requested (optional) |

Before engaging the classes in my 4-C creativity workshop for Canada, I held planning sessions with the instructors, both tenured full professors. The instructor in teacher education taught both master's courses in which I did workshops whereas the other in higher education taught the doctoral course.

Having initiated 60-minute planning sessions with both professors, I learned about the course, program, and culture. In turn, I clarified the purpose and focus of my activities, conveying highlights from Fig. 4.1, Appendix 4.2, and Appendix 6.1. After completing my workshops in the classes, I followed up with a brief postreflection.

In advance of my workshop, these teaching faculty also took the opportunity to learn about the planned creative exercise that applies an educational theory of creativity (i.e., Kaufman & Beghetto's [2009] 4-C model). They shared crucial contextual information, expressed ideas, and subtly communicated expectations. At the workshops, both faculty introduced and closed my activity. They also spontaneously interjected ideas during the session, sharing creative connections that may have stimulated their class and influenced 4-C responses.

At the preplanning session, I went over the electronic copies previously provided of my activity-based materials—introductory PowerPoint (PPT) slides, handouts, and the 2009 article describing the creativity typology (available for class distribution following the workshop.) I said that I would summarize the theory from the article during my lecture portion of the workshop and set the tone for ideas to be generated collaboratively and authentically by teams. The three classes did not have access to my materials in advance, precluding the possibility of preparing responses and consulting sources (like the Internet). Grades/points were not associated with my visit, which I clarified with the classes.

In sum, at the intensive planning meetings, dynamics such as aims, contexts, roles, and responsibilities were covered, specifically:

1. The roles and expectations of the facilitator (myself) and professor (participant)
2. The focus and nature of the course and its function and value within the departmental and university context, extending to general class demographics, the classroom culture, and any strengths and challenges from the professor's perspective
3. The aim(s) of the workshop and how it fit with the learning objectives and topical sequence of the course, extending to the content of the facilitator's lecture (PPT presentation), research materials, and 4-Cs activity
4. How much time would be afforded for the "lesson" (workshop) and what the facilitator would be doing and when, such as to engage the students and encourage their interaction
5. What the facilitator needed in terms of the spatial arrangement, materials, and anything else to ensure a beneficial learning experience
6. When the postreflection would occur, its aim and focus, and what was required from each party (the facilitator and professor)
7. Results from the data analyzed based on the workshop/lesson and the deadline for the facilitator to share these

At the postreflective sessions, I met with the course professors to review questions from my field notes. My record was based on in-class sources: student team responses on the 4-C activity sheets and my summary of written and verbal communications from the class. I solicited clarification in marked areas of omission and confusion. As a one-time facilitator, this was my best shot at faithfully checking for understanding and having my interpretative record improved and verified. In actuality, the reflective conversations propelled two-way learning, with the two professors expressing interest in reading educational creativity research to inform future classes.

The seasoned bilingual teacher educator who taught both master's-level preservice courses welcomed the 4-C workshop. We organized her classes into teams with approximately four students. She was open about her struggle at the course level with accommodating graduate students from the 2-year master of teaching (MT) program, owing to its merger with the master's of education (MEd) program. This fundamental change to the teacher education program was not appealing to her because (1) the merger increased enrollments beyond a workable class size; (2) it watered down what was historically a rigorous program of study (i.e., the MEd); and (3) it jeopardized the academic success of both populations (MT and MEd). She also differentiated the teacher aspirants partaking in the merger: there were those for whom advanced English posed difficulty (it was their second language), compounding their grasp of the academic Canadian culture, and those with acceptable, even strong, scholastic language capabilities who were culturally adjusted. Among the latter were students already teaching full-time in public schools.

With a comparatively modest enrollment in the higher education program, this professor recommended that her doctoral class of eight be engaged as a single group for the 4-C brainstorming activity. Her international students, mostly from the East, were likely to benefit, she thought, from my collective activity and discussion in that my approach typified her seminar style; also, my subject interest was deemed a good match for the specialized attention on international studies and dissertation research. A request was that I listen to students' research updates, including presentations, and provide verbal feedback, thus the timeframe was extended.

In the three classes, the 4-C prompts (research protocol) assisted students in generating responses, organizing their ideas, and sharing aloud. Validation of brainstorming (alternatively question-asking) as a creativity technique—endorsed by Craft (2002) and originated by Osborn (1979)—is a credible technique in creativity (and educational) research. With respect to the brainstorming practice, to aid team activity, I provided context and guidance by interactively presenting my PPT slides. I covered basics of the 4-Cs and its disciplinary context before turning to the activity because educational psychology was *not* included in participating students' programs of study and because academic English was ostensibly a challenge for some.

(The 30-minute individual interviews in faculty offices began with the 4-C theory and a handout delineating the four creativity types, followed by the interviewee's silent reading. As the interviewer, I wrote responses in my notebook and verbalized key points to confirm meanings.)

Prompts went beyond *creativity* in the 4-C theory to pairings with *accountability* and *Canada*, resulting in seven categories: creativity, Mini-c, Little-c, Pro-C, Big-C, accountability, and high-stakes testing cultures. My context-neutral protocol was designed to elicit authentic feedback, so *education* (and related usages) was avoided.

For the in-class activity, students worked as teams after being introduced to the 4-C creativity theory. When finished, volunteers read their team responses aloud, so written and oral data were obtained from all group interviews in a 90- to 120-min timeframe. While listening to the highlights, I produced six summaries. When comparing my summaries to participants' handwritten notes, I noticed gaps between the two sets of documents, which the course professor was able to resolve.

(I asked the individual interviewees, "What does creativity look like in a Canadian context from your perspective?" As they spoke to this open-ended prompt, I took notes.)

6.5.3   Data Analysis

For this Canadian study, the data analysis process and procedures follow the explanation provided. Areas of uniqueness in this regard, specific to the Toronto site, are described here.

During the coding of data from this glocality only, additional keywords were identified. As such, a total of 12 codes resulted, expanding the initial 7 precodes. The 4-Cs, appearing constantly, contributed significant weight to *creativity* and its preexisting codes (*Mini-c*, *Little-c*, *Pro-C*, and *Big-C*). The data analysis process occurred deductively, owing to the coding of language in my main research question, as well as inductively, due to the emergence of words that repeated in the interview data. Thus, nine additional words achieved the keyword/code status: *art*, *teaching*, *learning*, *testing*, *education*, *performance*, *culture*, *colonialism*, and *responsibility*. The listing of codes in this table was used for an initial data search (see Table 6.1).

To demonstrate the coding process known as "in vivo" described in the "Methods" chapter, a preservice teacher group wrote this barebones sentence: "Mandated testing does not dampen creativity in Ontario's public schools." Here, *testing* and *creativity* were coded for frequency count. In the Excel spreadsheet I recorded *testing*—Ontario public schools—mandated; *creativity*—not-dampen (*testing* did not decrease *creativity*). Initial subcodes associated with the sentence were: *testing*, *mandated*, *Ontario*, and *public school*. (These all showed up across the data, with *testing* eventually gaining the status of a keyword/code.) Echoing this participant view, another preservice group stated, "Toronto education culture focuses more on fostering creativity in classrooms than testing." Besides recording the primary codes *testing* and *creativity*, I included *culture*, which eventually became another keyword/code, albeit not appearing as frequently in the data as the two other terms. For both of the coded sentences, in my field notes, I wrote, "Monitor researcher bias— my assumption that teachers think mandated testing is a barrier, if not oppressive, to creativity in the classroom—the testimonial viewpoint does not 'feed' my bias." My additional notation for the second coded statement was, "Search the data for meanings of *culture*, specifically any explanations or perceptions of 'Toronto education culture'—why is it being described as a culture and how? Does anything make it unique or special?"

Independently, the teacher educator who welcomed my "teaching" of two of her preservice classes (in her presence) functioned as a qualitative rater. She completed a word-frequency count on a sample data set in Excel, and we made constant comparisons during a data session, identifying two tentative themes. Another decision was to highlight the teacher candidate responses in the analysis and write-up—owing to their prevalence/weight in the student and overall data—and incorporate others' salient points as applicable. We agreed that because the two data-based themes were unevenly projected across the raw data sets reflecting both student and faculty voices, these should be arranged according to their substantive emphasis: socially just pedagogy as creativity (theme 1) and creativity as educational entrepreneurialism (theme 2).

6.5.4   Place, Participants, and Programs

The university housing the graduate education building has a world-class reputation for being liberal minded. Hence, I assumed that participants would have some awareness of creativity in education and possibly within relation to reform or policy.

Canadian and non-Canadian students, faculty, and leaders in education ($N = 80$) partook in-person through onsite interviews or a brainstorming activity within a regularly scheduled semester in 2017. Students were racially and ethnically diverse (master's and doctoral level; $n = 65$); most were preservice and inservice teachers (57), fewer of whom were in the higher education program (8). Others, mostly Canadian citizens, were tenured faculty and leaders (unit coordinators; $n = 8$). Alumni and visiting professors were from Asian countries ($n = 7$). Group participation spanned six data collection venues: three credit-earning courses and three public seminars. The students, in face-to-face classes, completed aspects of the 4-C program. My seminars were sponsored by an international professional development center and department.

Ethnically, more than half of the students were Asian, born outside of Canada; others were Black, Middle Eastern, Indian, and Latinx. The few Canadian-born students did not identify as "ethnic." "Internationals" (a term faculty preferred and used instead of "immigrants" for identifying newcomers to Canada or persons without Canadian citizenship) were mostly recent arrivals; the preservice teacher immigrants were not yet interning or teaching in schools. Strikingly, 42% of these classes were Chinese and mostly female. The gender was 86% female in the two preservice classes, an imbalance that Canada's teacher education programs reflect (Hernandez, 2016). (The place-bound racial/ethnic descriptors appearing in this passage are consistent with those used by participating teaching faculty at the site to describe select student populations; thus, the racial/ethnic characteristics were not self-reported by students.)

Both teacher education courses contained master's students enrolled in the teacher development program either full- or part-time. One course's focus was language, culture, and identity in teacher development, and the other's was literature in a multicultural context. Students enrolled full-time (primarily immigrants from Asian countries) were studying with certified novice teachers earning the MEd degree part time. The MT program that qualifies graduates to teach in Ontario schools reflected this pattern; the classes wherein my workshops occurred reflected the student ethnic mix, the demographics of which typified the teacher education program.

In the third class, doctoral students in higher education were 78% Asian (mostly from China, with two from Japan) and otherwise Canadian-born of White or ethnic descent. Gender was mixed.

At my public workshops, participants were mainly female and Asian, predominantly Chinese. Canadian citizens joined in smaller numbers.

Most participating graduate students were from the curriculum department, where teacher preparation is developmentally and culturally oriented. This unit attracts prospective teachers seeking preparation for careers and professional advancement. Social justice principles underlie their education in this unit. The course curricula reflected the departmental mission and seemed consistent with the faculty syllabi and publications analyzed. Based on sources inspected (program bulletin with course descriptions, syllabi of the two preservice courses and six other courses, and faculty vitae and publications), the academic culture was steeped in basic social justice tenets of human dignity, respect for life, rights, and responsibilities, and so forth. The principle of the common good referenced value for establishing social conditions that allows people to reach their full potential. Preferential options for underrepresented populations in public schools, extending to the poor and vulnerable, another tenet, upheld the belief that these groups deserve equitable treatment, justice, and dignity. In the higher education program, those students partaking in my creativity program were from international studies where leading concepts (e.g., globalization, leadership, and interdependence) were also social justice oriented.

Most participants whose identities are anonymized (like the university and education building's name) engaged in my program and interviewed once due to their busy schedules. However, postreflection with two faculty followed my workshop in their (total of) three classes.

6.6 Results: Creativity and Accountability

Keyword citation frequency of the 4-Cs from the Canadian data analyzed as a whole suggests certain patterns relative to the creativity concepts. As seen in Fig. 6.1, there were 60 Mini-c responses/usages, 55 Little-c, 36 Pro-C, and 19 Big-C.

Table 6.2 is a summary of the 4-C results (prompts 2a through c) reflecting usage of the 4-Cs. Most (but not all) of the entries on the chart are expanded upon in the

"Discussion" section relative to the main themes: socially just pedagogy and educational entrepreneurialism. As next explainedthese ideas reflect perspectives shared on creativity within policy reform contexts

6.7 Discussion

Here I interpret the 4-C numerical results across all data sets, with some of the results displayed (Figs. 6.1 and 6.2, and Table 6.2). This descriptive analysis is followed by discussion of the overarching themes that associate creativity with socially just pedagogy and educational entrepreneurialism. As the narration conveys, the

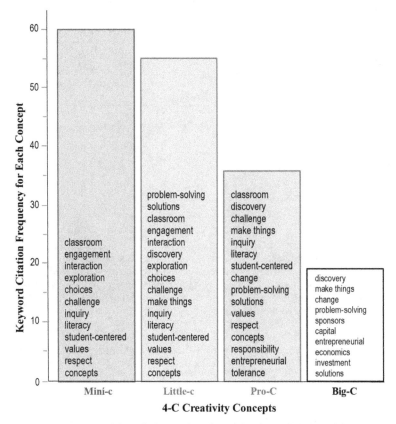

Note: Breakdown for keyword citations assigned to each 4-C creativity type:
Mini-c = 60 citations; Little-c = 55 citations; Pro-C = 36 citations;
Big-C = 19 citations (N = 170)

Fig. 6.1 Keyword citation frequency of the 4-Cs from Canadian data. (C. A. Mullen)

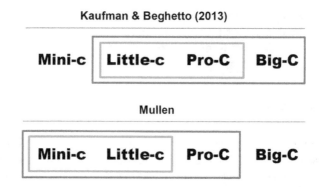

Fig. 6.2 Comparison of Kaufman & Beghetto and Mullen's 4-C Results. (C. A. Mullen)

Table 6.2 Keyword/code frequency from interviews and activities with Toronto-based educators ($N = 80$). (C. A. Mullen)

Keywords/Codes	Frequency
Creativity/CREAT	170
Canada/CAN	157
Art/ART	137
Teaching/TEACH	125
Accountability/ACCOUNT	118
Learning/LEARN	117
Testing/TEST	116
Education/EDU	115
Performance/PERFORM	110
Culture/CULT	19
Colonialism/COLONIAL	19
Responsibility/RESPONS	18
TOTAL RESPONSES	1221

Note. Keywords/codes, highlighted in bold, were preexisting based on the primary research question and literature review results. Keyword/code creativity was composed of *Mini-c* (60), *Little-c* (55), *Pro-C* (36), and *Big-C* (19). The nine keywords/ codes (regular font) were generated inductively. Keyword/code frequency reflects all citations of a search term by participating educators. Total responses = total keyword/code frequency

themes embody tensions between creativity and accountability, with culture implicit and, at times, explicit.

6.7.1   Description of 4-C Numerical and Written Results

My data-based interpretation incorporates keyword citation frequency (Fig. 6.1) and 4-C Canadian usages (Table 6.2). Being enacted is a numerical and descriptive analysis of the data in relation to the 4-C-informed prompts.

6.7.1.1   Mini-c Results

Mini-c, at times cited by itself, took a slight lead in the sheer number of times it was named (35%), amounting to being distinctive enough to be "favored" as a creativity concept. Mini-c, often tied to Little-c, suggested that the graduate students, in particular, gravitated toward both types of creativity, tending to see them as identical (Fig. 6.1). Their value statements and numerous examples suggest a strong identification with Mini-c, even though it was frequently joined with Little-c (Table 6.2). Mini-c examples of creative products of theirs included "identity project; small-scale presentations, story creations, and tangible self-expressions" (Table 6.2).

The pre/inservice-participants envisioned Mini-c as being ignited every day by creative people whom they identified as classroom teachers. These individuals, they wrote, create learning spaces that are conducive to Mini-c/Little-c, engage in meaningful inquiry, interact with others, and make discoveries through "inquiry-based learning." Creative curriculum and assessment can be expected to take such forms as "hands-on activities, exploring with technology, role-playing, storybooks, story-telling, collaborations, innovations, dramatic arts, and cultural projects," they explained. Such Mini-c experiences of creativity center "subject matter in student interest to foster creative learning," and these bring about "happiness" and propel creative expressions of "one's self and culture" (Table 6.2).

6.7.1.2   Little-c Results

Little-c was most often combined with Mini-c in the responses, and it was less frequently cited as a stand-alone concept. Also unfolding in everyday creativity, Little-c shared the same elements as Mini-c, except for "discovery," "mak(ing) things," "problem-solving," and finding "solutions." Problem-solving (e.g., "designing a project connecting local and family history with events"), according to the participants' descriptions, is stimulated through such dynamics as "teacher facilitation of inquiry-based learning" and curriculum design that is "culturally relevant" (from Table 6.2). Although they did not point this out, as explained in Chap. 3, all such status attributes, as assigned to Little-c, reflect a Western conceptualization (and bias) of creativity's problem-solving orientation, a human proclivity widely understood in creativity studies (e.g., Collard & Looney, 2014; Gardner, 1991; Li & Gerstl-Pepin, 2014).

6.7.1.3   Pro-C Results

Pro-C was distinguished by the students, faculty, and leaders, but the student tendency was to blend conceptualizations of Pro-C with those of Mini-c and Little-c. Among the distinguishing elements of Pro-C were "change," "responsibility," "entrepreneurial," and "tolerance," which were cited more frequently by the faculty and leaders.

A portrait emerged of creative teachers who are entrepreneurial and succeed at innovative projects. They make a difference without losing sight of social justice tenets (responsibility and tolerance), which they use as beacons of change. Portraiture specifics for Pro-C (see Table 6.2) depict a "notable achievement by a professional to a field/discipline," such as a preK–12 classroom teacher. "Examples of [such] creative products" include the "First Montessori school in Canada, Individualized Education Programs, and customized lessons." Creative people include "teachers who create learning environments and adapt curriculum for struggling pupils." About creative curriculum and assessment, imagined by participants were Pro-C contributions like "differentiated instruction and assessment, equitable practices of assessment and reporting, cross-curricular content; teacher evaluations and observations, and choices in content and assessment." Creativity, as specified, is experienced through "teacher–student relationships, liberty and responsibility, creative literacies, and testing ideas from inservice trainings."

Like Mini-c and Little-c, for Pro-C "classroom" was the prevailing context for generating ideas about creativity types. Teacher–student and student–student relationships were a natural extension and prioritized "student-centered" learning in the realm of creative activity. Catalysts of such activity, within Mini-c and Little-c creativity-rich worlds, were identified as "engagement," "interaction," "exploration," "challenge," "choice," and more. Interestingly, all such associations are consistent with creativity studies that include description of the 4-Cs and value "creativity in the classroom." These particular results, and certainly the grounding with learning environments, might come as no surprise, given that 81% of respondents were students immersed in a guided but open-ended activity. While their responses were prompted around culturally situated, accountability-linked responses to each of the 4-Cs, all associated notions and descriptions were of participants' own making.

6.7.1.4   Big-C Results

While Big-C was given far less importance than the other Cs by the students, whose Big-C commentary was sparse, together with the faculty and leaders' remarks it was recognized as a distinct category of creativity. Big-C was tied to "economics" and "investment," namely by "sponsors," such as the Government of Canada, for which "capital" was invested and generated (see Fig. 6.1). Like Little-c and Pro-C, Big-C was "entrepreneurial" in nature and "discovery" and "change" oriented; this "big splash" form of creativity was rooted in "problem-solving" and "mak[ing] things," but at the level of educational and societal "change." Missed was the connection between Big-C and Mini-c and the notion that major breakthroughs come from, and are ignited by, Mini-c (e.g., Kaufman & Beghetto, 2009). The disconnection from creativity's Mini-c origins was evident in associations that were lacking for Mini-c (e.g., "discovery," "entrepreneurialism," "mak[ing] things"; Fig. 6.1) but not for Little-c and Pro-C. In education, it seems particularly important that educators invest in the belief that personal and everyday meaning-making has the creative potential, like Little-c, to give rise to significant creative discoveries. Such thinking can reinforce the value of Mini-c for Little-c experiences, in addition to creative professional creativity that has the potential to become a Pro-C achievement.

In the across-group participant data, Big-C was defined as "groundbreaking creativity that changes a culture," exemplified by such creative products as "Canada's 150 symbol of its birthday, Blackberry (BlackBerry Ltd.), and Cirque Du Soleil (entertainment)" (from Table 6.2). Big-C creative people in Canada included "Margaret Atwood (literature), Michael Fullan (creativity in reform), and Pierre Trudeau (politics)." Also on this graphic, creative curriculum and assessment were illustrated as the "achievement of multiracial immigrant populations in school-based curriculum and national testing," as well as "entrepreneurism via twenty-first-century innovative school reform models." Experiences of Big-C creativity tended to highlight what was perceived as the nation's unique standing in the world: "Canada, as a model of diversity and tolerance, has a creative culture; also, it absorbs immigrants and refugees and offers asylum."

6.7.1.5   Mullen's Outcomes Compared with Kaufman and Beghetto's

Like Kaufman and Beghetto (2013), of particular interest in my study were "people's conceptions of creativity" and whether they can "recognize the four Cs" (p. 229). These creativity researchers' survey-based exploration provides evidence for the "theoretical assertion that Mini-c creativity is viewed as a unique and legitimate form of creativity" (p. 229). The empirical grounding of their 4-C theory inspired my research orientation, although the methodology, population, and context differ.

Comparing our particular methodologies, Kaufman and Beghetto (2013) "tested" their 4-C model by surveying undergraduates (details appear in Chap. 3), whereas my data were generated from an open-ended, 4-C semistructured protocol (Appendix 6.1). My tool was used with 80 educators (after piloting it in China). Additionally, I "paired" creativity with accountability on the prompts, thereby infusing the accountability construct across all creativity types. I was curious to find out how Canadian-based educators viewed creativity, particularly in relation to accountability within policy reform contexts. The college population involved in their investigation did, in fact, make some distinctions in the creativity types, a result that I found encouraging, which inspired me to apply their model within the Canadian landscape.

Figure 6.2 offers a graphical comparison between Kaufman and Beghetto's (2013) and my 4-C results. It seems prudent to keep in mind our numerous study differences when considering our approaches and outcomes: location (United States versus Canada), methodology (survey versus activity/interview), and participant group (undergraduate students versus graduate students, extending to faculty/leaders; even the racial/ethnic demographics were dissimilar).

Notably, Kaufman and Beghetto (2013) found that Mini-c was distinct, like Big-C, in regard to how the students conceived creativity; also, Little-c and Pro-C were not only fused but also linked with Big-C. In contrast, while Mini-c was perceived as distinctive in my data, Mini-c and Little-c were repeatedly fused, which graduate students signaled as "Mini-c/Little-c" (see Fig. 6.2). Across all of my groups, Pro-C, recognized as its own category, was differentiated. Students, however, typically blended Pro-C with Mini-c and Little-c, although they did cite value for the "entrepreneurial" eminence of professional creators (whom they presumed to be teachers). For them, "classroom" was the common denominator unifying Mini-c, Little-c, and Pro-C. One effect was the association of all Pro-C achievements with preK–12 classroom environments in which teacher–student interactions gave rise to creativity. Importantly, Pro-C was mostly restricted to everyday creativity within classrooms and exemplary teachers who innovatively foster creative thought and action within stimulating environments.

An element unifying Mini-c/Little-c/Pro-C in the data was "respect." As mentioned previously, student-participants cast responsible, reflective teachers as agents in thinking through mitigating factors that help explain undesirable pupil behavior. Mitigating factors are circumstances (e.g., family or personal situations) that enable understanding of conduct, and accountable teachers take the time to investigate. (A contrast was made between this kind of teacher and someone who defaults to strict enforcement of regulations and bans.)

Canada may be somewhat unique for the level of attention given to student and teacher rights. As examples from education and schools, it has active, influential teacher federations that advocate for educationally-related interests and rights not only of teachers but also children and youth. National Respect Day sets the tone for people being respectful of others and developing respectful relationships. The National Day of Silence puts social justice rhetoric into action, with "students across the country vow[ing] to take a form of silence to call attention to the silencing effect of anti-LGBT bullying and harassment in schools" (e.g., Decorah High School, 2012). Presumably, the pre/inservice teachers were aware of, or exposed to, such cultural influences, although there were no indicators (in the data).

Big-C was discerned as a separate category across participant groups. But, in the student responses, Big-C seemed disconnected from Mini-c, minimizing the importance of everyday creativity and its effect on Big-C. Among the few examples of professional creativity in Canada that have transformed disciplines, even world knowledge, students named Canada's Montessori schooling as Pro-C (see Table 6.2). Processes that could aid the transformation of a Pro-C achievement into Big-C one, however uncommon in reality, were pondered by several faculty members only. They underscored the need for sponsors to invest in the Pro-C creator (person, idea, or product) with the capital for testing/fine-tuning the creative idea or product (Table 6.3).

At a meta-level, like the student-respondents from Kaufman and Beghetto's 2013 study, mine viewed the 4-C categories as (somewhat) distinct, but without the textured particularities that give character to each category, as conjectured by the 4-C theory. The students in Canada seemed to favor Mini-c, appreciating it on its own merits while decidedly attending to perceived aspects that Mini-c shares with Little-c (e.g., "classroom," "exploration," "inquiry," "literacy," etc.; Fig. 6.2).

Table 6.3 Select Canadian usages of Mini-c, Little-c, Pro-C, and Big-C. (C. A. Mullen)

	Mini-c	Little-c	Pro-C	Big-C
Scope of creativity	Personally meaningful in learning and life	Daily creative problem-solving that has value/benefit	Notable achievement by a professional to a field/discipline	Groundbreaking creativity that changes a culture
Example of creative product	Identity projects; small-scale presentations; story creations; tangible self-expressions	Problem-solving (e.g., designing a project connecting local and family history with events)	First Montessori School in Canada; individualized Education programs; customized lessons	Canada's 150 symbol; Blackberry (BlackBerry Ltd.); Cirque Du Soleil (entertainment)
Example of creative person and collective	Mini-c learning; creation of spaces; engaging in inquiry; interacting; discovering	Teacher facilitation of inquiry-based learning; making curriculum culturally relevant	Teachers who create learning environments and adapt curriculum for struggling students	Margaret Atwood (literature); Michael Fullan (creativity in reform); Pierre Trudeau (politics)
Creative curriculum and assessment	Inquiry-based learning; hands-on activities; exploring with technology; role-playing; storybooks; storytelling; collaborations; innovations; dramatic arts; cultural projects	Problem-solving curricular modifications; making classrooms culturally relevant; resolving issues (e.g., access) for differently abled students; designing creative learning spaces	Differentiated instruction and assessment; equitable practices of assessment and reporting; cross-curricular content; teacher evaluations and observations; choices in content and assessment	Achievement of multiracial immigrant populations in school-based curriculum and national testing; entrepreneurism via twenty-first-century innovative school reform models
Experience of creativity	Happiness; subject matter centered in student interest to foster creative learning; express one's self and culture	Teacher solution-seeking for differently abled and behaviorally challenged students; trying to creatively bridge with parents	Creativity in teacher–student relationships; liberty and responsibility; creative literacies; testing ideas from inservice trainings	Canada, as a model of diversity and tolerance, has a creative culture; absorbs immigrants and refugees, offering asylum

Outcomes from our studies suggest that Mini-c was distinguished as a category of creativity by college students. Perhaps my exploration reinforces the "empirical basis" they provided for asserting that "Mini-c creativity is viewed as a unique and legitimate form of creativity" (p. 233). Creative action involving activity-based engagement via reflection, brainstorming, and collaboration was also a contribution ignited by my inquiry.

6.7.2   Overarching Themes: Creativity as Justice and Entrepreneurialism

Creativity as social justice and educational entrepreneurialism were two perspectives revealed across the data sets. Students and educators' comments during the creative activity and interview, respectively, referenced policy reform contexts. In no way simplistic, the themes invite unpacking to reveal their creativity–accountability dynamics, with linkages to culture. In the way of a quick overview before narrating each theme, participants' associations with creativity included "problem-solving, critical thinking, innovation, and twenty-first-century learning" (prompt 1 of the research protocol; Appendix 6.1). Accountability had different meanings as well, such as taking creative and responsible action on behalf of all learners and resisting neoliberal influences in education (prompt 4). To clarify, my use of *team* in what follows refers only to preservice and inservice responses; *group* is otherwise the default.

As analyses of responses conveyed, students adhered to the 4-C protocol in their reflections, whereas faculty exhibited a nonlinear or holistic approach. The latter reflected a more liberal train of thought with respect to critical and political ideas; the notions of education expressed were not restricted to preK–12 education, although it was a touchstone for a few faculty (former school leaders). Like the students, no professor remarked on the 4-C model; however, this respect makes sense, considering that Kaufman and Beghetto's (2009) conceptual scheme, while serving as the framework in my introduction to all classes, seminars, and interviews, was not listed as a prompt on the protocol/activity sheet (the 2009 citation was listed). Instead, I geared focus around the 4-Cs in Canada (e.g., Mini-c in Canadian settings).

6.7.2.1   Socially Just Pedagogy as Creativity (Theme 1)

Drawing heavily upon preK–12 schooling contexts, the teacher education classes described creativity through an educational lens. "Liberties" and "responsibility" were seen as catalysts for "creative learning" in classrooms. An overarching idea is that creativity "challenges norms." Going against the grain, Pro-C curriculum "cuts across math, the arts, and all subjects." Students hinted that creativity extends beyond arts classes and programs.

Characteristics assigned to creativity, although numerous, highlighted "spontaneity," "flexibility," "self-expression," "innovation," "imagination," "discovery," "diversity," "heterogeneity," "choice," "inquiry-based learning," and "thinking outside of the box." Many of these are descriptors of creativity in the literature cited; added was "listening to student voice," a point to which I return. Of note, "inquiry-based learning" was the lubricant for Mini-c and Little-c: "Learners from kindergarten onward" experience "innovation," "collaboration," "play," and "hands-on activities," encouraging "technology exploration and research online." "Having a platform to safely ask questions and express oneself" assists learners with "creative discovery."

Classroom creativity was not at the mercy of high-stakes or standardized testing, according to those teaching full-time and interning in preK–12 schools. Put differently, the required testing does not adversely affect creativity in Ontario's public schooling (a preservice teacher team). Other teams also espoused that creativity in classrooms familiar to them was not hindered by testing, although no one stated that testing eases creative learning. Another clarification was the province's standardized test (EQAO) was actually "emphasized more" than high-stakes tests in their schools.

With testing not proving disruptive to the inservice teachers' classrooms, they could experiment with creative pedagogies to support new learning. With real-world teaching experience, these graduate students could describe creative practices: "We make resources, design activities, and incorporate new ideas by consulting books and the Internet." They also gave Pro-C examples of investigatory learning and authentic assessment. It was as though Pro-C had to affect learning, engage learners, and even harmonize with pupil's Mini-c and Little-c to have intrinsic value: "In my classroom, I transfer what I learned from my Canadian arts high school where creativity was in every subject—teachers modeled Pro-C by allowing us to choose our topics and readings for projects."

Teacher facilitation of creativity and assurance of equity was all-important to these developing teachers in graduate school. Mini-c and Little-c industry make creative learning available to every pupil. They named advocacy and guidance, and planning and adaptation as equity-minded teacher behaviors. A belief was that teachers should pair "liberties" with "responsible action" across learners' developmental stages. Gaining familiarity with freedom and responsibility, pupils experience "choices in content and the classroom," "open-ended activities," and "interactive opportunities with peers."

In all such workflows, the next phase of reform positions teachers as partners helping pupils design their own learning (Fullan & Langworthy, 2013). Intriguingly, preservice comments reveal a subtle twist on this view of facilitation, advancing the interactive environment. In this worldview, it is the creative learning space in which teacher assistance takes place that enables youngsters to engage in discovery, interact with others, and collaborate on projects. Developing creative skills, pupils "resolve issues and make decisions that are meaningful—a higher-order challenge to every kid's creative process" (a preservice team).

Within dynamic settings, the teacher–student relationship is the magnet for creative nurturance. To these developing teachers, new learning calls for a reflective, adaptive, responsive, and empowering "Pro-C teaching style." At the teaching–learning interface, professional creativities paradoxically manifest and are indiscernible. Within nuances of interchange, Pro-C takes form: "Creativity means allowing my pupils to suggest project ideas and lead whole-group activities where there is no single answer." The learning environment is permeable; the pupil, while primary stakeholder, is not the only one. As such, a teacher's Pro-C challenge summoned parental engagement: "Being creative with how I respond to parent inquiries about their child's behavior is a goal. Teachers need to find creative ways of explaining difficult concepts to parents." The social interactive nature of teaching generates teacher–student interdependence (Beghetto, 2006) to which we can add environmental and social influences.

Returning to listening, creative teaching is not just student centered—it is also listening oriented. Like "listening to student voice," "happiness" is conceptualized as a deliberate pedagogic strategy: "Happiness in my classroom is about centering subject matter in student interest to nurture creative learning (Mini-c)." Rather than simply being a byproduct of learning experiences, student interest, voice, and happiness are all valued dynamics in creative spaces.

Fostering flexible and tolerant environmental dynamics struck a chord. This creative challenge would be met, preservice teachers thought, with teachers using pupil-centered pedagogies, some justice oriented. For these candidates, flexibility within Ontario's K–12 schools shows up as cross-curricular content that forces critical thinking. An example cited links classroom creativity to differentiated instruction on behalf of special populations: "Teachers are being creative when they adapt their instruction to curriculum expectations." Besides custom-designed lessons, creative strategies for differentiating instruction were "cooperative learning using the small c's," "Mini-c explorations using technology," and "Little-c problem solving."

Teaching creatively is associated with equity-mindedness and involves "making on-the-fly changes to help pupils discover connections with the world." Creative action entails pedagogical modification for differently abled learners and curricular adjustment for struggling learners. Pro-C teachers design content for struggling pupils: "We express our creativity with lessons that meet learner needs and by finding new ways to engage all of them" (a public school teacher). Another shared, "I work in a unique special education school, grades 7 to 12—it's a [creative learning] solution for anyone forgotten in public schools" (a private school teacher). Safeguarding diversity fosters community, compassion, justice, liberty, tolerance, and responsibility. Within Pro-C socially just contexts, Mini-c and Little-c learning thrive.

Further, principles of community, including ethical tenets, were voiced: "In our system we value respect and responsibility among teacher–student–parent." An example referenced school practices said to support tolerance (e.g., alternative reactions to infractions of rules): "We've moved away from zero-tolerance policy to weigh mitigating factors that come from knowing our pupils." Detrimental effects of standardized and international testing on teacher creativity and morale were not stated. In fact, socially just attitudes were attributed to the organizational cultures they knew, reflected in school policy. A healthy school culture evidencing a range of accountabilities emerged from this depiction.

Starkly contrasting with developing teachers' stances are multiple education stakeholders. Notably, teacher federations in Ontario express concerns about a testing culture that is overtaking creative teaching and learning (e.g., Ontario Teachers' Federation, 2014). Citing a growing teacher consensus within the province, unions claim that EQAO testing wastes classroom time, supplants creative pedagogies, and deprives pupils' creative and critical capacities. Faculty members in Toronto voiced similar criticisms in my presence, and researchers attest that high-stakes account-ability undermines micro and macro creativity (Beghetto & Sriraman, 2017) and jeopardizes equity for under-represented student populations (Triplett, 2017). Canada's PISA testing follows this very trajectory of making tested subjects homo-geneous across student groups (Kempf, 2016). Corroborating evidence challenges developing teachers' optimism.

A disparity was also evident across the student-generated data. Outside teacher education, creativity was perceived as inaccessible and exclusive—it was "usually found in the visual arts" and expressed "a world belonging to artist types." Pigeonholing creativity in all such ways confines it to the arts and humanities and only certain segments of society. But Kaufman and Beghetto's (2009) consciousness-raising theory underscores that daily occurrences of personal and professional cre-ativity are neither confined to subjects or people nor knowledge domains. Regarding equity, the nonteachers made few connections, unlike their preservice counterparts.

6.7.2.2   Creativity as Educational Entrepreneurialism (Theme 2)

Besides socially just pedagogy, creativity was paired with entrepreneurial innova-tion, specifically educational entrepreneurialism. Across the respondent pool, entre-preneurialism connoted a mixed message. While a positive social change for some participants, for others it posed a threat to the integrity of educational systems. In this regard, conflicting opinions suggested extreme positions, if not an epistemo-logical divide, over the purposes of education.

A "liberal" place where creativity thrives was one such prevailing view of Canada: "As immigrants, we think creativity is ingrained in Canadian cultures, making it Big-C" and "Canada attracts diversity and has creativity everywhere." Such perceptions speak to the lure of some immigrants to freely experience creativ-ity: "Professionals who are entrepreneurial gain advantages; free to think and act—their Pro-C can become Big-C and make a big splash!" Immigrants residing for a short time in Toronto while enrolled in the teacher education program conceived creativity in Canada differently than their peers. An unconditional idealism of Western democracies in which creativity thrives without constraint was projected. At the time of the study, they had very little experience of schools and likely with barriers to their participation in Canadian society, such as racism, xenophobia, and homophobia (Goldstein, 2013; Henderson & Wakeham, 2009; Mullen, 2020).

Also optimistic but knowledgeable of accountability-driven creativity trends in the nation was a program director. Referring to "Ontario and Canada's entrepre-neurial spirit," this Canadian-born retired school superintendent saw the nation as being "at a good point to excel as a creative leader on the world stage." Illustrating an empowered teacher culture in Ontario's K–12 public schools, she talked about assessment and evaluation: "Measurement, such as of creativity, works differently than in the U.S. It's more about a measure of teacher performance showing up implicitly in the curriculum than being top-down. Our teachers work well with sub-tle directions of change." To her, they absorb reforms without feeling "put upon."

Perhaps this director was implying that Ontario teachers' unionized protections help them maintain perspective on change. Teacher resiliency in the face of reform could prove beneficial with the "big wave ahead—the assessment of creativity—that's coming due to PISA's world influence. In 2018 PISA will measure creativity and drive creative financial literacy, globally." Concluding, she said, "A good thing is that Canada's a world leader in creativity and literacy."

PISA's nationwide reform was causing a groundswell. Paraphrasing a memo dated 2017, she described its 2018 operation: "In 2017 field testing was adminis-tered in Canadian schools; 15-year-old pupils were randomly selected in the thou-sands for the 2018 assessment. Besides reading, financial literacy is the domain added for Canada." Responding to PISA's testing priority for Canada, creativity was the expected focus of measurement and assessment. Such changes were propelling the momentum of high-stakes testing. The only participant who talked about PISA in the Canadian context, she was confident that the nation would rise in international rankings and shine in literacy and creativity. Welcoming Canada's global leadership status and participation in PISA 2018, she advocated measuring creativity on a large scale: "We need to assess creativity in our schools. But we should only ever measure what we value, so we'd have to value creativity first. This is where teacher buy-in comes in. Teachers shouldn't and can't be forced." As such, policy reform should respect teacher culture and values.

With an entrepreneurial take on solutions, she turned to a creativity initiative in Canada: "Fullan's NPDL model is certainly an example of educational entrepre-neurialism that proposes preK–12 learning solutions. It promises to be highly influ-ential in pedagogy and learning around creativity and innovation." Educational entrepreneurialism within schools, she continued, could "take off" with this reform and boost Canada's global proficiencies. Asserting that "prescriptive mindsets belong to the past," she credited "creative literacies and arts experiences" as "teach-ers' global competencies." To her, "storytelling, role playing, and dramatic arts" nourish Mini-c and Little-c student development.

However, creativity has been fraudulently repurposed, according to other faculty. To them, "entrepreneurial innovation" and "commercial value" are bedfellows, with carryover into "Canadian education." Someone remarked, "In today's world, if your idea is innovative and you can sell it, you're creative." Another professor relayed how "pupils are being taught problem-solving protocols for creative thinking con-nected to the EQAO testing program." The demand for outcome-based education was disrupting creativity even more by "requiring that, for assessment purposes, rubrics include questions that can be responded to using these protocols." About the EQAO, "Creativity means you need to work within the protocols that are scored." EQAO testing was blamed for "hammering creativity" into a "lackluster" form in Ontario.

At a public seminar of mine, professors expressed their view of the fate of cre-ativity in accountability-driven contexts. Creativity was at risk in Canada's educa-tion system (as opposed to morphing into new forms)—the liberal scope of creativity around discovery, engagement, and inquiry has been clamped down, at least in Ontario. A professor explained that with economics and competition as a national priority, creativity across the professions has been "reduced to an economic and competitive function." The new norm for being accountable as a worker "ties creativity to profits and economic entrepreneurialism." Another added that creativity serves neoliberal, not democratic, liberties. A quiet but resounding rejoinder in the room was that curriculum testers and other entrepreneurs have hijacked public education and with it creativity.

On the global Canadian front, a different faculty member declared, "There's no real entrepreneurship in Canada. We lack venture capital for educators' creative ideas and don't have Big-C breakthroughs. Much important work by Canadians is in collaboration with Americans and U.S. sectors—so *our* creators go *there*." A colleague of his had "exported" a creative idea to the United States where it's being developed in anticipation of having impact: "Canada is *not* willing to make this expensive investment—it wants from us but won't invest." Being depicted was leaders' "lack of entrepreneurial vision and will."

6.8 Reflections and Implications

Differences in thoughts about creativity in the global era were profound at times between students and faculty. Developing teachers' attention was clearly on preK–12 teaching and learning, with passing interest in policy dynamics that affect creativity. With some already in the trenches of Ontario schools (inservice teachers) and others preparing to teach (preservice teachers), these graduate students addressed the role of learning environments, particularly teacher–student relationships, in facilitating Mini-c, Little-c, and Pro-C. Adaptations for struggling and special-needs pupils posed a creative challenge for which they conveyed concern and responsibility. Fostering global competencies of creative and critical thinking within relational contexts was also apparent. Other than parents and pupils, these preservice and inservice teachers did not mention influential stakeholders (e.g., teacher federations and corporations). Not known is what they thought about resistance to EQAO testing by stakeholders (like professors and Ontario teacher federations) or federations' efforts to return creative teaching and learning to schools (e.g., Mullen, 2019c; Ontario Teachers' Federation, 2014).

For all but one faculty participant, creativity has been distorted beyond recognition in the education sphere. Tied to profit-seeking commercial interests, products, and services—and made into curriculum and assessment regimens that track productivity using narrow metrics—a new (unwelcome) global culture has been birthed (see Ball, 2012). Without proper vetting, frameworks, systems, and rubrics became fixtures in Canadian schools. Neoliberal interests have gained traction to such an extent that the expressed role of the faculty is to resist any further colonizing of public education or retire from higher education.

Canada's commitment to sustaining its global superpower status through PISA testing was stated only by the former superintendent, despite being field-tested across Canada in 2017. A PISA supporter, she did not mention PISA's neoliberal bias that favors the economic role of public (state) schools or mounting concerns that academics worldwide express about the impact of PISA tests on education and creativity (e.g., Frick, 2013; Tienken & Mullen, 2016).

While faculty at the research site spoke of the takeover of economic priorities in education, graduate students proved reticent on the subject. Little was said by them across programs about international pressures to compete and potential effects on creativity and accountability. However, the faculty participants attributed to co-opted creativity such functions as global competency, accountability tools, and economic measures. Neoliberal goals being served were economic prosperity, social improvement, standardized testing, international rankings, student proficiency gains, and pedagogic control. They seemed deeply disapproving. Perhaps their voices can be added to the growing international chorus of academic critics who oppose what they see as the neoliberal takeover of public schools, the undermining of the "dignity" and "integrity" of the teaching profession, and the discounting of the public school mandate to educate every child (e.g., Ball, 2012; Ravitch, 2014; Tienken & Mullen, 2016).

Canada's multicultural record—impressive by world standards—has a dark side: The marginalization of visible minorities (Hasmath, 2010) and colonization of Indigenous tribes depriving Aboriginal pupils of effectively implemented, racially honed creative cultural curriculum (Henderson & Wakeham, 2009; Mullen, 2020). Yet immigration is a "success story" of global proportions in public discourse (Conference Board of Canada, 2008). While Canada's superpower title arose from its 2016 PISA ranking, the spike has been largely attributed to migrants, many of whom test well (BBC, 2017). Societal tolerance has a bedfellow—negative racial bias toward the First Peoples of Canada, a visible minority.

6.8.1 Research Risk-Taking

Unknown was whether educators in Toronto would share their conceptions of creativity in education's present-day reform context. Many did. Although the word *education* was not used during the live study, it was presumed. Driving home this point, one preservice teacher team actually annotated a correction on the research protocol, inserting *education* in prompt 1 with an underline: "What does creativity look like in a Canadian *education* context?"

The intentional absence of *education* in my open-ended research prompts generated the hoped-for effect. Without being led by me, all participants spontaneously made connections between creativity and education and at times connecting policy reforms (e.g., standardized testing) and creativity dynamics (e.g., corporate control). Written and oral perspectives on creativity in education were generated in accordance with the 4-Cs in all three classes.

Another risk I took was not knowing if the educators would open up to an outsider. They did but with less collective knowledge of, or interest in, high-stakes testing issues than one might expect. Upon reviewing this study, a Canadian professor responded,

> If this were the United States, United Kingdom, or Australia where high-stakes tests are on the rise, then one would expect more knowledge of testing. With fewer of these assessments in Canada and over a decade of sustained attention to formative assessment in our jurisdictions, I'm not surprised by your results. (personal communication, 2018)

Interestingly, this view is not in step with Kempf's (2016) international study of high-stakes testing and finding—accountability through PISA testing is intensifying in Canada, owing to global pressures to compete. Standardized tests also remain strong in certain provinces, although alternative forms of testing have also taken hold elsewhere. Participating faculty attributed these trends to high-level support of PISA. While the scale of my study is certainly modest, it brings "voice" to these issues and a valuable policy perspective on them.

6.8.2 Reform Trends

Amid harmful reports of high-stakes testing, some provincial governments in Canada have taken charge, as summarized at the start. Generating their own public school reforms, such jurisdictions have performed a curriculum overhaul across all or most grades and subjects. While student-centered authentic learning is resulting in creative classrooms, other jurisdictions have simply turned to less regimented testing.

In these times of dramatic political change, Canada pursues testing priorities hand in glove with market-driven pedagogies. With reforms to education being part of a broader agenda for change, the nation looks to creative innovation for building competitive capacity and economic prosperity. The "new normal" of competitiveness and economics as creativity's gears will likely remain, which faculty participants considered detrimental for education.

Those of us who contribute creativity research take creativity's plight in the quickening hands of reform trends seriously, especially when it comes to preK–12 public education, but also postsecondary public education. Academics, mainly in higher education and across disciplines, pursue this broad problem—the creativity challenge and crisis—by advancing resistive theories, practices, and actions for renewing creativity and people's commitment to it (e.g., Beghetto, 2019; Beghetto & Karwowski, 2019; Frick, 2013; Kim & Chae, 2019; Mullen, 2019b; Tienken & Mullen, 2016). A sad irony is that education reforms do pursue student knowledge but through erasure, as in the arts, play, and recess from children's school day, clarified Frick, all of which fuel reflection and creative moments, insights, and strategies (Mini-c and Little-c).

Educational researchers encourage exercise of our imaginations and the creation of "freedom-loving" publics (e.g., Bogotch & Waite, 2017). Our experiences of dynamic creativity, and abilities to produce creative achievements under duress, depend on our imaginative and (inter)subjective capacities (Corazza, 2016). "Imagining identities," a potentially powerful manifestation of these dimensions, reveals young people's capacity for constructing discourses of race and community in polemical urban contexts (Tucker-Raymond & Rosario, 2017). Such creative actions may honor student knowledge holistically and facilitate voice and agency.

6.9 Parting Words

This chapter gave me the opportunity to story some Toronto-based educators' views about creativity and accountability in the Canadian culture and educational policy context. The theoretical background presented the frames of creativity, standardized testing (and the standardization of teaching), and multiculturalism. Linkages (and tensions) between and among the frames were also described. The data collection and analysis, systematic in nature, was eclectic, allowing for elements to be creatively drawn from classes, interviews, and public seminars. Outcomes suggest that perceptions about creativity ranged from being explicitly to implicitly linked to the 4-Cs, with strong value for Mini-c, Little-c, and Pro-C, and with a blurring of Mini-c/Little-c, and Pro-C with the small "cs." Less emphasis was given to Big-C (and the potential for the smaller c's to become Pro-C, and Pro-C to transform into Big-C).

To faculty who contributed ideas, Big-C in Canada summoned barriers to creative innovation. The main attribution was to transnational cultures in which risk-taking is not supported, to the detriment of the educational field and innovators in general. Negative influences in the world of education were identified as test-centric learning goals, the co-opting of creative problem-solving in standardized assessments like Ontario's EQAO testing program, and a perceived lack of vision at all levels of leadership. Investing capital in creative and innovative thinking could propel breakthroughs for Canada as a whole, according to the critics.

Finally, creativity was linked to accountability, at times tacitly, in deeper clusters of ideas around socially just pedagogy and educational entrepreneurialism. These creativity dimensions served to deepen study outcomes. Quite possibly, they enhance the educational discourse around the social justice and neoliberal dimensions of creativity. A new idea contributed to the field involves the application of the 4-C conceptual scheme within a glocality (Toronto, Canada). Connections made with culture were also grounded in data and awakened by participant voice. Perhaps readers will find new openings for experiencing, expressing, and enlivening creativity.

Acknowledgments and Notes This Fulbright project was funded in 2017 by World Learning: Global Development & Exchange, a program of the U.S. Department of State, Bureau of Educational and Cultural Affairs (grant #FSP-P000185).

I'm grateful to the Canadian university for hosting me as a Fulbright Scholar and visiting professor. Institutional Review Board approval was granted in 2017 from my home institution.

Appendix: 4-C Classroom Activity and Interview Protocol for Canada (C. A. Mullen)

1. What does creativity look like in Canada's local/regional/national/global context from your perspective?
2. What examples spring to mind for each component of the 4-C creativity framework?

   (a) Mini-c (creativity)?
   (b) Little-c (creativity)?
   (c) Pro-C (creativity)?
   (d) Big-C (creativity)?

3. In each example, what does accountability look like or what forms does it take?
4. When you think about creativity and accountability on a global scale, how might Canada compare with other nations' (testing) cultures?

References

Baker, F. S. (2013). Shifting sands in the United Arab Emirates: Effecting conceptual change for creativity in early childhood teacher education. *Teacher Development, 17*(1), 72–91.

Ball, S. J. (2012). *Global Education Inc.: New policy networks and the neo-liberal imaginary.* New York, NY: Routledge.

BBC. (2017, August 3). How Canada became an education superpower. *Education News.* Retrieved from http://www.educationviews.org/canada-education-superpower

Beghetto, R. A. (2006). Creative self-efficacy: Correlates in middle and secondary students. *Creativity Research Journal, 18*(4), 447–457.

Beghetto, R. A. (2019). Structured uncertainty: How creativity thrives under constraints and uncertainty. In C. A. Mullen (Ed.), *Creativity under duress in education? Resistive theories, practices, and actions* (pp. 27–40). Cham, Switzerland: Springer.

Beghetto, R. A., & Karwowski, M. (2019). Unfreezing creativity: A dynamic micro-longitudinal approach. In R. A. Beghetto & G. E. Corazza (Eds.), *Dynamic perspectives on creativity: New directions for theory, research, and practice in education* (pp. 7–25). Cham, Switzerland: Springer.

Beghetto, R. A., & Sriraman, B. (2017). *Creative contradictions in education: Cross disciplinary paradoxes and perspectives.* Cham, Switzerland: Springer.

Bogotch, I., & Waite, D. (2017). Working within radical pluralism: Reconstructing educational leadership. In D. Waite & I. Bogotch (Eds.), *The Wiley International handbook of educational leadership* (pp. 1–13). Malden, MA: Wiley.

Boily, P., Chapdelaine, N., Hartley, M., Kent, L., Suurkask, K., & Wong, J. C. (2014). *Creativity unleashed: Taking innovation out of the laboratory and into the labour force.* Retrieved from http://www.actioncanada.ca/wp-content/uploads/2014/04/ac-tf3-creativity-report-en-web.pdf

Butler, R., & Nissan, M. (1986). Effects of no feedback, task-related comments, and grades on intrinsic motivation and performance. *Journal of Educational Psychology, 78*(3), 210–216.

Canadian Heritage. (2017). *Creative Canada: Policy framework.* Retrieved from https://www.canada.ca/content/dam/pch/documents/campaigns/creative-canada/final%20backgrounder_en.pdf

Castagno, A. E., & Brayboy, B. M. J. (2008). Culturally responsive schooling for indigenous youth: A review of the literature. *Review of Educational Research, 78*, 941–993.

Ciuffetelli Parker, D., & Craig, C. J. (2015). An international inquiry: Stories of poverty–poverty stories. *Urban Education, 52*(1), 120–151.

Collard, P., & Looney, J. (2014). Nurturing creativity in education. *European Journal of Education, 49*(3), 348–364.

Conference Board of Canada. (2008, August). *Valuing culture: Measuring and understanding Canada's creative economy.* Ottawa, CA: Author. Retrieved from http://www.conferenceboard.ca/e-library/abstract.aspx?did=2671

Corazza, G. E. (2016). Potential originality and effectiveness: The dynamic definition of creativity. *Creativity Research Journal, 28*(3), 258–267.

Craft, A. (1997). Identity and creativity: Educating teachers for postmodernism? *Teacher Development, 1*(1), 83–96.

Craft, A. (2002). *Creativity and early years education: A lifewide foundation.* New York, NY: Continuum.

Decorah High School. (2012, April 19). Decorah high school gay–straight Alliance observes day of silence. *Decorah News..* Retrieved from https://www.decorahnews.com/archived-stories/2012/04/2508.html.

De Fina, A., & Georgakopoulou, A. (2012). *Analyzing narrative: Discourse and sociolinguistic perspectives.* Cambridge, UK: Cambridge University Press.

Edmonston, B. (2016). Canada's immigration trends and patterns. *Canadian Studies in Population, 43*(1–2), 78–116.

Education Quality and Accountability Office Act. (1996). *S.O. 1996, c. 11.* Retrieved from https://www.ontario.ca/laws/statute/96e11

Frick, B. (2013). Fostering student creativity in the era of high-stakes testing. In J. Hattie & E. M. Anderman (Eds.), *International guide to student achievement* (pp. 231–233). New York, NY: Routledge.

Fullan, M., & Langworthy, M. (2013). *Towards a new end: New pedagogies for deep learning.* Retrieved from http://www.newpedagogies.nl/images/towards_a_new_end.pdf

Gardner, H. E. (1991). *To open minds.* New York, NY: Basic Books.

Goldstein, T. (2013). *Zero tolerance and other plays: Disrupting xenophobia, racism and homophobia in school.* Rotterdam, The Netherlands: Sense Publishers.

Hart, D., & Kempf, A. (2018, June). *Public attitudes toward education in Ontario 2018.* Retrieved from https://www.oise.utoronto.ca/oise/userfiles/media/media_relations/oise-public-attitudes-report-2018_final.pdf

Hasmath, R. (2010). *A comparative study of minority development in China and Canada.* New York, NY: Palgrave Macmillan.

Hernandez, J. C. (2016,. February 6)). Wanted in China: More male teachers, to make boys men. *New York Times.* Retrieved from http://www.nytimes.com/2016/02/07/world/asia/wanted-in-china-more-male-teachers-to-makeboys-men.html?emc=eta1&_r=0

Henderson, J., & Wakeham, P. (2009). Colonial reckoning, national reconciliation? Aboriginal peoples and the culture of redress in Canada. *English Studies in Canada, 35*(1), 1–26.

Ibbitson, J. (2014, July 2). Why is Canada the most tolerant country in the world? Luck. *Globe and Mail.* Retrieved from https://www.theglobeandmail.com/news/politics/why-is-canada-the-most-tolerant-country-in-the-world-luck/article19427921

Kaufman, J. C., & Beghetto, R. A. (2009). Beyond big and little: The four C model of creativity. *Review of General Psychology, 13*(1), 1–12.

Kaufman, J. C., & Beghetto, R. A. (2013). Do people recognize the Four Cs? Examining layperson conceptions of creativity. *Psychology of Aesthetics, Creativity, and the Arts, 7*, 229–236.

Kempf, A. (2016). *The pedagogy of standardized testing: The radical impacts of educational standardization in the US and Canada.* New York, NY: Palgrave Macmillan.

Kim, K. H., & Chae, N. (2019). Recapturing American innovation through education: The creativity challenge for schools. In C. A. Mullen (Ed.), *Creativity under duress in education? Resistive theories, practices, and actions* (pp. 215–233). Cham, Switzerland: Springer.

Li, Q., & Gerstl-Pepin, C. (Eds.). (2014). *Survival of the fittest: The shifting contours of higher education in China and the United States.* Heidelberg/Baden-Württemberg, Germany: Springer.

Mertz, E. (2013). Alberta gets rid of Provincial Achievement Tests. *Global News.* Retrieved from https://globalnews.ca/news/548713/alberta-gets-rid-of-provincial-achievement-tests

Mullen, C. A. (2017). What are corporate education networks? Why ask questions? *Kappa Delta Pi Record, 53*(3), 100–106.

Mullen, C. A. (2018). Creative learning: Paradox or possibility in China's restrictive preservice teacher classrooms? *Action in Teacher Education, 40*(2), 186–202.

Mullen, C. A. (Ed.). (2019a). *Creativity under duress in education? Resistive theories, practices, and actions.* Cham, Switzerland: Springer.

Mullen, C. A. (2019b). Dynamic creativity: Influential theory, public discourse, and generative possibility. In R. A. Beghetto & G. E. Corazza (Eds.), *Dynamic perspectives on creativity: New directions for theory, research, and practice in education* (pp. 137–164). Cham, Switzerland: Springer.

Mullen, C. A. (2019c). Global leadership: Competitiveness, tolerance, and creativity – A Canadian provincial example. *International Journal of Leadership in Education, 22*(5), 629–643.

Mullen, C. A. (2020). *Canadian indigenous literature and art: Decolonizing education, culture, and society.* Leiden, The Netherlands: Brill.

Ontario Teachers' Federation. (2014). *Response of the Ontario Teachers' Federation to the EQAO Assessment Advisory Committee.* Retrieved from http://www.eqao.com/en/about_eqao/eqao-online/communication%20documents/ontario-federation-teachers-feedback.pdf

Organization for Economic Co-operation and Development (OECD). (2019). *About the OECD.* Retrieved from http://www.oecd.org/about

Osborn, A. F. (1979). *Applied imagination: Principles and procedures of creative thinking* (3rd ed.). New York, NY: Charles Scribner's Sons. (Original work published 1953).

People for Education. (2017). *EQAO testing.* Retrieved from https://settlement.org/ontario/education/elementary-and-secondary-school/evaluation/eqao-testing

Plucker, J. A., Beghetto, R. A., & Dow, G. (2004). Why isn't creativity more important to educational psychologists? Potential, pitfalls, and future directions in creativity research. *Educational Psychologist, 39*, 83–96.

Ravitch, D. (2014). *Reign of error: The hoax of the privatization movement and the danger to America's public schools.* Toronto, ON: Alfred A. Knopf Canada.

Stinson, W. (2014). Government of Saskatchewan eliminates plan for standardized testing. *Global News.* Retrieved from https://globalnews.ca/news/1266875/government-eliminates-standardized-testing

Tan, A.-G. (2013). Psychology of cultivating creativity in teaching and learning. In A.-G. Tan (Ed.), *Creativity, talent, and excellence* (pp. 27–42). Cham, Switzerland: Springer.

The Guardian. (2014). *OECD and PISA tests are damaging education worldwide – Academics.* Retrieved from https://www.theguardian.com/education/2014/may/06/oecd-pisa-tests-damaging-education-academics

Tienken, C. H., & Mullen, C. A. (Eds.). (2016). *Education policy perils: Tackling the tough issues.* New York, NY: Routledge.

Tolerance. (2020). *Wikipedia.* Retrieved from http://www.dictionary.com/browse/tolerance

Toronto. (2020). *Wikipedia.* Retrieved from https://en.wikipedia.org/wiki/toronto

Triplett, N. P. (2017). Conceptions of equity in an age of globalized education: A discourse analysis of how the program for international student assessment (PISA) discusses equity. In R. M. Elmesky, C. C. Yeakey, & O. Marcucci (Eds.), *The power of resistance* (pp. 3–30). Bingley, UK: Emerald.

Tucker-Raymond, E., & Rosario, M. L. (2017). Imagining identities: Young people constructing discourses of race, ethnicity, and community in a contentious context of rapid urban development. *Urban Education, 52*(1), 32–60.

Van de Vliert, E., & Murray, D. R. (2018). Climate and creativity: Cold and heat trigger invention and innovation in richer populations. *Creativity Research Journal, 30*(1), 17–28.

World Economic Forum. (2019). *What is competitiveness?* Retrieved from https://www.weforum.org/agenda/2016/09/what-is-competitiveness

Chapter 7
Australia Case: Revealing Creativity and 4-C Responses

7.1 Overview: Purposes and Foci

"As Indigenous people, we've been trying to get written into constitutional law but not in the way the Australian government wants. So, we remain at a standstill, unlike other global countries' constitutions," uttered an Aboriginal leader. A student team in a gender studies class (independently of this source) similarly stated, "Australian society should be combatting racism and structural discrimination."

In this chapter, I describe creativity and accountability in Australia, probe how they align or conflict with accountability-based conceptions of creativity, and explain how education stakeholders at a culturally diverse public university in Sydney conceive creativity and accountability. Framing the creative intervention was the pedagogic research question, Can diverse college students and educators in Australia discover creativity when encouraged under educational constraint? Participating were Indigenous and non-Indigenous stakeholders, including students,

© Springer Nature Switzerland AG 2020   157
C. A. Mullen, *Revealing Creativity*, Creativity Theory and Action in Education 5, https://doi.org/10.1007/978-3-030-48165-0_7

in the social sciences. Rooted in the Four C (4-C) Model of Creativity (Kaufman & Beghetto, 2009), undergraduate classes engaged in creativity, and individuals contributed to 4-C conversations. Regarding creativity and the 4-Cs, three themes emerged:

1. Political and legal expression of Australian Indigenous causes
2. Environmental reform manifesting as protest and action
3. Breakthroughs in technology, medicine, culture, and media

Contextualizing the information gathered and analyzed, I highlight the first two themes and specify how they overlap—notably, environmental reform is a significant Australian Indigenous cause, as well as legal reform. (Educational reform was barely mentioned.) The third theme is succinctly addressed in the results. Crossover was evident among all themes, with Indigenous-related issues favored by lecturers and leaders and environmental change by students. Perspectives elicited on educational creativity and accountability magnify the importance of culture in contemporary Australia. A description of concepts relevant to the literature provides a framework for this account, with some participant commentary interwoven.

7.2 Concepts from the Literature

Creativity, understood as a process, facilitates critically important concepts and movements, satisfying its definitional scope. Runco (2019) persuasively reasoned that the definition of *creativity* should not be limited to "product" and "process" and can be valued as an end unto itself. An alternative way of seeing creativity is to consider reform efforts (e.g., national) that manifest creativity and change. I approach this idea as social (tribal and climate) justice.

> Bell's (2016) description of social justice resonates with tribal justice as a world in which the distribution of resources is equitable and ecologically sustainable, and all members are physically and psychologically safe and secure, recognized, and treated with respect. … Individuals [would be] both self-determining (able to develop their full capacities) and interdependent (capable of interacting democratically with others). (p. 3)

Interestingly, Indigenous scholar Writer (2008) responded to Bell's statement (originally appearing in 1997) in a way that explicates links with tribal justice:

> [Bell's] social justice definition works to the advantage of Indigenous Peoples; it is here that the disruption of colonization can occur. As both process and a goal, social justice advances the interrogation of the manifestations of power and the dynamics of oppression, such as in the distribution of resources. … [resulting in] a plan of action … to transform systems of oppression. (p. 5)

Tribal and climate justice are each an important form of social justice in their own right. Within this chapter, besides describing aspects of tribal and climate justice in the global Australian context, I also trace a few of their intersections. Notably, both types of justice strive for restorative legal change to remedy power imbalances, and each frames a pervasive societal issue as a political and ethical violation of the tallest order.

As defined herein, *tribal justice* seeks racial equality, Indigenous rights and protections, decolonization of societies, reparations for stolen land and generations, and responsibilities to the Aboriginal people of a nation; colonial injustices, to be combatted, dehumanize tribes, assuming ownership of their territories while exploiting natural resources (Mullen, 2019, 2020).

Climate justice is a response to global warming, owing to human activity that affects the planet's most vulnerable populations, and associated negative effects on equality, collective protections, and communities' rights; of great concern, industrial expansion disrupts rural communities' livelihood and commodifies cultures by endangering the inhabitants and our planet (Robinson, 2018).

7.2.1 Tribal Justice and Creativity in Australia

The Australian Constitution offers a substantial reference point for reflecting on tribal justice and creativity. What is essentially a complex, unfolding story around this legal document contains a vital thread—the Indigenous push to enact a second referendum to change the text. Going a step further to completely decolonize the national document as it stands today requires that it be subjected to a radical re-imagining (Saunders, 2011). Constitutional change could affect the nation's identity and its aims and values, or at least this is the idea behind Indigenous and ally legal activism. Constitutional identity is serious business indeed—as the story of Australia's Constitution conveys, it can include or exclude racial groups, empower or disempower societal institutions, and offer or forego human rights protection.

As of late 2019, the Australian Constitution, coming into effect in 1901, the same year the Australian National Flag was first flown, carries embarrassing remnants of the settlement ideology in which it was enshrined. Constitutional perspectives of British and American colonial powers were the main influence, as the colonies were subject to the British Parliament (Reconciliation Australia, 2017a). Withholding equal rights and respect to Indigenous Australians, and even declaring that they should not be counted in the census, the Constitution still contains "provisions authorizing discrimination on grounds of race" owing to "Australia's continuing colonial status" and actions taken "to preserve a white Australia" (Saunders, 2011).

Historically, the Constitution permitted "racial discrimination" against Aboriginal and Torres Strait Islander Australians (Reconciliation Australia, 2017a, p. 4; also, Albeck-Ripka, 2019). The 1967 national referendum mentioned earlier successfully landed a majority vote to change two sections of the Constitution that made the invisibility and subjugation of Aboriginal people legal:

> The Parliament shall, subject to this Constitution, have power to make laws for the peace, order, and good government of the Commonwealth with respect to . . . the people of any race, *other than the aboriginal people in any State*, for whom it is necessary to make special laws." And Section 127 stated: "*In reckoning the numbers of the people of the*

Commonwealth, or of a State or other part of the Commonwealth, aboriginal natives shall not be counted. (Reconciliation Australia, 2017a, italics in original)

However, despite constitutional changes that followed, racism persists. The Australian Constitution still does *not* recognize Aboriginal and Torres Strait Islander Australians, thereby disallowing creative breakthrough in recognition of the nation's first peoples—and their remarkable contributions for the betterment of society—at the level of Big-C. Also, references (in Sections 25 and 51) allow the commonwealth or state governments to discriminate against people on the basis of race. Australia is the only nation with a Constitution allowing racial discrimination against its first peoples (Reconciliation Australia, 2017a; Saunders, 2011). Tribal justice is being thwarted and, consequently, eminent creativity in the form of legislative change blocked.

Specifically, Indigenous and ally leaders seek to (1) "remove references to race [in the Constitution] to ensure that equal rights and respect are given to all Australians including Aboriginal and Torres Strait Islander Australians in law" and (2) make amendments that bring the "Constitution into line with the values and aspirations of contemporary Australian society" (Reconciliation Australia, 2017a, p. 4). Legal protections and constitutional justice require changes to the preamble to acknowledge Australia's original inhabitants by tribal name and add non-discrimination clauses (Reconciliation Australia, 2017a).

In my ongoing conversations with an Indigenous leader at the university in Sydney (whom I shall call "Tjukurpa," "TJ" for short), he conveyed that his circle of university leaders openly supports such constitutional change as part of a campaign to advance racial reconciliation and healing. Referring to my original homeland (Canada), he added that Canada, unlike Australia, has a national Constitution that recognizes and affirms First Nations' rights and its reconciliation efforts incorporate Aboriginal treaty-making.

In Australia, creativity geared at political and cultural change is ripe on many levels. Activists' perspectives are generations deep and future-oriented, but the work involved in trying to make the Constitution comply with global standards necessitates consensus among eligible voters. Unlike the increasing diversity of Australia, and Sydney in particular, where the 2016 census confirmed that 40% of the population was born overseas, "Australia's power structure is [still] overwhelmingly White, nowhere near as diverse as the country." In fact, almost all federal and state government leaders are of "Anglo-Celtic or European heritage," and 94% of Parliament is White, making it more homogeneous "than the U.S. Congress and the British Parliament" (Cave, 2018). Shaw (2007) described Sydney itself as a city of Whiteness, despite its multiculturalism, owing to its British settlement heritage that still drives lawmaking.

Treaties successfully negotiated with governments in other countries focus on Indigenous sovereignty, land rights, shared power, recognition, and so forth (Whitmore, 2012). At a deeper level, the Australian constitutional change and treaty efforts signal an ongoing *attempt* to transform colonialism. These large-scale, deeply rooted Australian Indigenous reform initiatives signify creativity, I believe, in that the effort to educate the public is reflected in a changing collective conscious, as evidenced by voters' majority support of the historic referendum. Creative breakthrough at the level of Big-C might (or might not) occur in modern times as a tangible "product" (e.g., an amended Constitution) of civic change on a significant scale. Accounting for this perspective, Big-C, accomplished in 1967, mandated constitutional reform.

Complex political and social change that re-creates laws, societies, and institutions is not always accompanied by a discernible creative product. This logic also applies to the ambiguities and complexities involved in advancing "voice, treaty, and truth" through "constitutional recognition" (National Aboriginal and Islander Day Observance Committee [NAIDOC], 2019). There might be points in time that crystalize as a product, such as another constitutional referendum resulting from Indigenous activism. Currently unknown, however, is if another such process-based outcome (referendum) and product (a changed Constitution) will materialize in these contested political times. Even a revised Constitution and Aboriginal treaties are not end points, as new and reformed policies and institutions can be expected to follow (Referendum Council, 2017). Social projects like the referendum and treaties emerge from the social Aboriginal imagination and generational action over time (Zittoun & Gillespie, 2016), making it difficult to "measure" the "success" of a human rights campaign. Simply put, profound societal change is simply not comparable to a tangible product like the invention of the electric car.

Quite possibly, then, Aboriginal declarations seeking constitutional recognition of Australia's first peoples and successful treaties are, in fact, peak enactments of creativity. The 2017 *Uluru Statement From the Heart* (*"Uluru Statement"*) is a well-known proposal from Indigenous leaders named in honor of a sacred Aboriginal place in Australia. This document goes beyond mere symbolism in identifying ways to establish Indigenous recognition within the Australian Constitution. Raising the bar on expectations for social justice, the *Uluru Statement* demands a constitutional voice ("First Nations Voice") for Aboriginal and Torres Strait Islander people by way of a "representative body" within the Commonwealth Parliament, in addition to "distributive socioeconomic justice" among Aboriginal people. (For the short original text, see Referendum Council, 2017; for timely news commentaries, see Chrysanthos, 2019; Snow, 2019.)

Disappointingly and perhaps predictably, in 2017, former Prime Minister Malcolm Turnbull rejected the *Uluru Statement*, negating both the product and process that sought a better, stronger, and more inclusive future. In fact, constitutional change as envisioned by this document is not the end activists have in mind but rather "the beginning of years of legal change, which seek to provide a socioeconomic future for Australia's First People" (Fleay & Judd, 2019, pp. 2–3). Wanting a participatory role in Australian governance and tying this to a request for a new referendum is an unprecedented future-minded vision. Those who authored and presented the *Uluru Statement* broke new ground, with ripple effects likely felt for a long time. According to NAIDOC (2019), the *Uluru Statement* shows Indigenous people's "desire to have their voice heard after being excluded when the Australian Constitution came into being, and have an enhanced role in decision-making in Australia's democracy." They would like "their fellow Australians [to] recognise that sovereignty has never been ceded, and their land was taken without agreement."

Creative resistance in support of legislative reform defies easy classification using Kaufman and Beghetto's (2009) 4-Cs. Contemporary colonial powers decide what "counts" as creativity and creative breakthrough by disallowing racial equality. But Indigenous causes are being propelled by dynamic vision through which social innovation unfolds, meaning that any discernible products (like statements requesting constitutional change) are important steps in the process. Human action imbued with purpose and meaning does not necessarily attain the status of a breakthrough—the long view might afford a different perspective altogether when today's proposed initiatives are carried forth by future generations.

Debatably, requests seeking constitutional recognition of Australia's first peoples and legal change might be Big-C, not in light of any recognition or product per se but rather the momentum that gave rise to it and that continues on behalf of redefining nationhood. As TJ revealed to me, "My people's *Statement* was rejected, even though we were prompted to provide our consensus on the subject. We wanted self-determination and sovereignty, not the small changes being accommodated." (p. 4). Hinting at White/Indigenous politics, TJ was referencing the *Uluru Statement* requesting that the Constitution empower the First Nations to govern their own affairs and for legislation to accommodate their voice, oversight, and powers (Referendum Council, 2017). Perhaps his message was that sometimes we have to give up something we have been fighting for (or is finally being offered) when we're being shaped by, and for, a greater purpose. The *Uluru Statement* takes a long view, offering a future-minded perspective:

> We seek constitutional reforms to empower our people and take a rightful place in our own country. When we have power over our destiny our children will flourish. They will walk in two worlds and their culture will be a gift to their country. (Referendum Council, 2017, p. 2)

Seeking "power over our destiny" conjures an image of the future. Powerful distinctions between *future* and *futurity* are made in Indigenous literature. Tuck and Gaztambide-Fernández (2013) theorized that the *future* and its "horizon" are constructed in relation to the past, whereas the future is fathomable with *futurity*. Not only anticipated, the future is, importantly, acted upon in the present through "calculation, imagination, and performance" by such means as safeguards, cautions, and preparations (p. 80). Sense-making and decision-making are active, purposeful processes for creating the future in the works I analyzed. One Indigenous view is that while settler futurity seeks to completely eradicate "the original inhabitants of contested land," Indigenous futurity "does not foreclose the inhabitation of Indigenous land by non-Indigenous peoples, but does foreclose settler colonialism and settler epistemologies" (Tuck & Gaztambide-Fernández, p. 80).

Self-determination in the context of the *Uluru Statement*, as referenced by TJ in our talks, is "accountable to Indigenous sovereignty and futurity" (Tuck & Yang,

2012, p. 35). Agents of tribal justice resist White entitlement, privilege, and supremacy *and* advocate Indigenous authority, humanity, and futurity (Fredericks, Maynor, White, English, & Ehrich, 2014; Mullen, 2019, 2020). They also battle "settler futurity"—the continuation of a settler future that inhibits "the possibility of an Indigenous future" (Tuck & Gaztambide-Fernández, 2013, p. 79).

Another Australian illustration of creative resistance and Indigenous futurity within the context of constitutional colonialism involves one Indigenous person's worldview and activism. In 2014 Murrumu of Walubara relinquished his Australian citizenship and identification—he was fed up with constitutional discrimination against "true and correct [Aboriginal] membership inside the Commonwealth of Australia." He declared the Great Barrier Reef (the Yidinji Territory), which spans over 6000 square miles, an Aboriginal nation. He has a council of ministers and plans for supporting Aboriginal education with independent schools and universities (Albeck-Ripka, 2019). Using peaceful means of reconciliation, he pursues a treaty with the government of Australia recognizing Indigenous sovereignty for this self-declared nation—over which Indigenous sovereignty was never surrendered.

The Australian Aboriginal flag and the Torres Strait Island flag are sources of pride. They appeared in various places during my time in Australia, including as paintings on hands in association with significant events like NAIDOC Week that build awareness of Indigenous cultures and the 1967 Referendum (Reconciliation Australia, 2017b). I felt inspired by the visual concepts of tribal justice—a reminder us that words have power and that reconciliation and healing are needed. Based on creativities around me, I artistically rendered the flags (Fig. 7.1).

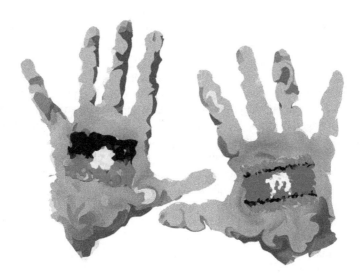

Fig. 7.1 Flags on hands honoring Australian Indigenous peoples (C. A. Mullen)

7.2.2   Climate Justice and Creativity in Australia

Climate justice and creativity within the Australian context are entangled with Indigenous communities and their homelands. Economic growth and expansion pose such serious threats to health and the environment as pollution, biodiversity, and greenhouse gas emissions (United Nations [UN] Environment Programme, n.d; Vincent, 2017; Whitmore, 2012). Opposition comes from the peril of agricultural homelands, destruction of ecosystems, and disruption of Indigenous ways of life.

Natural resource extractions worldwide have "cultural and spiritual impacts" resulting in "loss of livelihood" in such critical areas as "Indigenous language and moral values" (p. 18). Particularly a problem for "Australian Aboriginal people," various "large-scale projects" have also destroyed "places of cultural and spiritual significance," including "sacred sites and archaeological ruins" (Whitmore, 2012, p. 18). Isolated, rural, and under-resourced Aboriginal areas in Australia attract extractive industries—oil, gas, and mining—and "multiple megaprojects," yet few Indigenous Land Use Agreements currently exist between corporations and Aboriginal people (Trigger, Keenan, de Rijke, & Rifkin, 2014). Creative bargaining is indispensable for Indigenous leaders pulled into negotiations with well-funded companies from the resources sector. While agreements might transpire, unsurprisingly, power imbalances typically favor corporate interest, regardless of contractual terms, which range and might include monetary payment, jobs, and cultural heritage management. With sights set on "cultural rights, land rights, and economic gains," such scenarios activate "Aboriginal politics" and local inhabitants' deep-seated concern for the safety of ecosystems and communities (Trigger et al., p. 178; also, Whitmore).

Aboriginal people struggle to be heard on their own terms (Whitmore, 2012). With each Indigenous Land Use Agreement, perhaps aspects of societal, regulatory, and legal systems slowly erode. But for every successful agreement, many more escape attention due to unresolved agreements caught in litigation (Vincent, 2017). Colonization is perhaps diminished when companies are forced to contractually settle with local residents who emphasize livelihoods above profits, and value for "country, group membership, cultural identity, [and] representation and governance in groups" (Trigger et al., p. 185). Quite possibly, mutually beneficial agreements signify creative resolution at the level of, say, Little-c or Pro-C, in that creative skills in negotiating, brainstorming, debating, and so forth are utilized along with (developing) expertise. Might Big-C be on the horizon as Aboriginal communities continue to contest industry values and actions, only striking agreements accountable to their own rights, values, perspectives, and aims? And, because custodians of the land tend to monitor industrial development where possible, its negative impacts on the habitat may be lessened (Whitmore). Reports by Indigenous communities document problems, indicating a lack of accountability to environmental scrutiny. Monitoring agencies may ignore water contamination and other environmental crises brought about by extractive industries (Vincent; Whitmore).

Pitfalls and Pipelines (Whitmore, 2012) examines socially responsible assessments of extractive industries in Indigenous areas of the world, including Australia. On behalf of the UN Permanent Forum on Indigenous Issues, experts in Indigenous peoples' rights, industrial development, and corporate social responsibility illuminate key issues, with first-person cases authored by local Indigenous communities. Take, for example, Gundjeihmi Aboriginal Corporation's account concerning the "nuclear threat in Mirarr Country, Australia" (as cited in Whitmore, p. 24). This Aboriginal company was founded by the Mirarr people "to represent their rights and interests" (p. 24), which is, notably, a creative idea and pushback motivated by tribal justice. Uranium discovered on their homelands in the 1970s put this Indigenous community in the position of "fighting to protect [it] from mining" (p. 24). The Mirarr people, who live in a World Heritage–listed park (Northern Territory), managed to stop a mine from being developed by securing the company's agreement, but this outcome took more than a decade to achieve. Moreover, the Ranger Uranium Mine was allowed to proceed when its own environmental inquiry overruled the Mirarr's position. With the eco-destruction and climate change, traditional values and culture have deteriorated; as of 2012, the Ranger mine was the second largest in the world, supplying 10% of the global "uranium market"; "toxic radioactive waste" (p. 24) posed serious health threats owing to contaminated water. Due diligence and preventive regulation, scrutiny and assessment were lacking from state regulators, common worldwide.

Authors commenting on the Mirarr case underscore that mining development often proceeds on Indigenous land despite opposition and the threats to lives: "The history of nuclear power has been one of discrimination and disregard for Indigenous peoples. Indigenous lands carry a disproportionately high proportion of uranium mines" (cited in Whitmore, p. 86). Uranium mining and Indigenous peoples are correlated in the authors' contributions to various cases (in the Whitmore text), implying a burden being carried by Aboriginal communities worldwide. From my 2019 field notes, I describe my conversation with an engineering education student whose identity I protect with the pseudonym "Alinta."

> Alinta shared a firsthand account of environmental and cultural issues for Indigenous communities based on her experiences: "Mining is here to stay, so there's no point in wishing it would stop and go away." To her, being realistic means asking, "How are we going to handle this situation in our Indigenous communities?" She clarified, "When communities don't want mining because it will disrupt their lake ecosystem and dependency on it, mines will just do a workaround and bring in helicopters or whatever it takes to get the job done." As such, there's a twofold issue: obstruction by local communities in the face of the inevitable and the irresponsible, if not disrespectful, company behavior toward those being directly affected.

Employed by a mine as a "mediator," Alinta works to "ensure mutual benefits with local communities" and their environmental and economic sustainability. A question guiding her role is, "How can custodians of the land benefit from mining, and what are the most creative paths forward?" In this capacity, she is expected to assist Aboriginal inhabitants with their negotiations. During the contractual process, she "sees to it that their needs are recognized and they're being set up to receive benefits like royalties." Indigenous herself, she has strong ties to Australian Indigenous communities like her own and advocates for Aboriginal self-determination and land rights. A belief of hers is that mining companies are responsible for working productively with communities to address their concerns and arrive at a mutual understanding.

Alinta referenced a real-world example of a mining company planting native plants as part of a sustainability project: "It can't be either/or in the contemporary world with how things are going—that's just not realistic—and, at the same time, ecosystems and homelands must be protected." Some might consider this student/ employee's solutions-oriented perspective realistic, even-handed, or fair to Indigenous communities. Others might even find her viewpoint future-minded and ecologically and economically sustainable. But dissenting voices might believe it concedes land to colonial powers that inevitably exploit the community and disrespect sacred places; deplete resources and harm natural cycles; and destroy livelihoods while further entrenching societal inequities through poor health, illness, unemployment, and so forth.

From Alinta's viewpoint, though, her role as a mediator can serve tribal justice and is Little-c, given her expertise with sensitive contractual negotiations and moral concern for Indigenous rights. Her perspectives on, and approaches to, climate justice are nonetheless controversial. The research on extractive industries and Indigenous peoples in Australia, and globally, indicates that remote and rural Indigenous communities do not receive much of the profits from industrial development and that these populations frequently carry the burden of costs (social and environmental; e.g., O'Faircheallaigh, 2013; Vincent, 2017). Possibly, another dynamic is that Indigenous peoples' marginalization socially and economically may lessen with the increasing recognition of Aboriginal rights internationally, and the "growth of corporate social responsibility initiatives among mining corporations" (O'Faircheallaigh, 2013, p. 20).

However, the welfare of land and water continues to be subjected to controlling non-Aboriginal interests worldwide. Globalization has amplified investment in mining projects in Australia from foreign enterprises. A mighty indigenous struggle is to have custodial control and care of homelands and resources while assuming responsibility for ecological renewal and recovery. Aboriginal land rights have improved with the 1993 Native Title Act, but the entanglements often pit tribal councils against intrusive companies and powerful corporate attorneys (Vincent, 2017).

The term *native title* describes the rights to land controlled by Aboriginal Australians under their customary laws that the Australian legal system recognizes. But the reality is that battles can and do persist with governmental and corporate entities (Vincent, 2017). Predictably, native title claims are often caught in lawsuits. The creative struggle of Australian Indigenous communities for native land title is, on a larger scale, a battle for country and identity, and environmental and cultural sustainability.

Native title is supposed to be a means for affirming Indigenous rights to, and claim over, land, not in the sense of possession but as moral keepers and traditional owners recognized as such. A fundamental struggle is that Indigenous people are expected to reimagine their nationhood and themselves on state terms. Thus, the native claims process forces the reorganization of aboriginal identities and social worlds in order to satisfy legislation centered on "recognition" and "redress." Native title land is commonly perceived among Indigenous people as a key for reclaiming, controlling, and revitalizing land and culture (Vincent, 2017). Many who are granted native title and many who are denied demonstrate creative resistance to an inherently unfair colonial system. An informal Indigenous leader named Aunty Sue (from Vincent's ethnographic account) perceives native title as a state imposition resulting in "affective dispossession" for Aboriginal communities and the expansion of resource industries into unrecognized Indigenous areas with little or no accountability. The system of native title actually gives holders like corporations the right to negotiate mining or other developments, a practice that institutionalizes both corporate interests and racial inequality.

The native title system has been widely criticized as unjust for using colonial epistemologies and strategies that put unwarranted stress on both tribes and ecosystems. According to Vincent's (2017) Australian Indigenous insiders, the native title system and legislation are implicitly racist and based on Western logic. For example, the onus is on Australian Aboriginal people ("traditional owners") to prove their "cultural continuity" on land based on ancestry, despite settler-imposed "dispossession" and "dislocation" of them throughout time (Vincent, 2017, p. 158). The long and draining process has been described as painful and unjust, as well as extremely frustrating. Native title does "not provide the means to address the history of colonial dispossession" (Vincent, p. 194). While it seems like a form of justice, including to some Aboriginal people, Aunty Sue and her "mob" (Australian Aboriginal term meaning extended family and/or one's people) refused to deal with the system. Quite possibly, this extremely strenuous effort by Aboriginal activists to change systemic racism is Big-C.

Arguably, climate injustice, within the Australian context, perpetuates the belief that lands can continue to be owned, invaded, destroyed, and colonized, including by overseas powers. Interestingly, a pervasive belief is that precolonial Indigenous people were merely hunter-gatherers, but if we knew otherwise, would Indigenous ecological knowledge(s) actually be consulted as creative resources for resolving the global climate crisis? Provoking critical thought along these lines, Pascoe (2014) debunked the hunter-gatherer myth by using early explorers' own journals to base his convincing analysis of an ecologically sound precolonial Australia. Within this world, one learns of the sophisticated agricultural skills of Australian Indigenous people who, for over 60,000 years, successfully managed land and food production while protecting and cultivating their territories. They creatively manipulated the landscape through gardening and farming, sustaining an economy using innovative agricultural methods until Europeans arrived, bringing disease. Native title reform could benefit from tribal and climate justice lenses, and such documentation that "proves" cultural continuity and a deep knowledge of land cultivation and environmental protection. These Aboriginal ecological sensibilities and know-how are indicative of responsibility for *country*, which Indigenous Australian barrister

Dodson described as "a word for all the values, places, resources, stories and cultural obligations associated with the area and its features describ[ing] the entirety of our ancestral domains" ("Mick Dodson," 2020).

My review of literature also extended to the dominant narratives produced by the very corporations responsible for worsening climate change around the world. Public broadcasts retrievable from the Internet carry the expected message that extractive industries' production of oil and so forth makes an invaluable contribution to economies and that resource extraction projects adhere to rigorous industry standards for environmental and social risk management. Industry perspectives monopolize the conversation, justifying actions presented as benefits (e.g., supplying the world with sources of energy and employing millions). Downplayed (and ignored) are costs to the environment and planet, and Aboriginal peoples' lives and home/land.

An alarm was sounded around climate change and its effects on Indigenous people in a recent assessment of Australia's human rights record independently conducted by the Extraterritorial Human Rights Obligations (EHRO, 2017), a global consortium monitoring "human rights beyond borders." About climate change, the organization expressed concern about

> the continued increase of CO2 emissions . . ., at risk of worsening in the coming years, despite the State party's commitments as a developed country under the UN Framework Convention on Climate Change. . . . [Also], environmental protection has decreased in recent years as shown by . . . the State party's ongoing support to new coal mines and coal-fired power stations. (p. 2)

Regarding the local Indigenous residents in affected areas, this oversight committee stated that "climate change is disproportionately affecting the enjoyment of Covenant rights by indigenous peoples" (p. 2). Climate change and cultural issues were recognized as interrelated, with particular impact of damaged ecosystems on Aboriginal communities. "Alternative and renewable energy production" (and prevention efforts around greenhouse gas emissions) and policy change involving Indigenous people were all strongly recommended (p. 3).

Next, I briefly describe the approaches that were unique to the Australian pedagogic context explored. My analysis illustrates how these intersect with, and depart from, the issues raised in this framework relative to tribal and climate justice. After that, I examine the information gathered and classes' responses to the 4-C educational activities.

7.3   Creative Approaches in Sydney, Australia

For this case, situated at an urban university in Sydney, I applied Kaufman and Beghetto's (2009) 4-C creativity model within humanities courses. Additionally, one-on-one conversations occurring with stakeholders were informed by this model and my adaptation of it. The work was intensive, taking 1 month in 2019.

7.3.1   Challenges and Influences

Once onsite, I was asked to refrain from using the word *research* when implementing my pedagogic program and engaging students in the 4-C activities. The reason given is that Indigenous communities have been heavily researched in the past, resulting in sensitivity around this issue. Besides honoring this request, I've also amended my associated lexicon in this chapter (e.g., study, data, etc.) to the extent possible without compromising the integrity of my longitudinal research. I use *participant* to refer to those who contributed to the 4-C project.

To succinctly unpack these core issues, I would like to reference Australian collaborators in health equity at the University of Melbourne (Melbourne, Australia). In their study, they explained that a long Australian history exists of exploitation in research targeting Indigenous communities in health, medicine, and anthropology—education was not listed (see Guillemin et al., 2016). In interviews they conducted with Indigenous and non-Indigenous people, motivations were sought for participating in (any) research, which was the actual purpose of their study. Clear distinctions were evident in the two groups' responses. For Indigenous participants, "taking part in research was primarily to benefit their communities," and for non-Indigenous participants, the decision to partake was for "personal interests." The Indigenous feedback was characterized as "cautious," indications being taking the time to decide and rejecting "researchers' claims on face value," in contrast with the non-Indigenous feedback, characterized as readily accepting and perhaps trusting (p. 1).

About my creativity project, participant demographics were non-identifiable at the individual level, and students' responses could not be tied to their creators, in contrast with the Guillemin et al. (2016) study. Students who engaged in my pedagogic activities simply reflected course and program demographics, mirroring my previous approaches in China and Canada. As before, information specific to individual students were not prompted or collected; instead, course instructors shared a general statistical picture of their classes. The continuity in my longitudinal study also meant that the creative intervention was not intended for, or designed around, a particular cultural ethnic group or even a specific program or postsecondary level, meaning that my 4-C activities were amenable to undergraduate and graduate student volunteers.

In Australia, mostly non-Indigenous students (90%) and fewer Indigenous students (10%) participated, owing to course enrolments. All students had the opportunity to decide whether to participate in the 4-C prompts and activity at the outset. (I was asked to verbally cover my informed consent form at the outset of workshops, which was consistent with my past practice.) I explained that involvement in the activities was strictly voluntary and that grades would not be impacted regardless. Also, I indicated my plan to take photographs of any completed artifacts created during the workshop, so students were not to pen identifiers (e.g., their names). I added that I would promptly return their originals through the course lecturer.

A particularly challenging constraint on the delivery of my creative intervention involved a permanent scheduling change to all university courses that, in effect, shortened the traditional semester. It had only begun yet lecturers seemed frustrated with the "content cramming" they felt forced to accomplish in their lectures. Two commented to me, "With the top-down curriculum change, there is no time in the course to give to creativity, making it difficult to fit you in," and "The tutorial part of my course, which follows every lecture, is going to suffer from the calendar change—that's where my classes could have benefited from your lecture and activities." Their students apparently did not welcome the tighter scheduling timeline either. A student from China revealed not knowing of it until after the term had started, causing her to worry about having insufficient time to absorb course content. I only became aware of the scheduling constraint and its potential impact on my creativity program, when faculty shared it. Ironically, these were the same lecturers who generously accommodated my creativity workshop and planning session.

7.3.2   Participants and Contexts

Participating university stakeholders were non-Indigenous and Indigenous, as well as "internationals" from China and other countries. These general demographics applied to the students, lecturers, and administrative leaders involved with my creativity program. It was only the second week of the semester, so students were unfamiliar with one another and had not yet worked in groups. In two undergraduate classes, I guided learning in creativity theory and application, thereby adapting the 4-C creativity model with 30 students in their 3rd year of humanities and general education programs.

Indigenous study was the focus of one course and the other gender, with the latter explicit about incorporating Indigenous issues. In the Indigenous studies course, 21 (of the 24) students present that day engaged in creative brainstorming and responses (4-C protocol containing question prompts [Appendix 7.1] and poster) in 6 self-selected teams for (up to) 80 min, following my 20-min interactive lecture. This was the first course on Aboriginal topics the students had taken. (They struggled with the professor's questions related to assigned reading on the syllabus, consulting their devices in order to respond before my workshop began.)

Considerably less time was allocated in the gender studies course (15-min lecture, 45-min protocol activity), with 9 students in 3 teams addressing the prompts (but not the poster activity). In both classes, I asked students to refrain from utilizing their technological devices (e.g., IPhones) during our workshop and instead rely on themselves and their teams for generating ideas. When I made this request in the Indigenous studies course, a concern expressed aloud was how they could be expected to be creative without consulting the Internet on their devices, to which a teammate swiftly retorted, "We *can* be creative and we *can* rely on each other!"

Interestingly, the team with these two classmates got caught up in creative flow (in Csikszentmihalyi's, 1996 sense of a peak experience) more than any. Having completed the joint response to the 4-C prompts, team members continued working on their (ungraded) poster for 30 min after the class ended. Observing this team harmonizing and even standing and shifting places to add to (and improve) each other's contributions to the poster, I saw "creative confidence," or signs of it, enacted in a dynamic way (Karwowski, Han, & Beghetto, 2019). It struck me that a creative group has the power to offset an impoverished sense of creative capacity and even to nurture the potential through social interaction and that, perhaps, for reluctant creators creativity can only be revealed to them through such opportunities. Another observation I made while circulating is that a few teams did consult the Internet, with someone mentioning they were simply fact-checking. While the use of devices had not occurred in China or Canada, the integrity brought to the creative tasks seemed intact in Australia.

With each lecturer, considerable planning took place: three meetings (90 min) for the Indigenous studies course and two meetings (45 min) for the gender studies course. Prior to these sessions, I read the course syllabus and reading assigned for the day of my creativity workshop. Through the planning discussions, we identified overlaps between the course content and my exercises. Both professors were intent on establishing continuity in the lessons, with follow-up ideas. Something I emphasized is that by giving students time to work interactively, and being available to address queries, we were sending the message that we were confident that they were capable of creatively applying the 4-C theory in relevant ways and being task focused.

The exposure to students' thought process as I moved among the teams in both classes was truly stimulating, opening my eyes to surprising connections and multiple ways to approach creativity and accountability. Closely attuning to the brainstorming proved indispensable to describing what they were saying, writing, and drawing in my field notes and herein, as time was not permitted for teams to share aloud with the class. Debriefing with the lecturers, I was able to clarify several abbreviations in the teams' depictions and "try out" a few interpretations of symbols from posters. No follow-up or continuation of the activities could be accommodated.

Participation from educators who were not students ($N = 8$) involved 4 lecturers and 4 administrative leaders (e.g., unit heads and deans) in a one-on-one conversation in their university offices, the stimulus being the 4-C theory. However, an Indigenous leader committed to multiple sessions, thus I was given a rare opportunity to reflect on our discussions and ask questions, check for understanding while developing insight, and make creative connections not otherwise possible. I asked that he point out missteps to propel my learning about cultural issues, which he did (e.g., he advised me to always capitalize "Indigenous" and "Aboriginal" to convey proper acknowledgment.) Our sessions were productive and mutually satisfying, as I assisted him with his academic tasks. TJ was the only Australian Aboriginal person in the cluster of participating lecturers and leaders (the others were White). Eight of the many hours TJ and I talked intensely fostered insight into the 4-Cs from his reference frames and experiences, and we met weekly. He credited me for building an authentic relationship with him by being "responsive" and "respectful," which has cultural importance for informally assessing the ethical fit of non-Indigenous persons, including outsiders.

7.4   Justice-Oriented Discussion Around Themes

Regarding creativity and the 4-Cs (Kaufman & Beghetto, 2009), three themes from all informational sources emerged regarding Indigenous causes, environmental issues, and creative breakthroughs. These patterns are selectively encapsulated in Table 7.1 with respect to all Australian-based participants' usages of Mini-c, Little-c, Pro-C, and Big-C in the creativity activities and conversations; the entries are further differentiated relative to four dimensions of creativity: (1) example of creative product, (2) example of creative people and collectives, (3) creative curriculum and assessment, and (4) experience of creativity. Many, but not all, entries appearing on Table 7.1 are narratively described.

7.4.1   Politically and Legally Expressed Australian Indigenous Causes (Theme 1)

Justice, healing, loss, and identity were associated with politically and legally expressed Australian Indigenous causes. Four teams (from both courses) responded to my prompts about accountability within Australian culture and relative to other nations' (testing) cultures (Appendix 7.1). They described Australia as needing to combat racism and dismantle structural discrimination targeting Indigenous people. Also, they wrote that "Australians must acknowledge White settler/colonial history and we need to do this not only about the past but the present"; a way to approach this social justice goal is "by giving more recognition in Australia of Indigenous populations previously owning/occupying land." Interestingly, similar statements were made by the undergraduates majoring in gender studies (although the course outline indicated that intersections between gender and Aboriginality were a focus). Examples of creative people and collectives ranged considerably. Strategies recommended by the classes that everyone should adopt for developing constructive racial relations are (1) building a respectful rapport with Indigenous people in all learning spaces, and (2) celebrating the Aboriginal and Torres Strait Islander flags elsewhere (using the traditional Indigenous dot technique).

The Aboriginal concept of "justice as healing" resounds in published and publicized statements of reconciliation. Legislation and laws need to be "premised on both justice and healing," according to a female Australian Aboriginal human rights lawyer (i.e., McGlade, 2012, p. 195). These ideas were also reflected in TJ's ongoing conversations with me. Like McGlade, he talked about healing's significance to justice as an issue of "Aboriginal identity," especially with the impact of so many different influences on Aboriginal people and their diverse identities. A prevailing influence comes from non-Indigenous people (settlers), as well as colonial institutions and paradigms. Take but one paradoxical riddle of Australian government that insists that Aborginality be proven for such purposes as being granted native title by establishing a community's knowledge of the title-seeking party.

Table 7.1 Select Australian Usages of Mini-c, Little-c, Pro-C, and Big-C (C. A. Mullen)

	Mini-c	Little-c	Pro-C	Big-C
Scope of creativity	Creativity that is personally meaningful	Personal creativity (Mini-c) credited for its value/benefit	Professional achievement that is recognized by a field	Groundbreaking creativity that changes a culture
Example of creative product	Composting and recycling daily; motivated by environmental benefits to the planet	Wi-Fi connection enabling interpersonal connectivity and sharing about life	Declarations seeking constitutional recognition of Australia's first peoples and legal change; notably, the Uluru Statement from the Heart in 2017	Wi-Fi, invented by Australian O'Sullivan and patented by CSIRO
	Video games developed in Australia based on books, with educational value	Academic writing on personal and cultural identity questions	Publications on the need for recognition of Indigenous peoples' knowledges and eco-friendly creative methods for coping with the global climate crisis	Penicillin was codeveloped by Australian Florey; discoveries of a cervical cancer vaccine and Alzheimer's treatment
	Reading Australian Indigenous books; watching films featuring major Australian events	Creativity methods used in the social sciences for engaging vulnerable Indigenous youth	Parkes's radio telescope in NSW televised *Apollo 11*'s historic moonwalk	Archaeological discoveries of Aboriginal artifacts
		Industry contracts satisfying the terms of local Indigenous communities and benefitting them; involving expert Aboriginal mediators		The 1967 referendum leading to Constitutional reform; the native title system
Example of creative person and collective	Building a respectful rapport with Indigenous people in all learning spaces	Global Climate Strike—a student-led rally where thousands protested in Australia	Publications and posts by Indigenous leaders calling for formal recognition of Indigenous Australians in the Constitution and with representation, the Australian government	Significant recognitions of Australia's first peoples forging social justice agendas (e.g., National Sorry Day); Invasion Day pushes back on celebrating European invasion
	Depicting the Aboriginal and Torres Strait Islander flags on protest posters and elsewhere	Genuine engagement by non-Indigenous people with Indigenous people in public, professional, and academic spaces	The Australian Football League, consisting of 18 teams, plays at home and abroad	Invented by surfers, Australia's Seabin Project cleans polluted oceans by collecting rubbish
	Vegemite, a famous food spread developed in 1922	First Indigenous-designed jersey worn in a sports game		

(continued)

Table 7.1 (continued)

	Mini-c	Little-c	Pro-C	Big-C
Creative curriculum and assessment	Working in studios and workshops to develop creative practice with a like-minded community	A student project on traversing Indigenous community rights in the face of mining corporations' development projects, with an Australian example of a viable outcome	Aboriginal knowledge and application in an undergraduate course on cultural heritage and environment; field-based Indigenous community experiences	Aboriginal Australian World Heritage sites examine environmental management and Indigenous/colonial relations in education
	Learning about Indigenous knowledges and specialized terms used in formal and informal discourse in Australia that imbue Aboriginal perspectives	Writing scripts and role-playing to educate health professionals to be interpersonally and culturally sensitive and resilient in the face of an adverse health care culture	Identifying influences that shape gender issues and relations in Indigenous peoples' lives in Australia is the focus of an undergraduate course in gender studies	Webb's disaster risk reduction initiative improves lives in low SES ruralites vulnerable to natural disasters and includes participating youth
		Integrating NAIDOC Week and other celebrations of the first peoples into the learning and assessment of academic courses	Offering a university program based on the tenets of pastoral care to foster Indigenous retention and success	Guidance for research involving Indigenous participants
Experience of creativity	Learning about Aboriginal and colonial heritage, Aussie slang, cultural foods and cooking, replacing pluggers on broken sandals with a bread clip, gardening and landscaping, playful uses of Hills Hoist rotary clothesline, surfing, barbecuing, playing video games	Performing musically and writing songs about Indigenous life; measuring aerial routes, which has never been done; donning Akubra Hats; the cork hat that wards off insects	*Maggie's Table* by Australian chef Maggie Beer celebrates local culture and produce; campus food options	Clean Up Australia Day; public transportation system lowers emissions
	Participating in Climate Strike 2019	Experiencing Aboriginal events and climate rallies with programs or schools as part of larger movements to sustain cultures/life	Grace Under Pressure, public health curriculum being produced by medical educators	Song lines from Indigenous cultures mark the route of creator-beings and Aboriginal memory and existence
			Affirmative action ("positive discrimination") hiring of eligible Aboriginal people	Australia's airline was the world's first commercial nonstop flight between Australia and Europe

When I asked TJ if there is a 4-C category (or categories) to which Aboriginal identity belongs, he implied Mini-c, Little-c, and Pro-C where Indigenous people are telling their own stories and making contributions to society, but certainly not Big-C. Claims of Aboriginal identity continue to be subjugated by a British colonial framework, preventing creative breakthrough. In other words, Big-C for the Australian Indigenous community is suppressed, with entanglements in politics and Western paradigms. McGlade (2012) also addressed Aboriginal identity as subject to colonial dispossession and disruption in Australia, explaining that Indigenous people are forced to redirect their creative energies toward "healing," "relearning," and "figuring out who they are [and] their responsibilities" so that the case for, and right to, "self-determination" can be advanced (p. 195).

With Aboriginal identity-making being ensnared in the legalities of self-determination, McGlade (2012) scrutinized Australia's legal system within global contexts, discovering that "Healing is an aboriginal justice principle that is becoming merged into Canadian criminal law through the use of sentencing circles and community-based diversion programs" (p. 195). While in Canada, she was apparently taken aback by the accountability "to individual and community healing": "Since 1998 the Canadian government has supported the Aboriginal Healing Foundation to support many community-based healing initiatives of Metis, Inuit and First Nations people, who were … affected by the legacy of physical and sexual abuse in residential schools" (p. 196). Drawing upon the Canadian Indigenous trends and partnerships, she indicated, in 2012, that this is not something seen in Australian governance. TJ similarly contrasted Canada and Australia with regard to the momentum of change in healing and justice, adding that Canadian First Nations' voice and power base are comparably stronger (to which I wish to add that Canada, too, has suffered a history of setbacks with rejected requests to change the Canadian Constitution to enshrine Indigenous self-government; Mullen, 2020).

"Stolen Generations" was a term used by two participants. For the dean who is a historian, this pivotal event was strictly described as something that had occurred in the past, and as an "Indigenous issue" involving "past mistreatment" and "forced assimilation." When TJ described the same event, he narrated how the loss of stolen children terribly affected families and communities and *continues* to be felt today—it is etched in *all* Indigenous peoples' struggle and collective memory, a "forever tragedy." The Western sense of time in the first scenario did not accommodate the Indigenous sense of timelessness in the latter.

The forcible removal of Aboriginal children occurred in Australia from the early days of European occupation. Stolen Generations is a particular event referring to the human rights violation of Australian Aboriginals who were victimized, set in motion by governmental policies overseen by the Aborigines Protection Board. In New South Wales, starting in 1905 and into the 1970s, at least 100,000 Aboriginal children were separated from their families under the policy of "protection"—placed into compulsory residential schools, many were sexually abused, some never seeing their families again (Hinkson & Harris, 2015; McGlade, 2012). A gross violation, this action was precipitated by state violence against Indigenous communities and "half-caste" children. The event and memory live on, with the effects multiplying in the face of other genocidal treatment. This was another way that TJ explained timelessness to me. Stolen Generations may have three meanings: those who were abducted, those who were affected by the loss, and those who will always feel this tragedy (also Shaw, 2007).

In my conversations with TJ and related readings (e.g., Potter & Schaffer, 2004), my impression is that the prevalence of specialized Aboriginal terms (e.g., country, Dreaming, Dream time, Indigenous sovereignty, mob, native title, songlines, Stolen Generations) in popular culture, nationally and globally, is Big-C. An Internet search confirms their usage within broader cultures and different media among non-Indigenous people and in academic disciplines. While the ideas are complex and not easily understood by non-Aboriginal people like myself, the fact that they are readily used (and misused) and in creative ways, including misappropriations of Indigenous intellectual property and commodification in capitalist marketplaces, says something powerful about the collective unconscious (and the ugly side of humanity). For example, Pilkington's (2006) novel that was made into *Rabbit-Proof Fence*, the Hollywood film that universalized a particular story about the Stolen Generations, in effect "trades on trauma" and "homogenizes and commodifies experience" but also deepens viewer empathy; viewers took it upon themselves to publicize parallel experiences of Indigenous dispossession, residential schooling, and violence against children in different countries (Potter & Schaffer, 2004).

A current Australian Indigenous cause that is politically and legally enacted by governments is "positive discrimination" in the workplace (known as "affirmative action" in the United States and "employment equity" in Canada). TJ was among the eligible and competitive Indigenous people hired in accordance with antidiscrimination laws. The Racial Discrimination Act of 1975 is intended to compensate for disadvantaged groups in order to promote equality around race, gender, and age in the Australian community (Workplace Law, 2018). Even though people who fit these descriptors secure jobs in higher education and other workplaces through this legal intervention, positive discrimination is "very controversial," stated TJ.

While TJ supports positive discrimination, he pointed out an unintended consequence of this measure. Apparently, there are Australian Aboriginal people who do not apply for positions outside job quotas, thereby restricting themselves to highly select, competitive slots. Coming to the realization from a mentor that he was inadvertently limiting his own horizons, TJ has decided to take the initiative to help others think through this problem and consider broader employment opportunities not reserved for special groups. Tribal justice became more palatable to him with the realization that job quotas can, paradoxically, limit prospects for the Indigenous community.

7.4.2 Environmental Manifestations of Protest, Action, and Pride (Theme 2)

Across the classes, teams illustrated the 4-Cs as environmental issues widely ranging from areas of reform to pleasure from their own knowledge, and direct and indirect experiences of Australia. Examples were described with words and visual images in the Indigenous studies course, and narratively in the gender studies course.

In the synthesis of results that follow, I elaborate on the relevant entries on Table 7.1 and account for team responses documented in both courses pertaining to environmental issues. When a particular entry pertains to one of the courses, I specify it. Regarding the three figures in this section, all offer a partial view of an entire poster (reflecting one segment only of the three artifacts) to reflect the particular environmental issue under discussion.

7.4.2.1   Mini-c Across Student Responses

Mini-c descriptions of personally meaningful creativity were numerous. Experiencing creativity through the 2019 Global Climate Strike with protest signs (some homemade like those shown at the outset of this chapter) was a common refrain. Activism was a stated motivation for this creative collective action on behalf of sustaining life on the planet, returning ecosystems to a healthy state, and ensuring that youth have a future. The Cool Squad's poster contains the slogan "Make Earth Cool Again," signified by a "protest sign" with "planet Earth" donning sunglasses and looking cool (pun intended). Sydney is labeled on a "map" with an arrow connecting it to the "sign," invoking the 2019 Global Climate Strike that overtook Sydney and its youth earlier that month (Fig. 7.2). The Mini-c climate depiction and place of protest follow on behalf of aggressively and collectively combatting global warming.

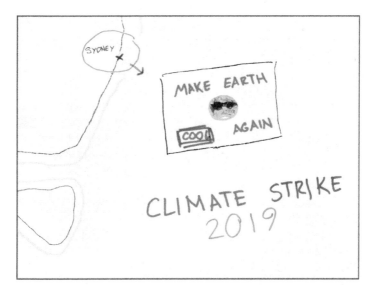

Fig. 7.2 Climate strike 2019—"make Earth Cool again" representing Mini-c (Australian student team)

Upon Googling "Make Earth Cool Again," the phrase/planetary symbol popped up in websites associated with youth activism and the commodification of Earth. Retail outlets that sell merchandise (e.g., T-shirts) incorporate this slogan/symbol, and it manifests in various world contexts, such as the 2018 midterm United States' elections encouraging youth to Make Earth Cool Again by voting for a party that will protect the environment and health—incidentally, this was a yogurt advertisement wherein youth looked "cool." The Cool Squad creatively channeled the slogan/symbol into Mini-c, thereby expressing the value of partaking in a strike that mobilized youth worldwide.

Describing creative products, both undergraduate classes indicated that composting and recycling daily, and using special bins, particularly the large-capacity contraptions on campus, had value to them in learning and life. Motivations given for this practice centered on environmental benefits to the planet and feeling good about themselves by doing their part. Such responses were more prevalent in the Indigenous course, with its focus on managing the environment (with respect to Aboriginal Australian World Heritage sites).

Creative people and collectives ranged considerably in the information gathered and include sources of pleasure. One such source is Vegemite, a famous canned food spread made from brewers' yeast extract developed in Melbourne in 1922. Students who are vegan like spreading it on toast. Also noted was the association of this food with a clever scientific discovery—that yeast cells could be broken down from breweries' waste and that the liquid extract, once concentrated, could be made into an edible paste.

Creative curriculum and assessment attracted fewer, somewhat cryptic but nonetheless intriguing responses about campus environments. Sydney's parks and beaches inspire outdoor living and creative approaches to curriculum and assignments, particularly in environmental management and art and design courses. Such experiences, perhaps extracurricular in nature, were strongly associated with nature and wildlife (e.g., surfing, camping, barbequing, gardening, and landscaping). Reference was also made to Sydney's 35 university campuses, some with studio space for developing creative practice with a like-minded community. Within the students' networks are those who have developed installations and other artifacts for exhibition, enabling sensory, social, and other creative experiences. International students may have been tapped for their reasons for choosing to be in Sydney or Australia, with mention of the "Aussie experience" and reputation for an active lifestyle, plus the state-of-the-art campus facilities and various accommodations for large international and study-abroad populations.

Other Mini-c examples were also particular to the environment (and Australian ethos): "mishmashing cultural foods and cooking in a variety of ways"—preferably outdoors; using a bread clip to replace pluggers on broken sandals; and, anywhere, anytime, playing video games. Playful uses of the iconic Hills Hoist rotary clothesline, manufactured since 1945 in Adelaide, South Australia, caught my attention. This compact invention, known worldwide, uses wind for drying laundry in backyards; because it's height-adjustable, it is creatively adapted for unintended uses, such as a children's swing. Because it replaces electric dryers, students depicted it as an environmentally smart decision of theirs.

7.4.2.2 Little-c Across Student Responses

Little-c responses continued the theme of the 2019 Global Climate Strike. Sydney pride had been broadly televised and publicized—unsurprisingly, it permeated narrative and graphical representations of Little-c in all artifacts. Participating in protests with one's program, school, or business as part of a larger movement received special mention. Perhaps the students from my two workshops were noting the allowance of many institutions for protesters to miss time from school or work. While the teams focused on Sydney and Australia, in accordance with my prompts, they were likely aware of other countries' engagement in the global phenomenon, especially as some were immigrants. If Mini-c is the personal value attached to the protest, then Little-c could be the credit given to protesters and those who enabled them. In this sense, there was also a return on, or multiplying of, the acknowledgment that students, albeit subtly, recognized the support they, friends, or others attracted for participating in the marches.

Also described were famous Australian cork hats—Akubra Hats—known for warding off insects and blocking harmful UV rays. Whether the participating students knew that melanoma is the most common cancer in young Australians and that more youth die from it than other cancers is unknown. As temperatures rise due to global warming, the risk of developing cancer increases.

Wi-Fi, a wireless radio technology, competed with the climate strikes as the most popular representation of Little-c. Overwhelming reliance on Wi-Fi was conveyed for daily interpersonal connectivity, in some cases with other countries. Acknowledgment in this creative space (i.e., the role of recognition in creativity and Little-c) was a new concept to the teams. Selecting Wi-Fi, the Surf's Up Aussie team sketched an "idea cloud" above the face (note the laptop, on the left of Fig. 7.3) to convey "I like your idea!" and "Great feedback, thanks!" They "got" that Little-c manifests with recognition of creativity, such as acknowledgments sent via text messaging.

7.4.2.3 Pro-C Across Student Responses

Professional achievement that is recognized by a field or discipline and has relevance to the environment was reflected in the domains of sports, science, community, education, and health. The Australian Football League, consisting of 18 teams, plays at home and abroad. The growing international reputation of the league was hinted at in the imagery (e.g., arrows directed outward from Australia toward other countries).

Fig. 7.3 Wi-Fi as global interpersonal connectivity representing Little-C (Australian student team)

In the area of science, students noted Parkes's radio telescope, located in New South Wales that televised *Apollo 11*'s historic moonwalk. (This example had been given on a slide during my lecture, complete with a photo of the telescope.)

A field-based Aboriginal community event was also described, a culminating educational experience in the Indigenous studies course. Anticipated was the first-hand discovery of cultural heritage and environment in a real-world setting where theories of environmental management of land and preservation of Indigenous heritage would come to life in a relatable way. While these ideas were expressed in the syllabus, the teams conveyed their own points of view, attributing value to the application of theory (referred to as "lectures") and especially the shared experience they were imagining while working on their posters. Sketches incorporated native bushland, such as caves, and wildlife that included kangaroos/"roos."

Australian chef Maggie Beer and her famous cookbook were acknowledged for celebrating local culture, health, and produce. Fresh, organic food options, readily available, were popular in the environment, with multicultural eateries also getting a Pro-C "thumbs up."

7.4.2.4   Big-C Across Student Responses

With respect to environmental issues, Big-C triggered events like Clean Up Australia Day (March of every year), with its widely known emphasis on environmental conservation and everyone pitching in to make local areas orderly. Clean Up Australia Limited is a not-for-profit Australian environmental conservation organization that bridges sectors of society "to address the environmental issues of waste, water and climate change" ("Clean Up Australia," 2020).

Fig. 7.4 Seabin for water protection representing Big-C (Australian student team)

Sydney's exemplary public transportation system earned a stamp of approval as a Big-C creative win for Australia (it's the only city in the nation with rapid transit). However, some of the heavy use of private vehicles has shifted onto buses and trains, with an overall reduction in greenhouse gas emissions. Road transport is a large generator of such emissions in Australia, and it currently lags behind other developed nations; instead of racing to reduce greenhouse emissions from transport, owing to policy inaction on pollution standards, it has seen a 63% increase since 1990 based on Climate Council reports (EHRO, 2017; Henriques-Gomes, 2018).

One team gave Big-C credit to Webb's disaster risk reduction initiative that improves lives in low socioeconomic status ruralities vulnerable to natural disasters (see Webb & Ronan, 2014). The Interactive Hazards Education Program is targeted at youth and incorporates their participation. Given that this project was in a pilot stage at the time of publication, it is likely a better candidate for Pro-C, in my estimation at least, unless something much bigger has come from this initiative.

The representation of Big-C I selected for visual purposes (Fig. 7.4) captures the hope and pride of environmental sustainability and the inspiration associated with youth leadership, creative entrepreneurship, and eco-friendly inventiveness. To quote the See-Ben Run team that identified just such an initiative, "Australia's Seabin Project [for Cleaner Oceans] is a solution to ocean pollution," so it's our Big-C winner—the bins protect "water ecosystem[s] by sucking rubbish out of oceans and filtering water back in." Sydney "birthed" this exciting initiative and its creators work at the Sydney Wharf Marina. The fact that two "Aussie surfers" invented this cleaning and recycling program possibly made the progressive stages of the 4-Cs more relatable to the young undergraduates than, say, the Big-C moon landing of generations past.

Sydney's fantastic initiative, formed through a community-based partnership, is still in the exploratory stage. Quite possibly, the Seabin Project is on the verge of becoming a Big-C invention and worldwide phenomenon, with its "global network of 719 units [removing] about 2000kg of waste each day." The goal is to "trial Seabin technology with cities around the world." Also, exclaimed the creators, education is "the key driver" of change and "real solution," not technology, thus educational programs are built into the initiative ("Seabin Project," 2020).

7.4.3 Breakthroughs in Technology, Medicine, Culture, and Media (Theme 3)

Across all contributing lecturers, administrative leaders, and students, Big-C breakthroughs and inventions were identified in technology, medicine, media, and other areas. Notably, most parties identified Wi-Fi technology, invented in 1997 by Australian electrical engineer John O'Sullivan. Released that same year, it was later patented by CSIRO (Morris, 2017). The importance of technology communications is an extraordinary global phenomenon, and connectivity was apparent across all stakeholders (they didn't even have to name Wi-Fi—"it" was in their hands or on a table). "It's like having the Internet in my hand," someone said, with another commenting, "With our kids, I have to be checking my device to arrange pickups and drop-offs."

When the lecturers and leaders' commentaries were considered apart from the students', penicillin equally came to mind as Big-C. This antibiotic was singularly viewed as a profound discovery. (Two student teams identified penicillin as Big-C.) While considered "life-saving," penicillin's discovery was incorrectly attributed by a student team to "Australian Howard Florey," who helped develop penicillin and bring it to people for treatment. However, Alexander Fleming discovered penicillin in 1928 in London, England. Other medical discoveries (creative products), such as the cervical cancer vaccine and a treatment for Alzheimer's disease, were also identified, with credit to Australian innovators (not identified by name).

Other Big-C creative products occupy the Indigenous domain of culture. Australia's archaeological discoveries of a wealth of Aboriginal artifacts and materials are a largely important initiative for establishing that Indigenous people have been around for thousands of years. This example was given by TJ (and Pascoe [2014] confirmed the explanation). A discovery TJ seemed excited about is the "overlapping hearths [camp fires] found on Rock Shelter, Balmoral Beach" in Sydney that were "used for almost 500 years in this shelter inhabited at least 3,600 years ago" (Hinkson & Harris, 2015, p. 48). Collectively, these findings could make a "Big-C" contribution, owing to their cultural significance and efforts to reconstruct the past and decolonize modern colonial mindsets. TJ added that this work needs to be painstakingly undertaken to "dispel the skepticism" around the longevity of his race.

The Indigenous cultural practice of ecological sustainability of land and natural resources (Bowman, 2016; Pascoe, 2014) is reflected in examples like the hearth discovery. Harmonious ways of existing with nature and recovering damaged areas was viewed as an Australian Aboriginal legacy by one student team. Fire had been observed by settlers in colonial Australia as Aboriginal people's universal approach for skillfully managing the landscape and tending to their needs, which included hearth fires for cooking, ceremonial rituals, and protection (Bowman). Indigenous fire ecology is highly attractive as a potentially important strategy for improved "fire management" and "biodiversity outcomes," Bowman explained. The question that remains is whether the ancient practices and principles can be applied to rapidly warming environments, such as fire-related emergencies, which he seems to doubt.

Media and video games in particular were seen as creative innovations by several teams: "Players need to use creativity and ingenuity, especially when pitted against others." Creative products developed in Australia included video games (e.g., Curious George) based on books with educational value. Products of value extended to famous Australian Indigenous books like *Follow the Rabbit-Proof Fence* (Pilkington, 2006) and/or films of major events in Australia (e.g., *Rabbit-Proof Fence* and *The Dish*). A lecturer thought that the international and study-abroad students (numerous in the classes) might be naming such sources. I wonder if a motivation was the same as mine as an outsider: to become better informed about Australian culture and history.

7.5   Reflections and Implications

Activism around big world problems like racial disparity and climate change was a dynamic unifying force for Australia, based on responses received and the literature reviewed. Spirited change and social improvement connected the three domains: Indigenous causes, environmental issues, and creative breakthroughs. These over-lapped in my analyses. For example, creative breakthroughs emerged from Indigenous causes—including in governance, policy, and society—with struggles around Aboriginal rights fueling consciousness-raising and reform.

College students contributed more topical ideas and examples (e.g., climate change) in the environmental domain. However, in Indigenous nomenclature the environment—in the sense of (home)land, country, heritage, and ecology—is ubiq-uitous, so I integrated notions of the environment in the discussions of Aboriginality and justice. Tribal and climate justice, each a type of social justice, were treated separately and together, depending on the context. Tribal and climate justice coalesce and are both high-priority targets for Indigenous cultures. In comparison, the students mainly deliberated on climate justice. There is room for growth and advocacy here; for example, ecosystem restoration and sustainability bridge climate justice with tribal justice, with potential for benefitting Indigenous communities more directly. Some breakthroughs in technology, medicine, culture, and media are relevant to Indigenous and environmental causes.

7.6   Summary

This chapter tackled creativity and accountability in Australia. Participating Australia-based students and educators contributed stimulating perspectives on Indigenous causes, environmental issues, and creative breakthroughs in various areas of society. Chapter 8 offers a case study synthesis of outcomes in the glocalities of Australia, Canada, and China, highlighting Hidden-c.

Acknowledgments and Notes   This Australian project was funded with a Niles Research Grant, awarded in 2019, by my home institution, with support from the university that hosted my stay as a visiting professor. In advance, ethics committees at my university and the overseas location reviewed the work plan.

Appendix 7.1: 4-C Classroom Activity and Conversation Protocol for Australia (C. A. Mullen)

1. What does creativity look like in Australia's local/regional/national/global context from your perspective?
2. What examples spring to mind for each component of the 4-C creativity framework?

    (a) Mini-c (creativity)?
    (b) Little-c (creativity)?
    (c) Pro-C (creativity)?
    (d) Big-C (creativity)?

3. In each example, what does accountability look like or what forms does it take?
4. When you think about creativity and accountability on a global scale, how might Australia compare with other nations' (testing) cultures?

References

Albeck-Ripka, L. (2019, September 13). The Indigenous man who declared his own country. *New York Times*. Retrieved from https://www.nytimes.com/2019/09/13/world/australia/indigenous-walubara-yidinji.html

Bell, L. A. (2016). Theoretical foundations for social justice education. In M. Adams & L. A. Bell, with D. J. Goodman, & Khyati Y. Joshi (Eds.), *Teaching for diversity and social justice* (3rd ed., pp. 3–26). New York, NY: Routledge. (1997, 1st ed.)

Bowman, D. (2016). Aboriginal fire management—Part of the solution to destructive bushfires. *The Conversation*. Retrieved from https://theconversation.com/aboriginal-fire-management-part-of-the-solution-to-destructive-bushfires-55032

Cave, D. (2018, April 10). In a proudly diverse Australia, White people still run almost everything. *The New York Times*. Retrieved from https://www.nytimes.com/2018/04/10/world/australia/study-diversity-multicultural.html

Chrysanthos, N. (2019, May 27). What is the Uluru Statement from the Heart? *The Sydney Morning Herald*. Retrieved from https://www.smh.com.au/national/what-is-the-uluru-statement-from-the-heart-20190523-p51qlj.html

Clean Up Australia. (2020). *Wikipedia*. Retrieved from https://en.wikipedia.org/wiki/clean_up_australia

Csikszentmihalyi, M. (1996). *Creativity: The psychology of discovery and invention*. London, UK: HarperPerennial.

Mick Dodson. (2020). *Wikipedia*. Retrieved from https://en.wikipedia.org/wiki/Mick_Dodson

Extraterritorial Human Rights Obligations (ETOs) for human rights beyond borders. (2017). *Concluding observations on the fifth periodic report of Australia*, pp. 1–12. [Committee on Economic, Social and Cultural Rights.] Retrieved from https://www.etoconsortium.org/en/search-results

Fleay, J., & Judd, B. (2019). The Uluru statement: A First Nations perspective of the implications for social reconstructive race relations in Australia. *International Journal of Critical Indigenous Studies, 12*(1), 1–14.

Fredericks, B., Maynor, P., White, N., English, F. W., & Ehrich, L. C. (2014). Living with the legacy of conquest and culture: Social justice leadership in education and the Indigenous peoples of Australia and America. In I. Bogotch & C. Shields (Eds.), *International handbook of educational leadership and social [in]justice* (Vol. 2, pp. 751–780). New York, NY: Springer.

Guillemin, M., Gillam, L., Barnard, E., Stewart, P., Walker, H., & Rosenthal, D. (2016). "We're checking them out": Indigenous and non-Indigenous research participants' accounts of deciding to be involved in research. *International Journal for Equity in Health, 15*(8), 1–10.

Henriques-Gomes, L. (2018, September 12). Transport emissions continue to rise as Australia lags behind other nations. *The Guardian*. Retrieved from https://www.theguardian.com/environment/2018/sep/13/transport-emissions-continue-to-rise-as-australia-lags-behind-other-nations

Hinkson, M., & Harris, A. (2015). *Aboriginal Sydney: A guide to important places of the past and present* (2nd ed.). Canberra, Australia: Aboriginal Studies Press.

Karwowski, M., Han, M.-H., & Beghetto, R. A. (2019). Toward dynamizing the measurement of creative confidence beliefs. *Psychology of Aesthetics, Creativity, and the Arts, 13*(2), 193–202.

Kaufman, J. C., & Beghetto, R. A. (2009). Beyond big and little: The Four C Model of Creativity. *Review of General Psychology, 13*(1), 1–12.

McGlade, H. (2012). *Our greatest challenge: Aboriginal children and human rights*. Canberra, Australia: Aboriginal Studies Press.

Morris, L. (2017, November 10). Did you know Australia invented Wi-Fi? *National Geographic*. Retrieved from https://www.nationalgeographic.com.au/australia/did-you-know-Australia-invented-wi-fi.aspx

Mullen, C. A. (2019). De/colonization: Perspectives on/by Indigenous populations in global Canadian contexts. *International Journal of Leadership in Education*, 1–20. https://doi.org/10.1080/13603124.2019.1631986

Mullen, C. A. (2020). *Canadian Indigenous literature and art: Decolonizing education, culture, and society*. Leiden, The Netherlands: Brill.

National Aboriginal and Islander Day Observance Committee (NAIDOC). (2019). *NAIDOC 2019: Voice, treaty, truth*. Retrieved from www.dca.org.au/blog/naidoc-2019-voice-treaty-truth

O'Faircheallaigh, C. (2013). Extractive industries and Indigenous peoples: A changing dynamic? *Journal of Rural Studies, 30*, 20–30.

Pascoe, B. (2014). *Dark emu: Black seeds, agriculture or accident?* Broome, Western Australia: Magabala Books.

Pilkington, D. (Garimara, N., Aboriginal name). (2006). *Follow the rabbit-proof fence*. St. Lucia, Australia: University of Queensland Press. (1996, original.)

Potter, E., & Schaffer, K. (2004). Rabbit-proof fence, relational ecologies, and the commodification of Indigenous experience. *Australian Humanities Review, 31*–32. Retrieved from http://australianhumanitiesreview.org/2004/04/01/issue-31-32-april-2004

Reconciliation Australia. (2017a). *Aboriginal and Torres Strait Islander Australians and the Constitution*, pp. 1–7. Retrieved from https://www.reconciliation.org.au/wp-content/uploads/2017/11/Recognising-Aboriginal-and-Torres-Strait-Islander-people-in-the-Australian-Constitution.pdf

Reconciliation Australia. (2017b). *Five fast facts—NAIDOC Week*. Retrieved from https://www.reconciliation.org.au/wp-content/uploads/2017/10/Five-Fast-Facts-NAIDOC-Week.pdf

Referendum Council. (2017). *Uluru Statement from the Heart: Information booklet*. The University of Melbourne (Melbourne Law School), pp. 1–7. Retrieved from https://law.unimelb.edu.au/__data/assets/pdf_file/0010/2764738/Uluru-Statement-from-the-Heart-Information-Booklet.pdf

Robinson, M. (2018). *Climate justice: Hope, resilience, and the fight for a sustainable future.* New York, NY: Bloomsbury Publishing.

Runco, M. (2019). Creativity as a dynamic, personal, parsimonious process. In R. A. Beghetto & G. E. Corazza (Eds.), *Dynamic perspectives on creativity: New directions for theory, research, and practice in education* (pp. 181–188). Cham, Switzerland: Springer.

Saunders, C. (2011). *The Constitution of Australia: A contextual analysis.* Portland, OR: Hart Publishing. (Kindle book).

Seabin Project. (2020). *Seabin Project.* Retrieved from https://seabinproject.com/sydney-wharf-embraces-seabin-technology

Shaw, W. S. (2007). *Cities of Whiteness.* Victoria, Australia: Blackwell.

Snow, D. (2019, January 26). Rediscovering the 'Heart': How Uluru statement got bogged in detail. *The Sydney Morning Herald.* Retrieved from https://www.smh.com.au/national/rediscovering-the-heart-how-uluru-statement-got-bogged-in-detail-20190125-p50tm3.html

Trigger, D., Keenan, J., de Rijke, K., & Rifkin, W. (2014). Aboriginal engagement and agreement-making with a rapidly developing resource industry: Coal seam gas development in Australia. *The Extractive Industries and Society, 1*, 176–188.

Tuck, E., & Gaztambide-Fernández, R. A. (2013). Curriculum, replacement, and settler futurity. *Journal of Curriculum Theorizing, 29*(1), 72–89.

Tuck, E., & Yang, K. W. (2012). Decolonization is not a metaphor. *Decolonization: Indigeneity, Education & Society, 1*(1), 1–40.

United Nations. [UN] Environment Programme (n.d). *About UN environment programme.* Retrieved from https://www.unenvironment.org/about-un-environment

Vincent, E. (2017). *Against native title: Conflict and creativity in outback Australia.* Canberra, Australia: Aboriginal Studies Press.

Webb, M., & Ronan, K. R. (2014). Interactive Hazards Education Program for youth in a low SES community: A quasi-experimental pilot study. *Risk Analysis, 34*(10), 1882–1893.

Whitmore, A. (Ed.) (2012). *Pitfalls and pipelines: Indigenous peoples and extractive industries*, pp. 1–414. Baguio City, Philippines: Tebtebba Foundation. Retrieved from https://www.iwgia.org/images/publications//0596_Pitfalls_and_Pipelines_-_Indigenous_Peoples_and_Extractive_Industries.pdf

Workplace Law. (2018). *Positive discrimination in the workplace.* Retrieved from https://www.humanrights.gov.au/quick-guide/12078

Writer, J. H. (2008). Unmasking, exposing, and confronting: Critical race theory, tribal critical race theory and multicultural education. *International Journal of Multicultural Education, 10*(2), 1–15.

Zittoun, T., & Gillespie, A. (2016). Imagination: Creating alternatives in everyday life. In V. P. Glăveanu (Ed.), *The Palgrave handbook of creativity and culture research* (pp. 225–242). London, UK: Palgrave Macmillan.

Part III
Enlivening Creativity-Deficit Educational Settings Worldwide

Chapter 8
Case Study Synthesis of Outcomes: Highlighting Hidden-c

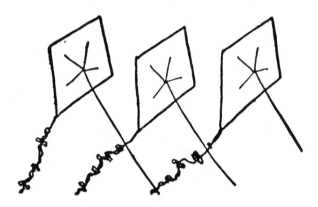

8.1 Overview and Study Implications

The countries to which I brought my 4-C creativity program each had their own cultures, politics, trends, values, histories, goals, struggles, creativities, innovations, and breakthroughs. Across glocalities, these layers were represented by those who took on the challenge of making sense of creativity and in relation to accountability. In general, I would say that China understood creativity as having collective values (e.g., nature, family, beauty, education), legacies deep; Canada associated creativity with multicultural diversity, tolerance, and inquiry-based learning; and Australia merged environmental issues and tribal justice with creativity.

In this chapter, I advance a synthesis of outcomes for the three glocal case studies and their commonalities and variations. Developments common to the Chinese, Canadian, and Australian cases are that (1) the Four C (4-C) Model of Creativity fostered creative engagement and dynamic creativity and (2) Hidden-c, the belief in one's creative capacity, nurtured (inter)personal powers for releasing creativity despite, or in light of, constraints.

© Springer Nature Switzerland AG 2020
C. A. Mullen, *Revealing Creativity*, Creativity Theory and Action in Education
5, https://doi.org/10.1007/978-3-030-48165-0_8

Highlighted is Hidden-c and how it enabled dialogical participation in open-ended activities while igniting a creativity paradox. The discussion of Hidden-c positions it as a level/ type of creativity unto itself—a shaping force that underlies the 4-Cs, potentially adding a fifth c to Kaufman and Beghetto's (2009) classic typology. My 4-C program of pedagogical activities—a process-based approach for dynamizing creativity—is summed up as Experience, Express, and Enliven Creativity (E^3C). In different countries, Hidden-c was cultivated by E^3C dynamics. Participants represented creativity in their contexts and cultures and engaged authentically in the 4-C program. Study implications are woven into the writing.

8.2 Developmental Outcomes of the 4-C Model

Primary developmental outcomes were parsed for the transnational cases. Across glocalities, the 4-C creativity model (Kaufman & Beghetto, 2009), methodologically interpreted and implemented, sparked creative engagement and dynamic creativity. In effect, the intervention did prove viable in places where creativity is repressed, ignored, or simply forgotten. From a "global perspective," the instances of creativity at the university sites were time-limited, yet interconnectivity and cultural communication existed among the actors. Corazza (2019) speculated that "this interconnectivity between creative instances" is, on one level, a dynamic snapshot in time and space and, on another level, part of "a never ending story" in that "the creativity process" is not reducible to a clean start or end (p. 299).

By tapping into networks and manufacturing teams, college students had the unique opportunity to engage creatively and relationally around a conceptual model (i.e., the 4-C framework). By *creative engagement*, my study utilized a "participatory process"; this served to embed the creativity project within "social relations" in which social–environmental factors shaped dialogical engagement in groups and dyads (Literat & Glăveanu, 2018; also Ness & Glăveanu, 2019). While the study involved "executory participation (a task-based contribution to a predesigned project)" (Literat & Glăveanu, 2018, p. 900), the creative process not only allowed for (inter)personal agency but also depended on it for cultural interpretation of open-ended creativity prompts rooted within a schema (the 4-C typology). Creators all enlisted their own entry points, stories, illustrations, and other creative strategies like "biographies" for vitalizing activities; in their responses to the 4-C prompts, participants pulled on their "diverse knowledge, experience, expertise, background experiences, and sociocultural perspectives" (Clapp & Hanson, 2019, p. 27) largely rooted within their sociocultural domains in China, Canada, and Australia. Team members built upon each other's ideas, negotiating meanings and brainstorming possibilities in relation to the 4-Cs, while interviewees engaged as such in relation to me (the interviewer) but to varying degrees.

In this book, all such creative processes have been cast as *dynamic creativity* (Beghetto & Corazza, 2019; Corazza, 2016; Mullen, 2019a, 2019b; Ness & Glăveanu, 2019; Runco, 2019). Students, faculty, and leaders' glimpses into creativity and accountability emerged from a dynamic interplay with their contexts, cultures, and creative selves. Such "supportive, exploratory approach[es]" to working with students, Beghetto (2019) explained, can nurture "creative potential" and "academic achievement." In my case studies involving educators, these approaches manifested as 4-C artifacts—creative performances emerged from cultural contexts. Artifacts were expressed as documented responses in words and images arising out of conversational flows between and among educators. Infusing each and every artifact were quintessential influences of culture and collaboration on creative learning.

As theorized about creative learning in sociocultural frameworks, when teams enact "group creativity," they creatively negotiate boundaries, interact, and generate something new by combining elements cultural contexts and multiple perspectives (Sawyer, 2012). Considering developmental outcomes associated with my 4-C application, a key notion is culture and creativity in relation to it. The meaning I brought to imagining, designing, and implementing this pedagogical study also resonates with Glăveanu's (2011, 2016) pioneering work in sociocultural theorizing. Human actors and contexts are seen as interdependent; in light of this codependency, "psychological processes 'extend' into the world through the means of action, interaction, and communication" (Glăveanu, Ness, Wasson, & Lubart, 2019, p. 63). Artifacts are a critically important signifier of creativity within cultural environments relative to Glăveanu's (2013) five A's Framework—actor, action, artifact, audience, and affordances. The 5As refer to Artifact (replacing "product") as shaped by an Actor (a sociocultural being whereas "person" overemphasizes the importance of the individual). Actors' thoughts and behaviors are not restricted to the internal workings of self (as "process" implies). The relationship of Actor to Audience and Affordances involves interplay, supported by resources, materials, and tools, and invites creative agency (whereas the sense of being limited by persons and resources is connoted by "press").

The 5As, and the interwoven strands of creativity that constitute its whole, arose as a dynamic alternative to the long-standing dimensions of creativity—person, process, product, and press (4Ps). Glăveanu's (2011, 2016) argument is that the 4Ps signify a disciplinary mindset that exalts the individual (actor) in bringing about creativity, in effect overshadowing equally important aspects (e.g., action). The proposal is to replace the 4Ps by giving weight to the sociocultural context of creativity and its dynamic, dialogical, relational, and interactional qualities. Based on Glăveanu's collaborative research (e.g., Glăveanu et al., 2019) and descriptions of studies upon which he builds, readers are transported, like the teachers and students who participate in virtual learning environments, to a universe that is supported by twenty-first century pedagogically-designed technologies and virtual worlds. Manifestations include the use of avatars in avatar-mediated creative learning and problem-solving tasks.

About collaboration, my case study outcomes of group creativity relied on creative collaborative performance in sociocultural learning environments. Sawyer's (2012) state-of-the-art conceptualization of "collaborative creativity" secured this direction in my thinking for the guidance it gave to participating groups and individuals. The artifacts produced in three countries in response to my 4-C pedagogical activities are expressive of the "creative process"—instead of being assessed or judged for their merit, the artifacts really need to be appreciated as emergences "within the context of culture" specific to actors' cultural and contextual interpretations of the 4-C schema (Helfand, Kaufman, & Beghetto, 2016, p. 24). In group situations, with the "collective social product" *not* being attributable to individuals (Sawyer, 2012, p. 67), the 4-C productions created in the Chinese, Canadian, and Australian glocalities cannot be separated from their environments, processes, or even creators.

Sociocultural theorizing as such resonates with Glăveanu's (2016) advocacy of "holistic" and "constructionist" ways of seeing "traditional dichotomies" like "individual and social," "creative potential and creative achievement," and so forth (p. 206). Creativity researchers, including 4-C originators Kaufman and Beghetto, describe the sociocultural contributions of Glăveanu's to the psychology literature and their 4-C theory in particular (see Helfand, Kaufman, & Beghetto, 2016). Both Glăveanu and Sawyer have been credited with conceptualizing creativity "as a process" (p. 226). In current times, their theorizing exists in tension with dominating assumptions and definitions of creativity that adhere to the belief that "creativity needs an output that can be evaluated" (a belief that Zittoun & Gillespie, 2016 propose is constricting, p. 226). Developmental outcomes of the 4-C model relative to my study necessitate viewing in the context of culture and collaboration and with the lens of creativity as process. To engage in meaning-making of the 4-Cs, my participants were led to closely consider their own transnational cultures and glocal contexts, which the artifacts all reflect (e.g., the moral and educational value of family, nature, friendship, and culture in China; see Mullen, 2017). The artifacts are expressions of cultural and contextual knowledge arising out of collaborative creativity for groups and relational creativity for interviews with individuals.

8.2.1   Activity-Based Creativity Phenomena

Dynamic developments across the glocalities stemmed from "action orientations" (Glăveanu, 2016) specific to three activity-based creativity phenomena that played out uniquely within each, whether highlighted in particular ways, fulfilled to a degree, or simply not accommodated:

1. creative achievement by student teams through intensive social interaction for a long interval (4-C responses/artifacts and three-dimensional [3D] creative posters, performances demonstrating highlights, creativity program assessment completed by students)
2. cognitive academic task completion by student teams through social interaction for a short interval (4-C responses/artifacts, with creative performances around sharing results in some locations)
3. content-relevant 4-C contributions (stimulating interviews/conversations with a broader constituency handled one-on-one and with groups)

In all glocalities, I was granted access to classes where considerable variability existed as to what components of my 4-C creativity workshop could be accommodated. The availability of, and access to, busy students, faculty, and leaders proved irregular everywhere, in no way surprising. Details also varied in the implementation of the creativity activities regarding, as examples, whether courses were at the undergraduate or graduate level, the curricular focus of these, and student demographics. Besides access, time—a source of pressure for all classes—was also a challenge for my accelerated course.

Interviews/conversations, too, were variable in that they occurred with individuals and groups, and the time allotted ranged somewhat; in Australia, a key insider (leader) devoted many hours to the 4-C conversation. Consequently, owing to all such variables, my 4-C program unfolded partially and differently in Chongqing, Toronto, and Sydney relative to the activity-based creativity phenomena. Even my own professional development and creative learning differed across sites.

To briefly illustrate activity-based creativity dynamics for each of the sites, with the unique opportunity afforded to teach the expedited undergraduate course in Chongqing, I was able to deliver the assessments I designed. These encompassed the 4-C activities and were built into the workshop. As described (Chap. 5), the Chinese preservice feedback indicated that the 4-C–steeped curriculum was appreciated, and, importantly, that the collaborative project activity performances were strongly preferred (over the individual ones). Content-relevant 4-C contributions from faculty and leaders at the location were not forthcoming.

Serving as a contrast, in Canada, only the cognitive academic tasks responding to the 4-C prompts were accommodated, not the production of the creative poster. However, I was able to carry out aspects of my creativity workshop with various graduate-level courses, including whole-class social interaction wherein teams were given a little time to share aloud key points. Professors whose classes I engaged in activities also participated in planning and debriefing around my activities, seeking a good fit with their lessons. Content-relevant contributions came from numerous sources, including my public talks/seminars. As such, the active conversational context encompassed faculty, leaders, and other constituents.

Australia differed still, with 4-C responses to prompts accomplished in two classes and, in the largest of these, the poster artifacts. While teams' social interaction was energetic and task-focused, time did not allow for communicating results across teams (unlike in China and Canada). Content-relevant contributions were made by lecturers and leaders; one leader (alluded to earlier) regularly shared his ideas and, with my communicative feedback, teased out their applicability to the 4-C typology. Like the Canada-based faculty, the lecturers whose classes I turned into a workshop were keen to establish the value of my creativity program to their curriculum.

8.2.2   Overall Creativity Patterns Across Sites

In light of these similarities and dissimilarities across the glocalities, the overall creativity pattern is this: *Developments and outcomes associated with creativity in general and the 4-Cs in particular transpired, revealing creativity as a progression from self to world.* In this experiential venture, Mini-c (and Little-c) did indeed turn out to be the key, especially for students, to sparking their meaning-making and grounding it contextually and culturally. Interestingly, this finding echoes Kaufman and Beghetto's (2009) value of Mini-c as the vital seedling upon which the other creativities depend; hence, Mini-c's role is foundational to both the creative process and progression of creativity. While Mini-c was portrayed as the 4-C model's centerpiece during my introductory lecture in all learning spaces, participants were nonetheless confronted with the theory for the first time. Complicating matters, I invited them to unpack my multifaceted abstraction (and set of prompts) that probes their perspective on creativity within their transnational context and with relevance to accountability.

Unsurprisingly, perhaps, more responses and depictions of Mini-c and Little-c were forthcoming from students than the other creativity types (Pro-C and Big-C were represented, but to a lesser extent). Resonance seemed strong with Mini-c, enabling everyday examples to be recalled from daily living and life practices, at times attached to social messages (e.g., recycling and composting is important to sustaining the planet). Because I had the opportunity to observe the work underway, thereby catching some of the brainstorming, it was evident where students seemed comfortable beginning the task. Starting with Mini-c, some even held up, pointed to, or sketched objects (like cell phones) to signify Mini-c (as Wi-Fi interconnectivity). They moved on from there, conceptualizing the 4-C theory from their own viewpoint, at times circling back to represent Little-c, Pro-C, or Big-C. Team members seemed to gravitate toward what they intuited as a progressive take on the developmental nature of creativity, thereby adopting Mini-c as their starting point to help build awareness of Little-c, Pro-C, and Big-C. A representation of Big-C for their country did not always readily come to mind, necessitating more time to ponder. Collectively across sites, students enacted "the personally meaningful way that individuals grow," which focuses on process and enables creative freedom given that Mini-c "does not require outside judgment" (Helfand et al., 2016, p. 18). Results from these case study situations in *Revealing Creativity* affirm Beghetto's (2019) description of Mini-c as the initial step in creativity and the model as a whole as a dynamic staircase one climbs.

To illustrate, one team's brainstorming revealed creativity as a developmental progression from self to world even though, paradoxically, the world is the self. (The self–world comes to mind as a way of reflecting an undivided or holistic way of being, which is fundamental to sociocultural theory [Glăveanu, 2011, 2016]). In one glocality, I had just completed my lecture on the 4-C creativity model and described the activities ahead. Zoe, who was studying my sheet with the 4-C prompts, turned to her teammates. Pointing at her hair accessory, she said,

"You see that my headband has salmon [a fish design] on it, right? What do you think it was, originally?" No one knew. "Wrapping paper made of fabric I stitched into a headband! Headbands are expensive—that's why I made this. But, it couldn't be any ol' design. I wanted to wear *this* one. Why do you think salmon matter to me?" Again, her team shrugged. "Because I'd love to become an ecologist working in water and fish protection. My 'fav' thing to do is signal environmental messages with my 'eco' style of dress, you know, like, 'Let's save the planet and protect endangered species.'"

Oliver nodded, responding, "So you converted the wrapping paper into something wearable and for an unintended purpose, which is a sign of creativity [referencing Mullen's lecture]." Fang chimed in, "And the fish design is meaningful to you, so it's Mini-c, right?" Jocelyn added, "Fang, because you're like—what's that word?—*recognizing* Zoe's creativity, we're witnessing Little-c?" "Yep," piped in Zoe, "I'm feeling good, so that's gotta be Little-c."

"How about Pro-C?," queried Jocelyn, to which Zoe replied, "Help me think this through, ok? I've been learning about extreme weather events. Climate change in Australia is getting worse. Our warming ocean ecosystems mean there's gonna be a huge reduction in our fish and food supply." "Do any sources of information stand out?" Oliver asked, to which Zoe responded, "By experts you mean? I like going to *The Conversation* [2019] where the stories link to published articles with data for different countries. I subscribe to its newsletter *The Conversation Australia.*" "On the Internet? We can't look it up right now on our devices," quipped Oliver. Fang pitched in, "What about using *The Conversation Australia* for our Pro-C and Zoe, can you figure out how to express it on our poster?" Zoe nodded.

"How about Big-C?" probed Zoe. Jocelyn chimed in, "Have any of you heard of Seabin, here at the Wharf?" Nodding, all seemed impressed with "Sydney's own" young entrepreneurs and their invention. While talking and recording their responses, and planning representational symbols for the poster, they took ownership of Seabin as their Big-C for Australia, all without consulting the Internet. Seabin elevated their theme of protecting marine ecosystems in the face of escalating environmental threats, as featured in Chap. 7. (field notes, with pseudonyms)

Across three nations, I witnessed some remarkable examples of creativity in action like this in which the 4-C model was actively and progressively interpreted. By synthesizing the results from the responses and materials generated over the years, what came into view is that *the 4-C model proved relatable and contextually and culturally meaningful within the pedagogical contexts studied, despite constraints and pressures.* Also, developmental outcomes associated with this typology and my methodological translation of it suggest that *creativity is universal—not a particular application, creativity, like good teaching and learning, can be observed anywhere, anytime, and under a range of conditions, including intense scrutiny and restrictions on creative experience and expression.*

An implication of the findings is that creativity challenges can help revitalize creativity-deficit educational settings. Further, *recovery of creativity was met head on within educational environments through a set of dynamic processes that can be summed up as Experience, Express, and Enliven Creativity (E³C).* Regarding the concept of enlivening, Corazza (2019) proposed that the impact for creators can continue beyond an isolated occurrence of creativity—"every creative instance has the potential to generate long waves of cultural interaction" (p. 300). With my project, the possibility of continued creativity resides on several fronts; for example, all artifacts were returned in their original form to their owners in a timely manner, and all lecturers who supported my workshop in their classes expressed interest in following up with the participating students and/or integrating creativity into a future class.

Taken together, these results imply that *creativity that is theory-informed and cognitively geared can absorb, enhance, disrupt, or even overcome constraints.* If so, then relevance for creativity and creative learning extends beyond China, Canada, and Australia and the exigencies of disabling global influences (e.g., standardized testing, bypassing of creativity in curricula, beliefs, stereotypes, neoliberal values, and colonialism). In fact, the importance of this creative intervention in college learning environments suggests the possibility of a fifth C—Hidden-c.

8.3 Hidden-c's Role in Nurturing Creative Potential

Releasing creativity under duress and despite constraints, or even because of them, is how I've operationalized my idea of Hidden-c. In *Revealing Creativity*'s case studies, Hidden-c was cursorily defined as a self-belief construct with a role in cultivating creative potential.

Quite possibly, before we as human beings can generate meaning and problem-solve, let alone contribute creatively to and beyond the professions, we must believe in our capacity to create. Alternatively, we can evolve in this direction or even find ourselves in a situation that requires creativity. In educational settings like those in this book, I've seen college students tap into creativity that might be hidden from themselves and perform creatively in seemingly impossible circumstances (also, Mullen, 2018). (I have also witnessed this phenomenon within preK–12 schools in China and published on it.)

Learning anew from such processes, perhaps creators unexpectedly make creative connections and find that they can go beyond fresh ideas to developing creative artifacts. Some might even have their production judged as novel and useful (e.g., Corazza, 2016), or perhaps more realistically as a clever remix derived from different sources (Ferguson, 2012), while others' contributions could prove educationally or socially beneficial.

Belief in one's creative ability can be personally and professionally empowering, and dynamic interactions can motivate, even inspire, other people. Creators—like Zoe and her team (from the vignette)—tapped into something, perhaps their Hidden-c. Sparking interpersonal chemistry, they (unwittingly) collectively modeled creative self-belief, confidence, self-image, and self- and group empowerment. This observation is true of a number of other participant contributions to this book, as signaled by the creative conversations and artifacts.

A big idea around Hidden-c, then, is that it builds on, and benefits from, existing theory and knowledge. Also, it can lie dormant or be experienced, expressed, and enlivened, and with others or in solitude. While an emergent term, Hidden-c's close association with established creativity knowledge calls for positioning my concept accordingly.

8.3.1 Hidden-c and the 4-C Creativity Model

Perhaps it can be ventured that Hidden-c intensifies recognition of Kaufman and Beghetto's (2009) framework by extending the 4-Cs and related theorizing. Substantiating this claim, the Hidden-c concept has been introduced in the context of a 4-C application involving educators, many working-class and, among them, immigrants struggling to adapt to a new country and unfamiliar norms and customs. My study reflects a growing trend in the literature. Creativity research as a domain is "shift[ing] away from elite, culturally dominant activities to activities found in a range of cultural, ethnic, and social class groups"; increasingly, the "everyday creativity" of "the working classes or the uneducated" is being studied (Sawyer, 2017, p. 354).

A bridging of educational disciplines (e.g., teacher education) with international education is another contribution of this longitudinal glocal study, with earlier publications setting the tone (e.g., Mullen, 2018, 2019a, b). In light of my transnational explorations and outcomes, quite possibly it can be claimed that Hidden-c foregrounds generative possibilities for adding a new C to the classic typology. My proposal is that Hidden-c is both a catalyst for creative endeavor—and thus a category of creativity unto itself—and a shaping force that underlies the 4-Cs. At all levels of creativity and across types, creators plagued by doubts, uncertainties, and unknowns might learn something valuable from making creative connections, taking unexpected turns, and even failing in the attempt.

8.3.2   Hidden-c and Dynamic Creativity

The 4-C typology is conducive to dynamic creativity, leading me to a countercultural belief in the psychology literature that questions whether creativity has to be achievement- and product-oriented. Previously mentioned, the opposing stance—articulated by Runco (2019) and other researchers (e.g., Glăveanu, 2016; Helfand et al., 2016) —is that creativity as a dynamic process can stand on its own and be appreciated without discernible results. Facilitative of Hidden-c, dynamic creativity is a resistive theory, practice, and action that counters static perspectives of creativity and their impact on educational cultures (Beghetto & Corazza, 2019; Beghetto & Karwowski, 2019; Corazza, 2016; Glăveanu, 2016; Mullen, 2019b; Runco, 2019). Static creativity has been attributed to the misunderstanding of creativity as "a thing" when it is "*a quality of human action*" (Glăveanu, 2016, p. 206; italics in original).

For years in educational systems, test-centric pedagogy, rote learning, standardized curricula, personal biases, cultural stereotypes, and more give way to static creativity, which characteristically lacks engagement with cultural knowledges through which the world is transformed and made "more humane and equitable" (Vadeboncoeur et al., 2016, p. 299). In "instructionist" classrooms, argued Sawyer (2013), workforce cultures and outdated pedagogies challenge the pedagogical capacity for creating constructivist environments, which are amenable to group creativity, student learning, and collaborative conversation. Collaborative teams actively engage in solving complex real-world problems, improvise and develop insight, and produce products that are refined. While collaboration can led to "collective creations," and collaborative cultures can renew systems (Sawyer, 2013), team-based creativity in educational environments can be difficult for students not accustomed to collaborative work; they need guidance and scaffolding to participate productively and creatively in groups (Sawyer, 2003).

While creating a collaborative culture beyond the one-time opportunities I had for guiding and scaffolding creative learning in classrooms was *not* an option at my research sites, a taste for group creativity may have been carried forth by the participants in their life worlds and futures. Creativity as a dynamic, interactive, and social process was the point of departure in my study; artifacts—creative responses, posters, and performances—resulted, despite pressures and unknowns. The artifacts and the performativity of them by the creators/actors arose out of challenging circumstances. To Sawyer (2013), all group creativity depends on interpersonal chemistry and "improvisation," and has "key characteristics" of "process, unpredictability, intersubjectivity, complex communication, and emergence." Like the team-based musical performances Sawyer (2003) analyzed, the performances that became artifacts in the glocalities I explored have an improvisational and eclectic quality. They also have an uneven quality, largely owing to contextual pressures (e.g., time limits on the creative tasks) and cultural restrictions (e.g. lack of attention on creativity in the milieu). In the end, there was variation in the quality of what was produced within the educational settings; yet, there was participatory involvement in the 4-C program. In fact, dynamic engagement in the creative process was likely satisfied as the greatest outcome associated with revealing creativity.

Teacher educators Kauper and Jacobs (2019) have explored the idea of "teaching as an improvisational performance" (p. 347), inspired by Sawyer's theorizing about creativity and collaboration. In an effort to make space for "creative expression" in their teaching within an increasingly rigid world culture of standardization and testing, they persisted despite having encountered resistance from their students to engage in creative acts. In an educational foundations course, they guided their class to create a 3D representation of their philosophy using materials (e.g., clay) to form sculptures. The activity followed students' personal essay writing about their beliefs, and the sculptures formed a "gallery walk" from which critiques emerged. Kauper and Jacobs came to see a dynamic of "creative subversion" at work that enabled all "actors" in the shared space to engage in "collaborative interactions" and co-construct a "creative improvisational process" that promised "meaningful change" (p. 347).

8.3.3   Hidden-c and Creative Self-Beliefs

Besides the 4-C typology and dynamic creativity, another crucial theory informing Hidden-c's compositional elements is "creative self-beliefs." These "shape one's creative self [and identity] and play a unique role in helping to determine a person's engagement and performance on creative endeavors" (Beghetto & Karwowski, 2019, p. 15). Three categories of creative self-beliefs these researchers outline are:

1. "creative confidence" (believing in one's creativity)
2. "creative self-awareness" (beliefs about one's capabilities)
3. "creative self-image" (beliefs about the fit of one's capabilities, goals, and strengths with one's self; Beghetto & Karwowski, 2019, p. 15; also, Beghetto & Karwowski, 2017)

"Creative confidence beliefs" facilitate "mov[ing] from creative potential to creative expression," explained Beghetto (2019), which is "moderated by the valuing of creativity" (p. 39). Creative self-beliefs are "triggered [in] . . . a performance situation," resulting "in a self-judgment about one's confidence to creatively perform an impending task at a particular level (e.g., 'I am confident that I can creatively solve three of these five problems')" (Beghetto & Karwowski, 2017, p. 7). Creative self-belief is itself rooted in the "perceived confidence to creatively perform a particular task" (p. 3). Hidden-c is also connected to "creative behavior" (e.g., Beghetto & Karwowski, 2017, 2019) or, better yet, *creative expression* (Beghetto, 2006) and *creative action*. These constructs fit my study well, with the emphasis on social engagement in creativity and expression of creative ideas in real time.

Illustrating the point that creative expression relies on self-judgment, Beghetto (2006) conducted a US-based survey of 1322 middle and secondary students' judgments of their creative abilities. Importantly, he found that "although creative ability is necessary for creative expression, it is not sufficient. Creative expression, like other forms of behavior, seems to be influenced by self-judgments of one's ability to generate novel and useful outcomes" (p. 447). Self-judgment then triggers one's Hidden-c.

Creative self-beliefs, judgments, behaviors, and actions can affect conditions (like authoritarian regimes and pedagogies and lack of attention on creativity) that constrain creativity and creative identity, and thus experience and expression, empowerment and performance. When hidden, as in suppressed, repressed, or even unknown, one's creativity can be influenced by self-doubts, uncertainties, resistances, hegemonic structures, repressive dynamics, or dominant forces. A scenario involving external influences is when the narratives, needs, interests, and experiences of traditionally under-represented groups are limited to dominant narratives and majoritarian agendas (Mullen, 2020). Activating Hidden-c in combination with cultural sensitivity and agency is vital for the well-being of humanity. Uncovering one's latent potential as creator and empowering oneself or others to explore creativity can reveal Hidden-c.

Paradoxically, the untold stories of creativity in Chinese students' early life, perhaps repressed or forgotten, served as the basis for what I came to name E^3C. Their personal essays formed the basis of the collaborative creative productions and future generative possibilities (Chap. 5). Pedagogic belief in others' potential for creativity can manifest, notably, through deliberate intervention and explicit instruction to be creative (as per Niu & Sternberg, 2001). These very conditions, inspired by Niu's takeaway from her studies, encouraged me to be as direct as possible with college students not only in China but also Canada and Australia.

The role of adopter and shaper of creativity theories is grounded in creative self-belief. Just such a belief of mine—that Hidden-c is potentially accessible to all, especially in social situations where creativity can be nurtured—took me from one country to another to "test" just how realistic this notion was. With explicit cognitive and methodological guidance, and emotional assurance, plus relatively supportive conditions, students tapped into their creative selves. Beyond theorizing, speculation, and analyses on my part, empirical validation of the hypothesis that self-belief is fundamental to creative processes is available (e.g., Beghetto, 2006).

8.3.4   Hidden-c and Creative Constraint

Creative constraint is another notion embedded within Hidden-c. As explained in this book, constraint has been theorized as a dynamic that exists in the experience of creativity and its operationalization within learning contexts and in life (Beghetto, 2019). When creativity's personal power is released, this does not somehow occur apart from restraints or even because barriers have been magically lifted or somehow defeated, although they may be traversed or overcome when building resiliency. The good news is that ideal conditions are not required for Hidden-c to manifest and cultivate creative potential—creators' E^3C powers can be triggered despite, or in light of, obstacles, and in ways ranging from the personal to the professional.

An extremely important point about constraints is that they do not necessarily negate creative energies and Hidden-c, even within environments that discourage or block creativity. In fact, individuals who create despite feeling unsupported can strengthen their capacity to be empowered creatively and even change their milieu or aspects of it (Beghetto, 2019; Mullen, 2017, 2018, 2019b). Concealed from many in education is the power of one's own creativity and capability for influencing and being influenced by our fields and domains, cultures and contexts. Hidden-c foregrounds personal and professional creativity and the creative potential to alter conditions or circumstances that affect authentic generative experience, extending to networks, contexts, and cultures.

Limitations on my creative intervention were many. These included, besides my being an unknown quantity, (a) insufficient time for engagement (workshop and int erviews/conversations), (b) uncertainty as to where educational creativity fits in existing curriculum and programs, and (c) an unstable sense of creative self-confidence. I found it striking that creativity was, in fact, discussed and represented in all three locations, given the mounting tensions. Besides the 4-Cs being meaningfully interpreted, my creativity program was also experienced, expressed, and enlivened, as conveyed by the responses I storied and the artifacts described.

8.3.5   Hidden-c and the E³C Continuum

Igniting Hidden-c dynamically and interpersonally through E³C was a programmatic implication. As such, expressing creativity in addition to experiencing it was a direct target of my 4-C program. One could say that the "enlivening" part of the E³C's experiential continuum has been left to chance and the imagination, owing to its unknown status as but a generative possibility, stretching beyond the end of my program. Corazza's (2019) macro-view of endings and beginnings, time and space, is intriguing: while outcomes associated with creativity have an endpoint, they can continue to have an impact (e.g., a product, like this book, leaves the creator's hands, marking an ending, only to begin a life of its own in the reader's hands).

As the international and study-abroad students return to their homelands, might they be more aware of their creative selves and their Hidden-c? Might they strive to have a personal project (e.g., essay) published or posted on the Internet so their ideas can be recognized and potentially have impact? Or, might they seek to contribute their unique talents to an inspiring initiative (like the Seabin Project) or even generate their own? As people unite and collectives grow across glocalities, could Hidden-c be in service of Hidden-C, for which a collective creative mindset can tackle the biggest problems in the world?

Interestingly, there were glimmers at all the sites of the enlivening of creativity. Professors divulged their interest in integrating creativity in some form into their teaching; it also struck me that when faculty welcomed my creativity workshop, they thoughtfully sought continuity with their lessons. At times, faculty and leaders approached me to add something new to our previous 4-C conversation. A striking occurrence was when the Australian Aboriginal administrative leader initiated ongoing dialogue wherein he not only responded to my 4-C prompts but also added reflections later. My 4-C analysis was something he invited of a foundational reading in his course, perhaps because his curiosity had been piqued.

Like Hidden-c, E³C sparks dynamic creativity in mysterious ways; when Hidden-c is kindled, latent creativity is aroused. In a state of receptivity, one can experience, express, and enliven creativity. Another way of discerning Hidden-c is through targeted self-report data, for which my project lacked capacity. If Hidden-c is being triggered in creative moments and within environments that directly or indirectly facilitate E³C, then presumably one's creative self-beliefs would be affected, such as by feeling more confident or being innovative.

Applications, interventions, and investigations of creativity all potentially support E³C, legitimizing its value for creative engagement as well as contribution. Attention on E³C could encourage self-transformation and desirable societal change.

8.3.6   Hidden-c and Creative Methods

The Hidden-c concept also intersects with my creative methods. Qualitative in nature, my study did not involve measuring creative self-beliefs. But in the Chinese context, students did assess the various creative activities, considering the extent to which they liked (or did not like) each one. After some confessed in their essays on childhood creativity that they lacked creativity, there were indications that everyone (or mostly all) had developed a level of confidence with their creative abilities—Hidden-c. The class rated the collaborative activities much higher (than the solitary ones), with a peak rating assigned to the challenging creative project (team poster).

Pedagogic attitudes supported creative methods. I felt confident in the young Chinese students' abilities even when they did not, having seen firsthand what they were capable of under duress. I constantly reminded them that we are all naturally creative, and together we identified examples at the outset. Also, I reassured them that they were *not* expected to show their artistry or become artists, but instead to tackle a cognitive challenge and creatively express themselves at the team level. Across all sites, I searched for signs of apprehension, especially involving insecurity about one's creativity (or artistry). Besides my comments to the class in China, I emphasized to students in Canada and Australia that they were not facing the creative challenge alone or being assessed. I entered the glocalities understanding that the prospect of taking on the unknown can stir self-doubts (just as it did for me). By presenting the creative tasks as smaller, manageable stages (e.g., each 4-C anchored to students' own contexts and cultures) and offering verbal reassurance, it became possible for the classes to apply the 4-C theory and *see results* in the process of moving among the 4-Cs. Using these and other creative methods, student creative confidence, self-awareness, and self-image seemed supported by the creativity challenge.

8.3.7 Hidden-c and Creativity Paradox

Up to this point, readers might be forming the impression that across sites students must have had some level of confidence in their creativity to even partake in the activities. However, in delivering the workshop from one place to the next and looking back on the creativity program as a whole, a paradox dawned on me: While not all students felt confident or comfortable enough to engage in the creative activities, they did in fact improve their creative self-beliefs. In China, Canada, and Australia, a number of them seemed uncomfortable with, or even intimated by, the "expectations" of an outsider, even though their course professor was present. While resistance and self-doubt were expressed culturally and emotionally, students produced interactively their creative responses and artifacts under pressure within short timeframes and without samples.

Contradictorily, as alluded to in the case studies, students spontaneously shared their concerns with the class during the question-and-answer segment of my lecture and/or while brainstorming with their teams. Hinting at low self-confidence in their creative abilities, such utterances included: "I'm not naturally creative"; "How are we supposed to be creative without using our devices?"; "I don't know how to draw or do art"; "We don't know each other well enough to do these tasks"; "Where do we start?"; "What does she expect us to submit?"; and, "What is supposed to be on our posters?" It was as though the creative activity felt out of reach. In China, disclosures along these lines transpired in their self-introductions and personal essays on creativity. Some wrote about having "a creative block" regarding their childhood, which paradoxically served as a prompt for eliciting the creative experience that had been obstructed.

In China, Canada, and Australia, when I explained that the 4-C activities were cognitive and collaborative in nature and that creativity was strictly dialogic and was *not* being judged, students may have felt somewhat reassured. I would add that I was an educator, not an artist, and that I was not qualified to judge art. In all teams someone seemed poised to tackle, initiate, or even lead the cognitive collaborative challenge, with others in tow. Peer synergies would ignite.

Against all odds, from one environment to the next, students proved creative and social, collaboratively engaging in discourse for which their representations of the 4-Cs were culturally and contextually unique. How is this possible? Previously, I have written about a particular barrier—high-stakes testing—a schooling culture common to the students involved in my creativity program, who were socialized as test-takers from the elementary grades. Thus, I was keenly aware that the creative intervention involved risk or uncertainty and likely seemed too open-ended. Yet, in nation after nation, students rose to the occasion despite similar conditions.

Observing students in creative action, it struck me how the capacity to function creatively can be expedited and even deepened through task-oriented social interaction in the face of multiple constraints. Perhaps, for some reluctant or resistive creators, creativity can only be revealed to them through explicit instructions to be creative. By adapting the 4-C classification system to group projects, students' creative self-beliefs may have changed; with every discovery of a small c and bigger C, they appeared to internalize the progression of categorical types and the message that they too can progress in their own creativity. In any grade or profession, it seems to me, then, creators can tap into the creativity that may be hidden from themselves and within seemingly impossible circumstances, building awareness and resilience in the process.

8.4   Reflection

Hidden-c is an implication of the longitudinal glocal study in that it cannot be "proven" but rather theorized and inferred from practice and outcomes. Through Hidden-c, creative discovery and risk-taking are empowered where creativity is experienced, expressed, and enlivened (i.e., E^3C). I brought E^3C forward as a named framework in this chapter for the first time to introduce creativity as a continuum. It emerged from my synthesis of the case studies wherein dynamics of experiencing, expressing, and enlivening creativity played out. Participants experienced and expressed creativity, with students more overtly experiencing it in my workshop than interviewees, for whom expression via conversation was the conduit of creativity.

With some stakeholders, enlivening creativity was hinted at through future-oriented generative possibilities, such as transference of creativity and creative learning to future teaching by preservice teachers and faculty alike. Otherwise, "enlivening" was barely discernible to me. Creativity carries on beyond identified outcomes through "continued exploration" by any of the agents involved (including myself), and other "mechanisms" contributing to "the extended development of the creativity process in the time and space domains" (Corazza, 2019, p. 300).

When teachers, facilitators, and leaders put personal creativity (Mini-c and Little-c) center stage in real time, this signals having confidence in potential creators' capacity to actively engage in exploratory experiences. Importantly, though, the creative process can be valued as an end unto itself for which greater understanding and deeper appreciation are needed (Runco, 2019). However, societies are increasingly mired in achievement, performance, and competition, valuing creativity that is original and useful, perhaps largely because it counts within the global marketplace and reflects individual achievement, and corresponding values, in Western cultures.

In service of creative thought and action, Hidden-c can be seen as a generative force affecting individuals, institutions, and cultures. The human condition through which creativity is revealed must remain within sight as a collective concern along with a planet that the young will want to inherit. On that score, based on what I've experienced and read by creativity researchers, universities and schools can better develop global-ready creative workers. Having said this, I acknowledge having learned a great deal about revealing creativity from my participants. At no point could I have anticipated the complexities and nuances of themes and their cultural significance, or even the kinds of examples that would accompany each C. I also did not know I was heading in the direction of E³C as a construct until I analyzed all results and had a meta-view. And it is only at this point of now being able to look back on the 4-year project that I can see that my creativity antenna have become better attuned to the power and strength of Hidden-c.

8.5 Summary

Outcomes were synthesized for the case studies, featuring developments around the 4-C creativity theory and Hidden-c. Points of explanatory focus were developmental outcomes of the 4-C model and Hidden-c's role in nurturing creative potential. The 4-C activity-based program was rolled out as E³C, with the future, imagined and unimagined, built into the continuum. The Hidden-c concept was unpacked relative to learning contexts and the potential for creative discovery even in the presence of constraints. Takeaways are addressed in the next and final chapter, geared around reflections and global influences on dynamic creative exploration.

References

Beghetto, R. A. (2006). Creative self-efficacy: Correlates in middle and secondary students. *Creativity Research Journal, 18*(4), 447–457.

Beghetto, R. A. (2016). Creative openings in the social interactions of teaching. *Creativity Theories–Research–Applications, 3*(2), 261–273. https://doi.org/10.1515/ctra-2016-0017

Beghetto, R. A. (2019). Structured uncertainty: How creativity thrives under constraints and uncertainty. In C. A. Mullen (Ed.), *Creativity under duress in education? Resistive theories, practices, and actions* (pp. 27–40). Cham, Switzerland: Springer.

Beghetto, R. A., & Corazza, G. E. (Eds.). (2019). *Dynamic perspectives on creativity: New directions for theory, research, and practice in education* (pp. 137–164). Cham, Switzerland: Springer.

Beghetto, R. A., & Karwowski, M. (2017). Toward untangling creative self-beliefs. In J. C. Kaufman (Ed.), *Creative self: Effect of beliefs, self-efficacy, mindset, and identity* (pp. 3–22). London, UK: Elsevier.

Beghetto, R. A., & Karwowski, M. (2019). Unfreezing creativity: A dynamic micro-longitudinal approach. In R. A. Beghetto & G. E. Corazza (Eds.), *Dynamic perspectives on creativity: New directions for theory, research, and practice in education* (pp. 7–25). Cham, Switzerland: Springer.

Clapp, E. P., & Hanson, M. H. (2019). Participatory creativity: Supporting dynamic roles and perspectives in the classroom. In R. A. Beghetto & G. E. Corazza (Eds.), *Dynamic perspectives on creativity: New directions for theory, research, and practice in education* (pp. 27–46). Cham, Switzerland: Springer.

Corazza, G. E. (2016). Potential originality and effectiveness: The dynamic definition of creativity. *Creativity Research Journal, 28*(3), 258–267.

Corazza, G. E. (2019). The Dynamic Universal Creativity Process. In R. A. Beghetto & G. E. Corazza (Eds.), *Dynamic perspectives on creativity: New directions for theory, research, and practice in education* (pp. 297–319). Cham, Switzerland: Springer.

Ferguson, K. (2012). Embrace the remix. *TEDGlobal 2012*. [Recorded talk]. Retrieved from https://www.ted.com/talks/kirby_ferguson_embrace_the_remix?language=en

Glăveanu, V. P. (2011). Creativity as cultural participation. *Journal for the Theory of Social Behaviour, 41*(1), 48–67. https://doi.org/10.1111/j.1468-5914.2010.00445.x

Glăveanu, V. P. (2013). Rewriting the language of creativity: The Five A's framework. *Review of General Psychology, 17*(1), 69–81. https://doi.org/10.1037/a0029528

Glăveanu, V. P. (2016). The psychology of creating: A cultural–developmental approach to key dichotomies within creativity studies. In V. P. Glăveanu (Ed.), *The Palgrave handbook of creativity and culture research* (pp. 205–223). London, UK: Palgrave Macmillan.

Glăveanu, V. P., Ness, I. J., Wasson, B., & Lubart, T. (2019). Sociocultural perspectives on creativity, learning, and technology. In C. A. Mullen (Ed.), *Creativity under duress in education? Resistive theories, practices, and actions* (pp. 63–82). Cham, Switzerland: Springer.

Helfand, M., Kaufman, J. C., & Beghetto, R. A. (2016). The Four-C Model of Creativity: Culture and context. In V. P. Glăveanu (Ed.), *The Palgrave handbook of creativity and culture research* (pp. 15–36). London, UK: Palgrave Macmillan.

Kaufman, J. C., & Beghetto, R. A. (2009). Beyond big and little: The Four C Model of creativity. *Review of General Psychology, 13*(1), 1–12.

Kauper, K., & Jacobs, M. M. (2019). The case for slow curriculum: Creative subversion and the curriculum mind. In C. A. Mullen (Ed.), *Creativity under duress in education? Resistive theories, practices, and actions* (pp. 339–360). Cham, Switzerland: Springer.

Literat, I., & Glăveanu, V. P. (2018). Distributed creativity on the Internet: A theoretical foundation for online creative participation. *International Journal of Communication, 12*, 893–908.

Mullen, C. A. (2017). *Creativity and education in China: Paradox and possibilities for an era of accountability*. New York, NY: Routledge & Kappa Delta Pi.

Mullen, C. A. (2018). Creative learning: Paradox or possibility in China's restrictive preservice teacher classrooms? *Action in Teacher Education, 40*(2), 186–202.

Mullen, C. A. (2019a). Creative synthesis: Combining the 4C and systems models of creativity. In C. A. Mullen (Ed.), *Creativity under duress in education? Resistive theories, practices, and actions* (pp. 3–25). Cham, Switzerland: Springer.

Mullen, C. A. (2019b). Dynamic creativity: Influential theory, public discourse, and generative possibility. In R. A. Beghetto & G. E. Corazza (Eds.), *Dynamic perspectives on creativity: New directions for theory, research, and practice in education* (pp. 137–164). Cham, Switzerland: Springer.

Mullen, C. A. (2020). *Canadian Indigenous literature and art: Decolonizing education, culture, and society*. Leiden, The Netherlands: Brill.

Ness, I. J., & Glăveanu, V. P. (2019). Polyphonic Orchestration: The dialogical nature of creativity. In R. A. Beghetto & G. E. Corazza (Eds.), *Dynamic perspectives on creativity: New directions for theory, research, and practice in education* (pp. 189–206). Cham, Switzerland: Springer.

Niu, W., & Sternberg, R. J. (2001). Cultural influences on artistic creativity and its evaluation. *International Journal of Psychology, 36*(4), 225–241.

Runco, M. (2019). Creativity as a dynamic, personal, parsimonious process. In R. A. Beghetto & G. E. Corazza (Eds.), *Dynamic perspectives on creativity: New directions for theory, research, and practice in education* (pp. 181–188). Cham, Switzerland: Springer.

Sawyer, R. K. (2003). *Group creativity: Music, theater, collaboration*. New York, NY: Routledge.

Sawyer, R. K. (2012). Extending sociocultural theory to group creativity. *Vocations and Learning, 5*, 59–75.

Sawyer, R. K. (2013). *Explaining creativity: The science of human innovation*. New York, NY: Oxford University Press. (Kindle book)

Sawyer, R. K. (2017). Creativity research and cultural context: Past, present, and future. *Journal of Creative Behavior, 51*(4), 352–354.

The Conversation. (2019). Retrieved from https://theconversation.com/ecosystems-across-Australia-are-collapsing-under-climate-change-99367

Vadeboncoeur, J. A., Perone, A., & Panina-Beard, N. (2016). Creativity as a practice of freedom: Imaginative play, moral imagination, and the production of culture. In V. P. Glăveanu (Ed.), *The Palgrave handbook of creativity and culture research* (pp. 285–304). London, UK: Palgrave Macmillan.

Zittoun, T., & Gillespie, A. (2016). Imagination: Creating alternatives in everyday life. In V. P. Glăveanu (Ed.), *The Palgrave handbook of creativity and culture research* (pp. 225–242). London, UK: Palgrave Macmillan.

Chapter 9
Takeaways: Global Influences on Dynamic Creative Exploration

Influence Shutterstock

9.1 Overview

Paradoxically, "creativity is a dynamic phenomenon" (Beghetto & Corazza, 2019a, p. 321) in accountability-bound world cultures. If it can be said that creativity acts and actions "use culture while, at the same time, renewing it" (Glăveanu, 2016, p. 1), then creativity research can be framed, designed, and operationalized with this perspective in mind. By dynamically adapting creativity frameworks to uncover perspectives on, and experiences of, education in creatively deprived cultural spaces, creativity becomes enlivened in exciting new ways, such as through advocacy for a cleaner world and better life. A chief precept in *Revealing Creativity* is that existing models of creativity—like the Four C (4-C) Model of Creativity—can be utilized to

© Springer Nature Switzerland AG 2020   209
C. A. Mullen, *Revealing Creativity*, Creativity Theory and Action in Education
5, https://doi.org/10.1007/978-3-030-48165-0_9

inform, interpret, and probe ideas of creativity in and across (testing) cultures (Mullen, 2019c). This assumption echoes Beghetto and Corazza's (2019b) viewpoint as articulated in *Dynamic Perspectives on Creativity* and the work being advanced on cultural creativity by an increasing number of creativity researchers using qualitative (and quantitative) research methodologies (e.g., Glăveanu, 2016; Karwowski, 2016; Ness & Glăveanu, 2019).

Another beliefs-infused foundational idea is that "creativity can be understood as a process rather than a product, and processes are by definition dynamic" (Runco, 2019, p. 182). As a (dynamic) process, creativity can be interpreted, approached, and studied as such. Applications and interventions of creativity support this notion, legitimizing it as a possibility for both understanding and experiencing preliminary work in glocalities. For example, new uses of research-informed creativity models can shed light on Hidden-c creativity, the potential to be discovered in all educational settings and places of learning under duress (also, Mullen, 2019c). Additionally, educational creativity can be experienced, expressed, and enlivened within glocalities applying Kaufman and Beghetto's (2009, 2013) 4-C typology.

In the journey that became this book, three global/world influences affected my 4-C creative intervention: creativity crisis, curriculum shortfalls, and creativity constraints. Counterforces—creativity process, dynamic adaptation, and creative exploration—also shaped the research and results. I describe these forces and counterforces, referring to the literature reviewed and research conducted. Because readers might be navigating these influences/forces within glocalities where restraints inhibit dynamic creativity, I expound on each influence keeping in mind that while we are influenced by global forces, we can in turn exert influence. Many scholars (e.g., Robinson & Aronica, 2015) characterize education in the creativity economy as largely accountability-bound, even bankrupt, within test-centered nations. I'm among those who nonetheless feel compelled to engage with and reveal creativity wherever and whenever possible. Considering a pessimistic outlook on the state of creativity in the world, it might not be surprising that despite the careful, intensive planning around my informal 4-Cs creativity program, in reality it could have failed. I placed myself in college environments that were foreign to me, among people unknown and amid unexpected institutional and world fluxes. The global influences on creativity I depict likely demand monitoring within rapidly globalized learning environments to enable conditions for experiencing dynamic creativity.

I shift to briefly convey my meta-reflection on the research questions and what was discovered from this pedagogical study before turning to the global influences on creativity.

9.2   Meta-Reflection on Research Questions

The three transnational contexts portrayed in *Revealing Creativity* were all examined to determine whether diverse college students and educators can discover creativity when encouraged under educational constraint. As per this line of inquiry, it was found that the populations studied were able to reveal creativity. With pedagogic guidance, creativity under duress was recovered and fostered, which implies that creativity can indeed be discovered in accountability-bound learning environments.

As far as new ideas that might be added to the social sciences canon, educational knowledge, and, specifically, the creativity paradigm, an overarching perspective is: *The 4-C theory-informed framework was meaningfully interpreted by participants neither familiar with it nor from educational psychology.* Because of this outcome, it appears that my 4-C creative intervention productively operationalized the creativity framework within the Chinese, Canadian, and Australian glocalities. A related takeaway is that *dynamic creativity was enacted, with identifiable creativity processes and learning outcomes, despite constraints from the global environment and those strategically "imposed" (by me) within the pedagogically designed settings.*

A second main message is that *the personal power of creativity—Hidden-c—was triggered by the 4-C creativity program of activities and animated through it.* High engagement was from activist oriented stakeholders involved in social movements. A lesson learned from the creative exploration is that *if creativity can be understood and appreciated as a process, even a "messy" one that is highly individualized from one person, context, and culture to the next, then the glimpses afforded can "count" as having value.* As such, authentic engagement in the creative process and space was the constant, not the production of things or exaltation of individuals. The social construction of creativity was evident in both undergraduate and graduate students' dialogical interactions and results, and in the connectivity between and among interviewees and me. This finding raises thought-provoking ideas deserving of contemplation. With culture as a point of reference, it comes to mind that the creativity typology adopted in this book might *not* fit when analyzing culturally specific responses or the cultural behavior of particular groups. One might wonder about the conceptualization of the 4-Cs when developed only with reference to the responses of Indigenous residents: Would a child who advocates climate change to rescue Indigenous habitats and restore life be thought of as displaying Big-C? Or, must the child be invited to a globally recognized platform to qualify his or her C?

On point, a reflection from the research is that creativity's "complex characteristic" allows for analysis "on many levels (e.g., from mini-c to Big-C) in various domains," making "it easier for people to accept the assumption that creative potential may be developed" (Karwowski, 2016, p. 167). Further, Karwowski (2016) asserted that the 4-C typology, like any popular theory of creativity, does not have to be "culturally universal"; for, "perceiving and defining creativity is reflected in [its] validity" and "in the quality of conclusions drawn on the basis of studies with the use of methods devised in different cultural conditions" (p. 177). Based on ethnographic studies that include their own, Ness and Glăveanu (2019) bring to the conversation about creativity and culture the importance of "social" and "cultural" dimensions of creativity. Dialogue proved essential among the organizational participants in "multidisciplinary groups" for engaging dynamically in creativity, collaboration, and learning. Advancing the concept of "dialogical creativity," they proposed from their fieldwork with organizations the "pre-condition of dialogue" in dynamic relationships within cultural environments (p. 189). Interestingly, they envision their conception of creativity as serving a purpose other than replacing creativity theories and approaches—they aspire to heighten awareness of "a social and cultural basis" in work others are doing (p. 203). In hindsight and with relevance for my 4-C transnational study, I ask, how might knowledge of cultural and social forces assist with culturally enriching creativity knowledge and paradigms? Might the power of Hidden-c that manifests in culturally distinct ways help stimulate possibilities for theorizing and reimagining creativity? Enhancing models and applying them? Renewing creativity and culture?

A third key idea takes us to E^{3}C, a continuum of creativity from experience, to expression, and enlivenment. A set of dynamic processes, E^{3}C can be approached in such a way as to trigger Hidden-c—the dynamic potential to be discovered in all educational worlds. The arousal of Hidden-c feeds one's creative capacity for authentically engaging in the experiencing, expressing, and enlivening of creativity. Instead of a one-off experience, possibilities can accrue from creativity that live beyond singular experiences and expressions to experiences and expressions that awaken, even exalt, the imagination and have impact. With the enlivening of creativity, visions can be animated of a future-oriented present (e.g., E^{3}C in Australia emerged as daily creative practice and breakthrough innovation in support of eco-smart, sustainable worlds that are inseparable from educational study). When we construe dynamic creativity as a continuum, it might be that opportunities increase for the experience, expression, and enlivenment of creativity to unfold. Current research findings and reflections of mine on others' studies create a possible boundary shift in theorizing creativity from the 4-Cs typology to a possible 4-Cs + Hidden-c + E^{3}C theory of dynamic and emergent creativity or creativity across boundaries. Taking my own transnational explorations as examples, future research can enrich the theorizing of creativity from exploring models, emergences, and actions.

Being intentional about igniting Hidden-c dynamically and interpersonally through E^{3}C and the 4-Cs has implications for theory, research, and practice. Theorizing dynamic creativity as a continuum (i.e., E^{3}C) could lead to research being designed around not only the experience or even expression of creativity but also the enlivening of it, such as through imagined worlds (e.g., the protection of oceans and marine ecosystems) and anticipatory human actions (e.g., creative activism through environmental protests, worldwide, on behalf of the planet). When creativity is implemented at the level of practice in classrooms and other learning spaces, it may be that the enlivening of it is not typically thought through or addressed. While enlivenment does summon the unseen and the unknown, it can excite new vistas previously unexplored that inform, perhaps even harness, powerful experiences and expressions of creativity. A curricular program built upon E^{3}C can even begin with enlivenment as the starting point for creative discovery, explicitly linking the imagination and future mindedness to the entire creative process and to hoped-for impacts (e.g., oceans purged of human waste).

Interestingly, Hidden-c was cultivated by E^{3}C dynamics in the glocalities I studied without my attention on anything other than authentic creative engagement and expression in different accountability-bound cultures and, as insight deepened, "the dynamic and evolving quality of the relationship we develop with others within a shared cultural environment" (Ness & Glăveanu, 2019, p. 189). This only serves to underscore the point that creativity-deficit places could stand to benefit from thought and design behind these ideas through which "social exchanges that are at the heart of creativity" are guided (Ness & Glăveanu, 2019. p. 189). Igniting Hidden-c dynamically and interpersonally through E^3C can be the target of a creativity program, practice, or study, affording more of a macro-view of creativity's intangibles like its unseen/unknown outcomes. As such, thoughtful consideration of E^3C could encourage theorizing, researching, and practicing around profound educational and societal change. A takeaway is, *E^3C as a concept and set of dynamics has the potential to enrich theory, research, and practice, and that a fuller excavation of it in accountability-bound cultures can extend the potential for impact while building greater capacity for dynamic creativity.*

A fourth central point concerns the notion that creativity "spans disciplinary boundaries" and that the work can be multidisciplinary and even transdisciplinary (Henriksen, 2018). Bridging the individual with the group, multidisciplinary teams, utilizing diverse perspectives, have proven innovative (Ness & Glăveanu, 2019). As a takeaway, *the very nature of creativity posed a challenge for faculty and leaders (non-creativity researchers), who struggled with the fit of creativity and my 4-C creativity program. Moreover, while giving public talks and even lecturing in classes as a visiting professor were recognizable discourse-styled actions in the university cultures, staging interviews with stakeholders and guiding students in dialogic activity-based groupings were not.* As underscored in qualitative creativity research in this vein, group creativity can support free expression and exploration, and dialogic exchanges can build creative cultures within educational milieus (e.g., Mullen, 2018) and organizations (e.g., Ness & Glăveanu, 2019). A final "lesson" is that *global influences on creativity can be usefully navigated within glocalities as well as confronted and transformed through counterforces.*

I now turn to the force–counterforce tension to describe and visually depict it. In the discussion of each global influence, the counterforces shine through at different points, with references to the educational literature and my research. You might consider it helpful to be aware of these influences on creativity and how I navigated them should you (or someone you know) similarly find yourself in a foreign college environment.

9.3 Global Influences on Exploring Creativity

Figure 9.1 introduces the next three sections by depicting prevailing global forces that influence creativity across the dimensions of understanding, experiencing, and exploring it. Three overlapping circles are on the graphic. In the upper left, the circle is labeled *creativity crisis*. The circle in the upper right is categorized *curriculum shortfalls*. The lower circle, just as important and equal to the other two, is identified

Fig. 9.1 Prevailing global influences on creativity and counterforces enabling it (C. A. Mullen)

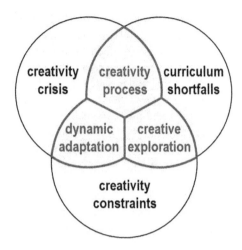

as *creativity constraints*. Counterforces across these domains are creativity process, dynamic adaptation, and creative exploration. While the global influences seemed formidable for nurturing creativity, these counterforces enabled creativity.

9.4   Creativity Crisis: Global Influence 1

A creativity crisis has been identified in the West and especially the East by the popular press and creativity and curriculum scholars worldwide. According to a crescendo of voices from schools and colleges, the crisis seems pronounced in nations where the Programme for International Student Assessment (PISA) has been adopted, classroom learning is rote, and standardized pedagogy and learning outcomes squelch creativity. Within PISA testing nations like Australia, Canada, China, and the United States, creative education has suffered. Consequently, creativity and other global competencies have been under strain, weakening nations along with individuals' creative capacities, educations, and futures. Ironically, by burdening schools and narrowing curriculum, testing regimes contradict the message of employers worldwide—creativity *is* a global competency expected of workers.

Educational creativity deficits plague the university cultures I researched. But these in no way characterize in absolute terms the state of creativity in China, Canada, and Australia. Considering participating educators' perceptions and capacity for authentically performing the 4-C creative activities, clearly there is hope. From the research I reviewed, while many aspiring and practicing preK–12 teachers value creativity, creative pedagogy and learning are not commonly cultivated in the twenty-first-century classroom. Of great importance in contemporary times, Kim (2011) found that student creativity has declined—from kindergarten through 12th grade—based on Torrance Tests of Creative Thinking scores. Across many personal creativity dimensions, statistically significant drops (approaching deficits) were detected in the capacity to be emotionally and verbally expressive, imaginative, energetic, passionate, perceptive, and unconventional; also affected was the ability to connect and synthesize things, and see from different angles. Creative interventions like mine show great promise for helping college students who have been socialized in stymied schooling systems express creativity.

As many college faculty likely realize, postsecondary education is intrinsically connected to, not divorced from, preK–12 schooling. At a systems level, governments in different nations push for intensified accountability and high-stakes testing, endeavoring to satisfy the public's need for answerability, confidence, and transparency in the standards and outcomes of schooling. However, an unintended consequence is the near extinction of creativity. In fact, performance-based accountability reforms have spread within accredited colleges. Reflected in curricula, assignments, expected learning outcomes, and testing, accountability measures are firmly entrenched in professional accreditation, licensure, and certification standards in teacher education. Thus, K–20 performance-based reforms overshadow program preparation of college students for work in the creativity economy, and teachers and leaders for careers within curriculum policy contexts.

As quick examples, consider Australia and Canada. Creativity is seen as desirable in schools, but guidance on what it is apparently lacks, along with "language about what practices actually sponsor creativity" (Henriksen, Creely, & Henderson, 2019, p. 8). High-stakes testing in Australia, and K–20 performance-based metrics, reduce the space for creative practice. These problems presumably continue in higher education, except when college faculty incorporate creativity in their programs. As another point of reference, note that high stakes are attached to the testing performance of preservice teachers in Queensland's education system—their test results in "literacy, numeracy, and science" are "tied" to "registration requirements" (Klenowski & Wyatt-Smith, 2012, p. 69); not coincidentally, "literacy and numeracy" assessments were mandated for "all students in Years 3, 5, 7, and 9" (p. 65).

These findings also resonate for other testing cultures, such as Canada's, based on studies of teaching. Kempf's (2016) large-scale study of Canadian trends in creativity and accountability identified a decrease in creative teaching and learning within the nation's preK–12 educational systems, largely attributed to the expansion in high-stakes standardized testing. (The United States and other countries remain more burdened by testing than Canada.) Without intentional creative intervention, the lack of creative practice inhibits education at the college level, particularly within professional programs that prepare preservice teachers and leaders. Across systems, creativity is suffering, from the early years of schooling through adolescence, affecting the future of societies.

A conviction shaping this book is that college students should have as many enrichment opportunities as possible to develop their creative and collaborative capacities. Under the leadership of creative educators, they can be encouraged to persevere and take risks. College students and graduates can transfer creative skills and knowledge from theory-informed quality teaching and learning to their current and future classrooms, thereby enriching countless pupils. To renew creativity, preK–12 and college teachers can generate opportunities even within the most regimented curricula.

For example, newly founded in 2019, the Creativity in Research Engaging the Arts, Transforming Education (CREATE) Centre at the University of Sydney, Australia, has brought together collaborators from education and the arts (e.g., theater companies) to change the tide so that creativity can thrive again, but in entirely new ways. The CREATE founders seek to "create dynamic places and spaces for imaginative learning and ensure our young people are equipped for [challenges]," based on recent Australian research that "suggests that re-imagining how we prepare for the world of work—and equipping our future workers with interpersonal skills and creativity—could contribute $36 billion to our economy" (Zaglas, 2019). The future might be right around the corner, but it is also a living construct. The future is acted upon in the present through demonstrable acts of imagination, vision, intention, and collaboration.

9.5   Curriculum Shortfalls: Global Influence 2

When creativity in academic learning is not explicitly promoted or connected with academics and courses, as is often the case, classroom teachers mirror these curriculum shortfalls. Even though preK–12 teachers tend to value creativity, they can feel blocked due to mounting external accountability pressures, being ill prepared to teach creatively and inspire originality, confusing creativity with the arts, and holding beliefs that affect how they see creativity and creative people. Without knowing creativity theory and research, and by misperceiving creative behaviors as, for example, "misbehavior," they struggle to identify creativity in others and facilitate creativity (Mullet, Willerson, Lamb, & Kettler, 2016). Teachers dealing with mandatory testing and test-centered curricula often feel confined pedagogically and overwhelmed, so it's not uncommon for them to relinquish creative activities valued and enjoyed in their classroom, including cooperative group work, the arts, physical activity, and recess. College faculty experience stress too and face some of the same barriers to creativity.

Not to be overlooked, though, are those preK–12 teachers (and college faculty) who cope creatively, and even courageously, with constraints that are imposed. Doyle's writings (e.g., 2019), based on her teacher interview study, recognize creative work with problems in the classroom. Deliberately facilitating their students' creative learning and artifacts, these teachers not only experienced a transformation in their understanding of the content but also of themselves. At all levels, teachers and faculty who create favorable conditions for creative engagement, expression, and collaboration mitigate unwelcome circumstances. Reclaiming the art of creativity in preservice teacher and leader programs necessitates change agency. Narey (2019) refers to this creative capacity as "questioning the status quo," especially in systems of standardization around social inequities and injustices (p. 325). Kauper and Jacobs (2019) referred to critical thinking aimed at social justice as "creative subversion," which involves "disciplined improvisation within the existing systems and frameworks of schools" (p. 347).

As Beghetto (2019) reminds us, constraints like controls are inevitable and these can be used to aid, if not structure, the "uncertainty" associated with creative experiences. Years earlier, he expressed the importance of not only acknowledging this dilemma but also finding a curricular balance. About the constraints on creativity, he stated:

> Current accountability movements in public education, marked by increased use of high-stakes testing, can contribute to teachers feeling pressured to quickly cover content. Teachers may feel that they simply do not have the time (or resources) to allow their students to adequately explore, interpret, and meaningfully engage in all of the topics that they teach. (as cited in Beghetto & Kaufman, 2007, p. 301)

In response to this dilemma, he asserted,

> [Nonetheless], we still believe that teachers can strike a balance between covering required content and encouraging students to explore, interpret, and make personal meaning of what they are learning. For teachers to move to this more balanced approach, educators must . . . develop a more interpretative view of learning. (as cited in Beghetto & Kaufman, 2007, p. 301)

Everyday creativity in (preK–12) classrooms—igniting as Mini-c and Little-c discoveries—is a conduit for striking a balance between creativity and accountability. Content that is regulated must be offset with exploratory subject matter and meaningful creative learning. As such, teacher "balance" between mandatory and "interpretative" content can help ensure quality educational experiences. Curriculum shortfalls can be offset through teacher questioning, challenging, and subverting normative expectations in support of creative adjustments.

9.6   Creativity Constraints: Global Influence 3

Constraints on creativity can be thought of as inevitable and natural. The very selection of theories/models/frameworks for pedagogical research is an example. Choosing a theory to unpack, framed as 4-C exploratory pedagogy in my case, triggered both restrictions and possibilities. The 4-C creativity typology (i.e., Beghetto, 2019; Kaufman & Beghetto, 2009, 2013) proved appealing as a conceptual organizer for interpreting, experiencing, and classifying creativities. My utilization of this model meant that I was taking on its embedded worldview and assumptions. Yet, with the 4-C framework, I could guide others' theorizing, brainstorming, collaborating, and creating while providing an opportunity for autonomous thinking and creatively connecting ideas—all while navigating controls (e.g., timed tasks). I had good cause to feel hopeful about implementing the model in glocalities unknown to me, for the value of the 4-C theory has been established. Also, the argument that creativity can thrive under constraint struck me as realistic. But I was also taking a creative risk. Making time for creativity goes against the priorities of busy people contending with life in performance-driven cultures.

Another layer is that when creativity is valued in education within such institutions, it's typically tied to prestigious disciplines like science and medicine and products with commercial promise. The creativity-as-product standpoint can drive creative processes in a particular way, thereby limiting the generative and possibility space. This steadfast Western conception of creativity as a thing, and "creative things" as products expected to be "original" and effective" is something Runco (2019) interrogated. Going a step further, he claimed that creativity does *not* even depend on a product or being recognized. In concert with these ideas, from the outset, the traditional standard for what counts as creativity—products and recognition—proved too narrow for my creative intervention. What came from the application in China, Canada, and Australia were responses and ideas, examples and artifacts—and even these "outputs" were uneven, variable, and individualized across the sites, thereby not satisfying the standard definition of creativity. All in all, my eclectic methods offer starting points for others.

A lesson is, creativity should *not* be avoided due to stresses and strains. When in the field, I kept in mind that I could both elicit and capture everyday creativity despite the constraints and uncertainties (Beghetto, 2019). While it might sound counterintuitive, restraints can be acted upon and used to facilitate creative thought and action, problem-solving, and process and artifact. We can even "story" interferences as dynamics of creativity, as I have attempted to do. Educators live with restraints every day—some we impose ourselves without thinking about it (e.g., course syllabi and readings, expectations for success, specified options and choices, and assessment rubrics).

To briefly illustrate constraints from Chapters 4, 5, and 6, the Chinese, Canadian, and Australian students, respectively, were invited to collaboratively apply the 4-C creativity model with peers (none of whom they knew). Also, they were restricted to a compressed timeframe (and, in two of the nations, a sheet of paper for artifact production). Discouraged from accessing technology or outside resources, they were "forced" to "show" creativity.

When any learning route or medium (e.g., paper) is chosen, constraints are naturally invoked. We just don't think about restraint this way, with its negative associations. Medium and its selection is an imposition known to artists: "Sculpture versus painting sets material affordances: opportunities and constraints" (Doyle, 2019, p. 49). "Parameters of success," also a constraint, are intended to help students "fulfill their creative potential and thrive" (Schmidt & Charney, 2018, p. 283). So, in the scheme of things, boundaries of one kind or another, whether imposed or summoned, can propel creative expression, innovation, and production.

In fact, entire domains of thought have been birthed through conceptual constraints that forge new directions. A classic example from the visual arts in American history is abstract expressionism. Valued was "expressivity" in opposition to realistic representation—the movement was created out of resistance to social realism (Doyle, 2019). Constraints—internal and external—range in their manifestations and effects on individuals, communities, and domains. Besides the arts, an example of a creativity constraint *in* educational research summons design elements serving as governing principles. When arts-based educational research was forming in the early 1990s, Tom Barone and Elliot Eisner proposed criteria for the qualitative paradigm, including uses of language (e.g., "expressive"), "personal signature" (of the researcher), "empathy" and its promotion, and "aesthetic form" (which they continued to update; see Barone & Eisner, 2012). The expectancy was that some of these be satisfied in arts-based work. These tenets are used today for recognizing, shaping, and assessing narrative and aesthetic research, including dissertations.

For my transnational project, I drew conceptual strength from the premise that creativity is accomplished in everyday worlds (e.g., classrooms) in the face of pressures. But I was also aware that monitoring constraints is important and that compounding psychological, cultural, political, and environmental constraints can aggravate creativity. Empirical research that closely links culture with creativity offered insight: In Niu and Sternberg's (2001) study, evaluators rated Chinese and American college students' artwork, finding the latter "more creative." The researchers concluded that the Chinese students' creativity was likely reduced due to "restrictive task constraints" or "the absence of explicit instructions to be creative" (p. 225). (Six years later, Niu, Zhang, & Yang's [2007] outcomes were the same.)

I absorbed this lesson in the development of my creative methods, first trialed in China. To cultivate creativity, I needed to mindfully attend to uninhibited task constraints and overt instruction on creativity. These pedagogic approaches to creative learning, encouraged by Niu and her coauthors, were said to be applicable with student populations in China. Restraints this population endures include hierarchical, standards-driven, and teacher-centered classrooms. The steadfast belief that one is not creative, undermining confidence is also a tenacious barrier; in Chongqing; remarkably, Chinese students' self-actualization through the creative process was the most glaring to me across the glocalities. While it was also the only place where I could teach a course and conduct self-reported assessments of learning, would one expect the highest creativity to come from the nation with the most rigid accountability?

With my research journey beginning in China, I took Niu's findings (i.e., Niu & Sternberg, 2001; Niu et al., 2007) to heart for *all* of my sites. In the three nations, I met many international and study abroad students, some from China, for whom English was a second language. As such, I sought to spark creative thought, engagement, and expression around the 4-Cs by providing a boilerplate, along with supportive materials. Creative and reflective responses were elicited in the constant presence of both limitations and uncertainties. Students were strongly encouraged to connect creativity to their own contexts, cultures, lives, and selves.

In Australia and China, students not only responded to my 4-C prompts but also developed the creative poster (artifact) in concert with the 4-C creativity model. For my own part, I was aiming for creative guidance, not direct instruction that scripts the learning process. (Hammond, Skidmore, Wilcox-Herzog, & Kaufman [2013] briefly explain these classic pedagogies and the distinctions.) This logic was reflected in a parallel way for individual interviewees with whom follow-up questions emerged spontaneously during the conversations.

Assessment is commonly believed to be a restriction on creativity. However, assessments that support the developmental aims of creative activity and learning (outcomes) are deemed a best practice. Like other creativity researchers, Beghetto (2005) refuted the widespread misconception that appraisal interferes with—or somehow disturbs—the creative process and endeavors. In fact, assessments that reflect theory and research, combined with a developmental perspective of creativity, have been effectively carried out. In universities, creativity assessment contexts include preservice teacher education (see Mullen, 2018) and theater education (see Schmidt & Charney, 2018), and in schools, these cross elementary, secondary, and postsecondary classrooms (e.g., Reilly, Lilly, Bramwell, & Kronish, 2011). A related issue is that the assessment of student creativity is underrepresented in the literature for both the postsecondary and preK–12 levels. Reviewing literature on teacher perception of creativity, Mullet et al. (2016) concluded,

> Teachers need an awareness of the variety of theories and definitions of creativity when selecting teaching and assessment tools. Teachers who misperceive creativity could unwittingly suppress creative expression in the classroom; negative or erroneous perceptions of creativity may prevent teachers from recognizing opportunities for developing creative potential in students. (p. 10)

Given that mistaken beliefs "cloud" creativity within the teaching profession, it makes sense that this problem extends to the assessment of creativity.

Creativity studies of college classrooms operationalize Beghetto's (2005) creed that assessments supportive of creative teaching and learning do not "kill" student creativity. At their home university in Texas, USA, theater educators Schmidt and Charney (2018) used three assessments (i.e., the Creative Achievement Questionnaire, reflective journals, and rubrics) to effectively evaluate student creativity in a learning lab. And they utilized recommendations from research on promoting student creativity in cooperative peer groups (just as I did for this book). Acting on their theory-informed belief that creativity should be assessed when it's "central" to a program's "learning outcomes" (p. 283), they studied students' responses. The information they gathered could "guide curriculum, improve learning outcomes, and help students of theatre reach their creative potential" (p. 271) (Table 9.1).

To the developing discourse on this topic, I would add that we as educators can be heartened that assessment supports genuine engagement, and even enhances ideas for future contexts. "Authentic positive feedback"—a basis for assessment—is vital for helping students with their motivation and development (Hammond et al., 2013, p. 294, also Beghetto & Kaufman, 2007). Relative to this book, assessment took different forms—in China, these were built into the course I taught, which was simply not possible within classes visited in Canada and Australia. In both English and Mandarin, assessment feedback was provided in China not only on the quality of students' creative accomplishments but also on the extent to which they had collaboratively, resourcefully, and imaginatively dealt with constraints. Underscored was the importance of twenty-first-century skills and capacities, and self-actualizing in this direction. I was also keen to receive feedback on the 4-C activities, especially the perceived value of them.

Table 9.1 Recommendations for future research and practice that build on the 4-C program (C. A. Mullen)

Investigate creativity in PISA nations (wherein creativity is apparently on the decline) to ascertain whether application of the 4-C model can trigger creativity in countries other than those featured herein (e.g., the United States)
Bring unique perspectives on, or different interpretations to, the 4-C typology to determine the potential for stimulating creativity (e.g., Hidden-c) in relation to this validated theory-informed framework
Explore the 4-C responses of university-based populations in educational disciplines not investigated in this book (e.g., educational psychology) or non-educational disciplines (e.g., science, technology, engineering, and mathematics); alternatively, direct attention at specific demographics (e.g., students of color, females only, international students)
Examine how school-based populations (e.g., children and youth; members of marginalized groups) interpret the 4-C program and engage in its activities; to do so, modify the 4-C application to accommodate curriculum, program, or standards expectations and ensure consistency with what is developmentally or culturally appropriate
Revise or redesign the 4-C program instructions and group activities (e.g., childhood essay; conversational prompts; poster activity; small/whole group performances; assessments by students of the tasks) or the interview prompts
Develop or incorporate performance measures (e.g., survey, self-report) to assess the effectiveness of the 4-C program and activities, such as the extent to which each task was valued; creative self-beliefs can be assessed as indications of participants' level of confidence with their creative abilities before and after experiencing the activity tasks
Engage the same class (or group) more than once, building on activities in such a way as to allow the program to be experienced as fully as possible; make time for teams to report results and for the researcher to seek clarification
Use your own classroom or someone else's in your "glocality" or a foreign location that satisfies the criteria of this 4-C application (e.g., embedded in creativity theory; occurs in a PISA nation; utilizes engagement techniques)
Change the physical classroom setting to an electronic classroom or learning space; utilize synchronous (live video) capabilities and software programs to assist with working in groups and creating in a paperless environment
Conduct a cross-cultural comparative study that controls for differences in methods (or modalities) to the extent possible so that outcomes can reflect educational, cultural, ethnic, historic, political, social, or other particularities
Instead of a macro-longitudinal approach to the 4-C program, adopt a "micro-longitudinal" one that enables numerous measurements of the phenomenon under study within short time periods (see Beghetto & Karwowski, 2019)
Devise a study that accounts for E^3C in an intentional way, thereby potentially generating insight into this continuum and "enlivenment," the future-minded aspect of educational creativity (beyond "experience" and "expression")
If a theory or model other than the 4-C typology is selected for study, ideas listed in this table can be freely adapted; in addition, it is recommended that feedback be pursued at critical junctures from creativity research experts

9.7 Farewell and the Future

Hopefully, a picture has emerged from this book that conveys how generative possibilities can come from creative exploration in accountability cultures. As the E^3C results indicate, educational creativity was experienced, expressed, and enlivened in the presence of constraints within transnational cultures applying Kaufman and Beghetto's (2009) 4-C typology. Through interaction, influences were navigated in the process of moving constructively from creativity theory to theory-informed practice and action. The 4-C framework was methodologically interpreted and converted into an application with human actors whose Hidden-c was triggered and creativity engaged. Activity-based methods like this allow for the enacting of theory and re-theorizing from practice.

I join other researchers who take the lead in college, school, and workplace settings "to reverse the creativity crisis" (e.g., Kaufman & Beghetto, 2013; Kim & Chae, 2019, p. 217; Mullen, 2019c). Some conduct investigations into creativity and education, while others apply creativity theory in real-world practice. These creativity pathways are evident in this book. An edited collection addresses these dimensions of creativity and change—creativity framework, investigation, and application—in various glocalities in which creativity is under duress (see Mullen, 2019a.)

Given twenty-first-century global pressures, I was keen to implement a creative intervention in different nations to explore possibilities for renewing and revealing creativity, despite the odds. Based on research and educational trends, I came to firmly believe that we as educators must go beyond acknowledging and criticizing the creativity crisis, curriculum shortfalls, and creativity constraints. By assuming personal and professional responsibility for interrupting these problematic trends, creativity deficits can be better managed and dynamic creativity experienced. If we ourselves do not plant the seeds of hope and forge opportunities for students (and others) to explore theory-informed creativity within learning environments, then how will creative applications, practices, and actions arise and become frequent occurrences, especially for children and youth?

Enrichment of theory and practice comes from discovering new places where we immerse others—and ourselves—in vibrant creative learning. Taking with us a model or method for creative discovery forges new kinds of engagement with theories and practices (Guerra & Villa, 2019). We make imaginative connections, develop insights, and refine methods within cultural contexts that help us cultivate creative capacities, including Hidden-c. With every form of creative and cultural experimentation we will not see perfection but rather possibilities for promoting, revealing, and releasing creativity. Doing this kind of work within unknown glocalities further excites all of these levels and dimensions of creative learning and risk-taking. Always a project in the making, creative investigations, interventions, applications, methods, and actions can both deepen understanding and advance knowledge. Having the opportunity to meaningfully engage students, faculty, and leaders around the world is truly a privilege and honor—who knows, they might just carry on as social-minded explorers of creativity.

Looking ahead as a field, we have before us a creative challenge—exploring creativity as a dynamic process in places carrying burdens. When thoughtful inquiry and creative learning are enabled, it becomes possible to re-theorize creativity models and ideas. The enrichment of theory, research, and practice that comes from creative discovery is anticipated for future frontiers of creativity. In this creative spirit, I ended with takeaways for future research that build on my 4-C program, itself organized to discover if there is any creativity left in PISA nations and, if so, what it looks like. Hopefully, these ideas and potential next steps for further developing research-based creativity interventions like my own can assist pedagogically oriented researchers with interest in pursuing this line of inquiry.

The winter of 2020 gives pause and a chance to see things differently amidst the growing uncertainty and unpredictability of these times. This book is being sent into the world during a deadly pandemic when global communities are contending with the rapid proliferation of the COVID-19 disease and when, as human beings everywhere, our lives are being dramatically altered. Academics are navigating the overnight transition to telework, online teaching, and virtual meetings. Concerning research exploration and activity, much needs to be rethought given the directive to cease our normal day-to-day lives and radically utilize online formats. In-person interaction has been reduced to cautionary, restrictive mandates to maintain social distance.

To ensure that human participants are not at risk of harm from data collection, the type of programming and face-to-face activities I developed could be reimagined for distance. To avoid putting research activities on hold, then, researchers/pedagogues could turn to remote technologies, such as video- and tele-conferencing, as alternatives for in-person data collection. For my own studies, I have had to think along these lines. My teaching, mentoring, and advising of graduate students are, increasingly, dependent on digital delivery. I use cloud-based course design (currently, Canvas and Zoom) for courses and pedagogic research. My work situation demands ongoing creative adaptation and improvisation in unforeseen circumstances. While I am located at my university's main campus in the rural Appalachian region of Virginia, our educational leadership students mostly reside in Washington, D.C. and Northern Virginia. So, I continue to retool, utilizing digital pedagogies for delivery of core curriculum at satellite campuses while investigating creativity and innovation (e.g., Mullen, 2019b). Creative improvisation, with its emphasis on unanticipated decision-making and action, offers a method of creativity research and a way of creating new knowledge.

Creativity explorations begin with a dream. Despite unknowns, dreams take shape in response to uncertainties, constraints, and realities. The metaphoric expression "working differently inside the box" conveys that students can thrive when presented "with opportunities to work through uncertainty in a well-planned learning environment"; similarly, in research situations, participants' "original expression" can be fostered while they "engage productively with uncertainty" and constraints that are unavoidable (Beghetto, 2019, pp. 34–36).

We are being called upon to reimagine our lives, including how we conduct work and interact, and teach and research. John Lennon's (2016/1971) beloved song "Imagine" invites dreamers to join in healing the world—and defeating the status quo. Dreaming something into being awakens possibilities imagined *and* unimagined. The edge of the present is the future.

References

Barone, T., & Eisner, E. W. (2012). *Arts based research*. Thousand Oaks, CA: Sage.

Beghetto, R. A. (2005). Does assessment kill student creativity? *The Educational Forum, 69*(3), 254–263.

Beghetto, R. A. (2019). Structured uncertainty: How creativity thrives under constraints and uncertainty. In C. A. Mullen (Ed.), *Creativity under duress in education? Resistive theories, practices, and actions* (pp. 27–40). Cham, Switzerland: Springer.

Beghetto, R. A., & Corazza, G. E. (2019a). Coda. In R. A. Beghetto & G. E. Corazza (Eds.), *Dynamic perspectives on creativity: New directions for theory, research, and practice in education* (pp. 321–324). Cham, Switzerland: Springer.

Beghetto, R. A., & Corazza, G. E. (Eds.). (2019b). *Dynamic perspectives on creativity: New directions for theory, research, and practice in education* (pp. 137–164). Cham, Switzerland: Springer.

Beghetto, R. A., & Kaufman, J. C. (2007). Intellectual estuaries: Connecting learning and creativity in programs of advanced academics. *Journal of Advanced Academics, 20*, 296–324.

Doyle, C. L. (2019). Speaking of creativity: Frameworks, models, and meanings. In C. A. Mullen (Ed.), *Creativity under duress in education? Resistive theories, practices, and actions* (pp. 41–62). Cham, Switzerland: Springer.

Glăveanu, V. P. (2016). Introducing creativity and culture, the emerging field. In V. P. Glăveanu (Ed.), *The Palgrave handbook of creativity and culture research* (pp. 1–12). London, UK: Palgrave Macmillan.

Guerra, M., & Villa, F. V. (2019). Exploration as a dynamic strategy of research-education for creativity in schools. In R. A. Beghetto & G. E. Corazza (Eds.), *Dynamic perspectives on creativity: New directions for theory, research, and practice in education* (pp. 101–116). Cham, Switzerland: Springer.

Hammond, H. L., Skidmore, L. E., Wilcox-Herzog, A., & Kaufman, J. C. (2013). Creativity and creativity programs. In J. Hattie & E. M. Anderman (Eds.), *International guide to student achievement* (pp. 292–295). New York, NY: Routledge.

Henriksen, D. (2018). *The 7 transdisciplinary cognitive skills for creative education*. Cham, Switzerland: Springer.

Henriksen, D., Creely, E., & Henderson, M. (2019). Failing in creativity: The problem of policy and practice in Australia and the United States. *Kappa Delta Pi Record, 55*(1), 4–10.

Karwowski, M. (2016). Culture and psychometric studies of creativity. In V. P. Glăveanu (Ed.), *The Palgrave handbook of creativity and culture research* (pp. 159–186). London, UK: Palgrave Macmillan.

Kaufman, J. C., & Beghetto, R. A. (2009). Beyond big and little: The Four C Model of Creativity. *Review of General Psychology, 13*(1), 1–12.

Kaufman, J. C., & Beghetto, R. A. (2013). Do people recognize the Four Cs? Examining layperson conceptions of creativity. *Psychology of Aesthetics, Creativity, and the Arts, 7*, 229–236.

Kauper, K., & Jacobs, M. M. (2019). The case for slow curriculum: Creative subversion and the curriculum mind. In C. A. Mullen (Ed.), *Creativity under duress in education? Resistive theories, practices, and actions* (pp. 339–360). Cham, Switzerland: Springer.

Kempf, A. (2016). *The pedagogy of standardized testing: The radical impacts of educational standardization in the US and Canada*. New York, NY: Palgrave Macmillan.

Kim, K. H. (2011). The creativity crisis: The decrease in creative thinking scores on the Torrance tests of creative thinking. *Creativity Research Journal, 23*(4), 285–295.

Kim, K. H., & Chae, N. (2019). Recapturing American innovation through education: The creativity challenge for schools. In C. A. Mullen (Ed.), *Creativity under duress in education? Resistive theories, practices, and actions* (pp. 215–233). Cham, Switzerland: Springer.

Klenowski, V., & Wyatt-Smith, C. (2012). The impact of high stakes testing: The Australian story. *Assessment in Education: Principles, Policy & Practice, 19*(1), 65–79.

Lennon, J. (2016/1971). *Imagine* (song, recorded by Apple Records, USA). Retrieved from https://www.google.com/search?q=song+lyrics+to+imagine&rlz=1C1GCEU_enUS820US820&oq=song+lyrics+to+imagine&aqs=chrome..69i57j0l5.3812j1j4&sourceid=chrome&ie=UTF-8

Mullen, C. A. (2018). Creative learning: Paradox or possibility in China's restrictive preservice teacher classrooms? *Action in Teacher Education, 40*(2), 186–202.

Mullen, C. A. (Ed.). (2019a). *Creativity under duress in education? Resistive theories, practices, and actions.* Cham, Switzerland: Springer.

Mullen, C. A. (2019b). Does modality matter? A comparison of aspiring leaders' learning online and face-to-face. *Journal of Further and Higher Education,* 1–19. doi:https://doi.org/10.1080/0309877X.2019.1576859

Mullen, C. A. (2019c). Dynamic creativity: Influential theory, public discourse, and generative possibility. In R. A. Beghetto & G. E. Corazza (Eds.), *Dynamic perspectives on creativity: New directions for theory, research, and practice in education* (pp. 137–164). Cham, Switzerland: Springer.

Mullet, D. R., Willerson, A., Lamb, K. N., & Kettler, T. (2016). Examining teacher perceptions of creativity: A systematic review of the literature. *Thinking Skills and Creativity, 21,* 9–30.

Narey, M. J. (2019). Who stands for what is right? Teachers' creative capacity and change agency in the struggle for educational quality. In C. A. Mullen (Ed.), *Creativity under duress in education? Resistive theories, practices, and actions* (pp. 313–337). Cham, Switzerland: Springer.

Ness, I. J., & Glăveanu, V. P. (2019). Polyphonic orchestration: The dialogical nature of creativity. In R. A. Beghetto & G. E. Corazza (Eds.), *Dynamic perspectives on creativity: New directions for theory, research, and practice in education* (pp. 189–206). Cham, Switzerland: Springer.

Niu, W., & Sternberg, R. J. (2001). Cultural influences on artistic creativity and its evaluation. *International Journal of Psychology, 36*(4), 225–241.

Niu, W., Zhang, J. X., & Yang, Y. (2007). Deductive reasoning and creativity: A cross-cultural study. *Psychological Reports, 100*(2), 509–519.

Reilly, R. C., Lilly, F., Bramwell, G., & Kronish, N. (2011). A synthesis of research concerning creative teachers in a Canadian context. *Teaching and Teacher Education, 27*(3), 533–542.

Robinson, K., & Aronica, L. (2015). *Creative schools: The grassroots revolution that's transforming education.* New York, NY: Viking.

Runco, M. (2019). Creativity as a dynamic, personal, parsimonious process. In R. A. Beghetto & G. E. Corazza (Eds.), *Dynamic perspectives on creativity: New directions for theory, research, and practice in education* (pp. 181–188). Cham, Switzerland: Springer.

Schmidt, M., & Charney, M. (2018). Assessing creativity as a student learning outcome in theatre education. In S. Burgoyne (Ed.), *Creativity in theatre* (pp. 271–287). Cham, Switzerland: Springer.

Zaglas, W. (2019, September 25). New CREATE Centre wants all learning infused with creativity and the arts. *Campus Review.* Retrieved from https://www.campusreview.com.au/2019/09/new-create-centre-wants-all-learning-infused-with-creativity-and-the-arts

Author Index

© Springer Nature Switzerland AG 2020
C. A. Mullen, *Revealing Creativity*, Creativity Theory and Action in Education 5, https://doi.org/10.1007/978-3-030-48165-0

Subject Index

© Springer Nature Switzerland AG 2020

C. A. Mullen, *Revealing Creativity*, Creativity Theory and Action in Education 5, https://doi.org/10.1007/978-3-030-48165-0

CPSIA information can be obtained
at www.ICGtesting.com
Printed in the USA
LVHW081335270720
661390LV00002BA/20

9 783030 481643